Politics, Markets,
and America's Schools

POLITICS, MARKETS, AND AMERICA'S SCHOOLS

John E. Chubb and Terry M. Moe

The Brookings Institution | Washington, D.C.

Copyright © 1990 by
T H E B R O O K I N G S I N S T I T U T I O N
1775 Massachusetts Avenue, N.W., Washington, D.C. 20036

Library of Congress Cataloging-in-Publication data

Chubb, John E.
  Politics, markets, and America's schools / John E. Chubb and Terry M. Moe.
    p. cm.
  Includes bibliographical references (p.   ).
  ISBN 0-8157-1410-6 (alk. paper)—ISBN 0-8157-1409-2
(pbk. : alk. paper)
    1. Public schools—United States. 2. Academic achievement.
  3. Politics and education—United States. I. Moe, Terry M.
  II. Title.
LA217.C48 1990   90-32187
371'.01'0973—dc20   CIP

9 8 7 6 5 4 3

The paper used in this publication meets the minimum requirements
of the American National Standard for Information Sciences—
Permanence of Paper for Printed Library Materials, ANSI Z39.48-
1984.

THE BROOKINGS INSTITUTION

The Brookings Institution is an independent organization devoted to nonpartisan research, education, and publication in economics, government, foreign policy, and the social sciences generally. Its principal purposes are to aid in the development of sound public policies and to promote public understanding of issues of national importance.

The Institution was founded on December 8, 1927, to merge the activities of the Institute for Government Research, founded in 1916, the Institute of Economics, founded in 1922, and the Robert Brookings Graduate School of Economics and Government, founded in 1924.

The Board of Trustees is responsible for the general administration of the Institution, while the immediate direction of the policies, program, and staff is vested in the President, assisted by an advisory committee of the officers and staff. The by-laws of the Institution state: "It is the function of the Trustees to make possible the conduct of scientific research, and publication, under the most favorable conditions, and to safeguard the independence of the research staff in the pursuit of their studies and in the publication of the results of such studies. It is not a part of their function to determine, control, or influence the conduct of particular investigations or the conclusions reached."

The President bears final responsibility for the decision to publish a manuscript as a Brookings book. In reaching his judgment on the competence, accuracy, and objectivity of each study, the President is advised by the director of the appropriate research program and weighs the views of a panel of expert outside readers who report to him in confidence on the quality of the work. Publication of a work signifies that it is deemed a competent treatment worthy of public consideration but does not imply endorsement of conclusions or recommendations.

The Institution maintains its position of neutrality on issues of public policy in order to safeguard the intellectual freedom of the staff. Hence interpretations or conclusions in Brookings publications should be understood to be solely those of the authors and should not be attributed to the Institution, to its trustees, officers, or other staff members, or to the organizations that support its research.

For our children
Adam, Rachel, and Rebecca
and
Caitlin

Foreword

BY MOST ACCOUNTS, the American education system is not working well. Children appear to be learning less in school today than they did a generation ago. Some 25 percent of the nation's high school students drop out before graduating, and in large cities—whose poor and minority children desperately need quality education—the figure can climb to 50 percent. On math and science achievement tests, American teenagers trail students from other nations—a pattern with alarming implications for America's ability to compete in the world economy.

More troubling still, these problems have stubbornly resisted determined efforts to solve them. During the last quarter century, successive waves of education reform have swept the country—most recently in the wake of the publication of *A Nation at Risk*—but, as a new century approaches, there are few signs of real progress.

How can government work so hard to improve schools yet make so little progress? In this book, John E. Chubb and Terry M. Moe argue that government has not solved the education problem because government is the problem. They contend that the political institutions that govern America's schools function naturally and routinely, despite everyone's best intentions, to burden the schools with excessive bureaucracy, to inhibit effective organization, and to stifle student achievement. The book documents these institutional influences in an analysis of more than 20,000 students, teachers, and principals in a nationwide sample of some 500 schools.

The nation's education problem, then, is an institutional problem. To overcome it, the authors recommend a new system of public education based on fundamentally new institutions. They propose a shift away from a system of schools controlled directly by government— through politics and bureaucracy—to a system of indirect control that relies on markets and parental choice. Although this new system is bound to be controversial, it is clear that less fundamental reforms have yet to turn American education around.

This book is the culmination of a large study that began nearly ten years ago, and the authors gratefully acknowledge the support they have received along the way.

The financial assistance of the following organizations is deeply appreciated: the Institute for Educational Finance and Governance at Stanford University, the National Institute of Education of the U.S. Department of Education, the Office of Educational Research and Improvement (Field Initiated Studies Program grant #G008610968) of the U.S. Department of Education, the Lynde and Harry Bradley Foundation, and the John M. Olin Foundation.

The authors would like to thank several people who worked with them in the design of the Administrator and Teacher Survey: John H. Bishop, Larry Hotchkiss, Gail S. MacColl, Fred M. Newmann, Stewart C. Purkey, Marshall S. Smith, and the able staff at the National Opinion Research Center at the University of Chicago. The authors are also grateful to their many research assistants: Matthew D. Berger, Elaine Carlson, David H. Fallek, Michael G. Hagen, Paul R. Joyce, Steven Neptune, Charles H. Stewart III, Julie Strickland, Paul M. Wright, and especially Karen L. Fuller who executed most of the statistical analysis and provided crucial assistance long after she left Brookings.

While the manuscript was being drafted, the authors had the benefit of advice from many readers: John E. Coons, Raymond J. Domanico, Chester E. Finn, Jr., Peter M. Flanigan, Seymour Fliegel, Coleman Genn, Nathan Glazer, William M.H. Hammett, Eric A. Hanushek, Ted Kolderie, Myron Lieberman, Robert J. Lytle, Thomas E. Mann, Joe Nathan, Mary Anne Raywid, Thomas T. Schweitzer, Joseph White, and particularly Denis P. Doyle, Paul E. Peterson, and James Q. Wilson who commented on the entire manuscript. The authors greatly appreciate this advice. They also wish to extend thanks to the many groups of teachers, administrators, and education policymakers who listened to presentations of this research and offered practical suggestions.

Theresa B. Walker edited the manuscript, Paul R. Joyce verified it, Susan Woollen prepared it for typesetting, and Max Franke prepared the index. The authors finally want to thank Renuka D.

Deonarain, Teresita V. Vitug, Eloise C. Stinger, and particularly Vida R. Megahed for typing the manuscript.

The interpretations and conclusions presented are solely those of the authors and should not be ascribed to the persons whose assistance is acknowledged above, to any group that funded the research reported herein, or to the trustees, officers, or other staff members of the Brookings Institution.

BRUCE K. MACLAURY
President

April 1990
Washington, D.C.

Contents

Tables

Chapter One

The Root of the Problem

FOR AMERICA'S public schools, the last decade has been the worst of times and the best of times. Never before in recent history have the public schools been subjected to such savage criticism for failing to meet the nation's educational needs—yet never before have governments been so aggressively dedicated to studying the schools' problems and finding the resources for solving them.

Whether the criticisms have come from average citizens, business leaders, public officials, or educators themselves, they have had a common thrust: the schools are failing in their core academic mission, particularly in the more rigorous areas of study—math, science, foreign languages—so crucial to a future of sophisticated technology and international competition. America's children are not learning enough, they are not learning the right things, and, most debilitating of all, they are not learning how to learn.[1]

The signs of poor performance were there for all to see during the 1970s. Scores on the Scholastic Aptitude Test headed downward year after year. Large numbers of teenagers continued to drop out of school. Drugs and violence poisoned the learning environment. American students consistently did worse than students from other nations on international achievement tests. An emerging awareness of national crisis hit with full force in the early 1980s, when widespread dissatisfaction with the state of American education was granted scientific legitimacy and political weight by a sudden flood of new studies and commission reports, all of them highly critical of the schools and arguing the urgent need for change.[2]

What followed has been called the "greatest and most concentrated surge of educational reform in the nation's history."[3] State after state imposed tougher academic requirements, introduced new tests for student achievement, and increased pay and certification requirements for teachers, among other things. Some states and school districts boldly pursued more innovative solutions, from career ladders and

1

merit pay to school-based management and magnet schools.[4] From the vantage point of those in the educational community—and most everyone else involved in the reform process, it seems—this was American democracy at its finest. The problem of declining academic performance had been met head-on with a revolutionary program of reforms that promised a brighter future for the nation's schools.

We take a very different view of these developments. While we too would like to be optimistic about the prospects for better schools, we think the reforms adopted thus far are destined to fail. Our reason, when all is said and done, is that they simply do not get at the underlying causes of the problem—which have little to do, at least directly, with graduation requirements or teacher certification or any of the other obvious characteristics of schools and their personnel that have so occupied reformers. It is our view that the most fundamental causes are far less obvious, given the way schools are commonly understood, and far less susceptible to change. They are, in fact, the very institutions that are supposed to be solving the problem: the institutions of direct democratic control.

This, in large measure, is what our book is about. For reasons we will elaborate and document at length, the specific kinds of democratic institutions by which American public education has been governed for the last half century appear to be incompatible with effective schooling. Although everyone wants good schools, and although these institutions are highly sensitive and responsive to what people want, they naturally and routinely function to generate just the opposite—providing a context in which the organizational foundations of effective academic performance cannot flourish or take root. The problem of poor performance is just as much a normal, enduring part of the political landscape as school boards and superintendents are. It is one of the prices Americans pay for choosing to exercise direct democratic control over their schools.

What we have to say about the public schools and their governing institutions is part of a larger perspective that we develop on schools in general—private as well as public—and why they look and perform as they do. It is our view that all schools are shaped in pervasive and subtle ways by their institutional settings, and that the kinds of organizations they become and how effectively they perform are largely reflections of the institutional contexts in which they operate.

The institutional perspective we develop here departs considerably from conventional wisdom on the subject, and, in particular, is very different from the theoretical foundations on which reformers have based their assessments of the schools' problems and what might be done to turn matters around. Reformers believe the source of these problems is to be found in and around the schools, and that schools can be "made" better by relying on existing institutions to impose the proper reforms. We believe existing institutions cannot solve the problem, because they *are* the problem—and that the key to better schools is institutional reform. This book is our effort to explain why.

The One Best System

Until the first few decades of the 1900s, there was really nothing that could meaningfully be called a public "system" of education in the United States. Schooling was a local affair. Basic issues of organization and control—issues that today would be classified as budgeting, curriculum, personnel, purchasing, accountability, and the like—were not so mind-bogglingly technical or bureaucratic then, and they tended to be handled by the people closest to each school: parents, interested citizens, and their elected representatives. In urban areas, party organizations sometimes had a hand in orchestrating all this, and they saw to it that their interests in patronage and the letting of contracts were furthered. But even in these settings, authority was highly decentralized and afforded the lower classes and ethnic and religious minorities control over their own schools.[5]

Education was about simple, important things that ordinary people cared about and could understand. Above all else, it centered on teaching, on how their children were to be taught and who would teach them. Because local schools were bound up with family, neighborhood, and community, and because teaching was intrinsically anchored in personal relationships and experiences, people naturally believed that they could and should be able to govern their own educational affairs. And as they proceeded—all across America, without plan or coordination—to fashion the kinds of schools they wanted for themselves and their children, the great heterogeneity of the nation came to be reflected in the diversity and autonomy of its local schools.[6]

This was not to last. Institutional reforms rooted in the Progressive era would revolutionize American education over the first half of the twentieth century, creating a true system of public schools—and eroding school diversity and autonomy. The traditional explanation for what happened is one of inevitable progress.[7] Reformers and educational leaders, dedicated to the goal of effective education and possessed of the best scientific knowledge about how to achieve it, succeeded in building a rational system of schools for the nation as a whole, triumphing over the parochialism, fragmentation, and party machines of an unenlightened past. The system they created was bureaucratic and professional, designed to ensure, so the story goes, that education would be taken out of politics and placed in the hands of impartial experts devoted to the public interest. It was the "one best system."[8]

This rosy account was widely accepted for many years, not least because the most influential books and ideas on the subject were generated by the reformers and professionals themselves.[9] During the last few decades, however, scholars have done a thorough job of demolishing their claims.[10] The new educational institutions imposed on the nation were neither inevitable nor uniformly progressive. They were the result of a haphazard series of political victories, slowly realized over a period of many years, in which social groups that benefited from and supported institutional reform gradually won out over those that were disadvantaged by it and had vigorously opposed it.

The winners were elements of business, the middle class, and educational professionals—especially the latter, for they would be running the new bureaucratic system. The losers included the machine politicians, who were so easily characterized as the enemies of effective education. But the losers also included a sizable portion of the less powerful segments of the American population: the lower classes, ethnic and religious minorities, and citizens of rural communities. Their traditional control over local schools was now largely transferred to the new system's political and administrative authorities—who, according to what soon became official doctrine, knew best what kind of education people needed and how it could be provided most effectively.

Throughout this period of conflict and change, the politics of education was driven by fundamentals. Powerful groups fought over the kinds of democratic institutions that would organize and govern the public schools. Virtually everything about American education was up for grabs. But the battle over fundamentals eventually came to an end. The winners won and the losers lost. New institutions were in place and functioning. And, as the decades passed, these institutions became deeply entrenched as an integral part of America's political and social life.

Today, this system is so thoroughly taken for granted that it virtually defines what Americans mean by democratic governance of the public schools. At its heart are the school district and its institutions of democratic control: the school board, the superintendent, and the district office. The school board is the district's legislative body and is almost always elected. The superintendent is its administrative head and is sometimes elected, sometimes appointed. The district office is the bureaucratic organization responsible for carrying out the policies of the board and the superintendent.

These district institutions gain their authority from the state government, which, under the United States Constitution, is the primary locus of public authority in the field of education. The state's specialized institutions parallel those of the district: it also has a school board or reasonable facsimile, a superintendent or "chief state school officer," and a bureaucracy, the latter taking the form of a department of education.[11] Finally, there is the federal government, whose role by law and custom has been distinctly secondary—although, as in many other areas of domestic policy, it has grown in fits and starts over time. The federal government has its own educational bureaucracy—since 1979, organized under the U.S. Department of Education—with various linkages to the more tightly integrated state-local hierarchy.

This system of governance has been firmly in place now for as long as most Americans can remember. Throughout, there have been plenty of conflicts in the politics of education. The issues strike so close to home—literally—for so many Americans, there are so many organized groups with direct stakes in the outcomes, and there are so many units of government with the authority to make policy decisions, that it could hardly have been otherwise. These political conflicts have almost always been struggles over policy. Should the government use forced busing as a means of desegregating the schools? Should the schools teach sex education? Should they be required to provide bilingual education for non–English-speaking students? Should the disabled be mainstreamed into conventional classroom settings? Should vulgar books be removed from school libraries?

Less frequently, political conflict has centered on the more fundamental issue of how power should be allocated within the system. During the 1960s, the struggle by minorities in urban ghettos for "community control" was a reaction against the insularity of bureaucratic professionalism and a demand for greater political responsiveness and control. The desegregation controversy of the 1960s and 1970s involved, among other things, a power struggle among levels of government as to which authorities would make basic decisions about local schools and their student bodies. The "teacher power" movement in the 1970s and 1980s was driven by demands for professional status and the autonomy, pay, and decisionmaking power that go along with it.[12]

But however heated the conflicts over educational policy and practice have been, however intense the struggles for influence and resources, the "one best system" has consistently stood above it all. It has provided the framework of democratic institutions within which demands are expressed, problems identified, solutions explored, and policy responses chosen. It has structured criticism and reform—but it has never been their target.

Academic Excellence and Educational Reform

The last decade has been a period of massive discontent with the public schools. It is tempting to say that all the various conflicts over race, equal opportunity, political responsiveness, teacher power, and the like have cumulated to crisis proportions, causing educational issues to skyrocket to the top of the nation's political agenda. And there is doubtless some truth to this, since these issues, like most in American politics, have never really been settled or even effectively addressed. But the stinging criticisms and widespread unrest that began in the early 1980s have generally been oriented by a distinctive, more narrowly focused theme: that the academic quality of the public schools is unacceptably low. The universal demand, at all levels of government, is for reforms that promote academic excellence.[13]

For those familiar with the history and politics of education, there is a certain sense of déjà vu in this riveting attention to academics.

Some thirty years ago, the launching of the Soviet *Sputnik* set off shock waves within the American educational community. Many became convinced that the United States was losing the race for space, and for technological and economic progress more generally, because the public school system was failing to provide American children with rigorous academic training, particularly in science and math. Influential critiques of American education—most notably, James Conant's *The American High School Today*—argued the seriousness of the problem and urged governmental action.[14] A frenzied concern for national security thus fueled a political movement to beef up the academic performance of America's public schools. The most tangible result was a major leap forward in federal aid to education, the National Defense Education Act of 1958: a policy "solution" that took the form of new money and new responsibilities for the federal government.[15]

The issue of academic excellence then rather quickly plummeted on the national agenda, to be superseded by others—notably, race and equal opportunity—that, by no coincidence, were closely bound up with the broader social controversies that animated the turbulent politics of the 1960s and 1970s. Meantime, there was no indication that the schools had actually improved. The problem of academic excellence remained. It simply lacked the ingredients of political salience.

This, of course, is the standard state of affairs for most social problems most of the time, whether they have to do with education or poverty or international trade. However serious they may be in some objective sense, they only take precedence over all the other deserving social problems and attract the special attention of policy-makers when the political stars happen to line up just right. Academic excellence fleetingly gained the national spotlight during the late 1950s, not solely because of its intrinsic merits, but because a spectacular technological achievement by the Soviets prompted a national fit of paranoia. It would be awhile before the political stars would come into alignment again.[16]

This time, however, the dissatisfaction with public education would prove to be genuinely widespread, the result of years of growing frustration among ordinary citizens about what they perceived to be the deterioration of their schools. The single most important symbol of the underlying problem came to be the monotonic decline, from the mid-1960s through 1980, in the scores of high school students on the national Scholastic Aptitude Test, or SAT. This was widely taken as tangible and dramatic evidence that something was wrong with the way American children were being educated. Exactly what was wrong was more complicated.[17] But Gallup polls throughout this period consistently showed that the public was concerned above all else with lax discipline—with permissiveness, disorderliness, drugs, violence—and, correspondingly, with the loose or nonexistent academic standards that had become fashionable among educators during those counter-cultural times.[18] In the cities, where poverty conspired to make these matters far worse, concerns were similar but more grave. Throughout the country, then, demands for order, structure, and rigor began to be placed on the schools.

Still, it is not at all clear that academic excellence would have burst back onto the political scene with full force and coherence had it not been for the sputnik-like effect of an essentially unrelated crisis, this time in the sphere of economics. The oil embargo, stagflation, and a serious deterioration in the United States' ability to compete in international markets all combined to light a political fire under those—particularly in the business community—most directly concerned with national economic policy.[19] What could be done to combat America's economic decline? Study, debate, and old-fashioned pressure trained the political spotlight on a host of issues most immediately connected to the problem, issues like protectionism, the opening of foreign markets, and the value of the dollar. But they also focused attention on the more fundamental, long-term determinants of economic success in a fast-paced world of competition and sophisticated technology.

The educational system, responsible for shaping America's "human capital," understandably attracted close scrutiny—and with scrutiny came severe criticism. Again, test scores provided concrete indicators of serious underlying problems: not only were SAT scores declining year by year, but American students consistently did worse, often dramatically and embarrassingly worse, than foreign students on internationally standardized tests, particularly in the areas—math and science—so crucial to technological sophistication. How was the United States supposed to compete effectively against economic powerhouses like Japan or Germany when its schools, by comparison to theirs, were so poorly geared to the human capital requirements of produc-tivity and innovation in the modern age?[20]

From an economic standpoint, America clearly needed better—and more rigorous—education. But beyond that, it also needed education of a different kind. Critics increasingly came to agree that a dynamic economy well suited to modern conditions requires workers who are not only technically knowledgeable and well trained, but who also have the capacity for creative, independent thought and action—since technology and the requirements of productivity are constantly changing and cannot be learned once and for all.[21] In the modern world, they claimed, productivity is keyed to knowledge, brain power, and flexibility in their application, not, as in Henry Ford's day, to disciplined labor and mindless rule-following. Americans must be taught how to think. They must learn how to learn.

In response to economic crisis, then, groups and individuals within the business community mobilized their formidable political resources behind demands for high-quality academic education—thus focusing and, in effect, serving as a vanguard for the broader, more diffuse constituency for reform at the grassroots. The combination amounted to political dynamite, and, by the early 1980s, politicians and educational professionals were tripping all over themselves to demonstrate their genuine interest in educational reform. The same old problem, however, hung on: what exactly could be done to promote academic excellence? The reformers had achieved enough power, it appeared, to pressure successfully for change, but they did not know what changes to pressure for.

This situation gave rise, over just a few years, to literally hundreds of official commissions empowered to study (or review studies of) America's schools and to explore and suggest ideas for reform. Some of these commissions were set up by the state and federal governments. Some were funded by private foundations, whose energetic participation in educational reform both reflected and reinforced the highly charged political atmosphere.[22]

The commissions' findings were on the whole scathingly critical of the public schools.[23] But as often happens in politics, a single event proved to be a watershed. In this case it was the April 1983 report of the National Commission on Excellence in Education, which almost immediately came to symbolize the nation's dissatisfaction with the quality of public education and its commitment to meaningful reform. The eighteen-member panel, appointed some two years earlier by Secretary of Education Terrel H. Bell, painted a grim picture of "A

Nation at Risk" and offered what is doubtless the most memorable characterization to have emerged from this period of formal assessment: "The educational foundations of our society," the panel warned, "are presently being eroded by a rising tide of mediocrity that threatens our very future as a Nation and a people."[24] The panel went on to recommend specific reforms designed to stem the tide and promote excellence in education. Besieged by requests for copies of the report, the Department of Education distributed some six million of them within a year.[25]

In their typically disjoint fashion, the states had been moving toward educational reform before "A Nation at Risk" appeared. Afterward, however, their piecemeal efforts coalesced into a forceful national movement for academic excellence, and the reforms that followed were far more extensive in breadth and magnitude than anything the nation had seen since the early years of Progressive institution-building. The pace of change was frenetic. State after state adopted some permutation of a laundry list of reforms that, in the course of public study and debate, had come to be associated with effective education: stricter graduation requirements, more rigorous standards for teacher certification, higher teacher salaries, career ladders and (occasionally) merit pay for teachers, stricter disciplinary policy, more homework, longer school days or years, and greater reliance on standardized tests of student performance, among others.[26]

Toward the end of the decade, this "first wave" of reforms was followed by public deliberation of more far-reaching proposals for engineering better schools—notably, through school-based management, teacher empowerment and professionalism, and controlled choice for parents and students. This "second wave" of the reform movement, still under way at this writing, has achieved political success in a limited number of school districts around the country—Chicago, Rochester, and Dade County are prominent examples—and, if anything, it appears to be gathering momentum. Reformers are excited and optimistic about the future.[27]

During the 1980s education became a powerful force at the federal level as well—although largely on symbolic grounds, since the federal government takes a back seat to the states on educational matters. William Bennett, who succeeded Terrel Bell as secretary of education, proved an articulate, hard-hitting spokesman for the cause of academic excellence, grabbing media headlines and urging policymakers at all levels to take aggressive action. During the presidential primaries and general election of 1988, educational reform took on the status of a motherhood issue for candidates of both parties and various ideological stripes—with the winner, George Bush, declaring amidst great fanfare his intention of becoming the "education president." In September of 1989, the president met with the nation's governors at a historic "Education Summit" in Charlottesville, Virginia, publicizing and promoting the cause of school reform.[28]

To many in the educational community, the last decade has represented a period of revolutionary change. And judged by the bench mark of the last several decades—the decades following the entrenchment of the "one best system"—this is perhaps a fair characterization. Viewed more generally, however, these changes do not add up to much of a revolution. While the sheer numbers and varieties of reform might somehow seem impressive, and while they certainly do call for serious changes in school organization, personnel, and practice, virtually all reforms, including those in the much-touted second wave, are cut from the same institutional mold.

As was true for earlier episodes of political conflict and reform, the struggle for academic excellence was played out in an institutional context that was itself taken for granted. This was not a struggle over whether the schools should be governed through direct democratic control. It was a struggle over *how* that control was to be exercised and thus over the kinds of rules that school boards, superintendents, district office bureaucracies, departments of education, and legislatures should impose on local schools and their personnel in order to "make" them better. The notion that these institutions might themselves be undermining academic performance, and thus that the pursuit of excellence in education might call for truly fundamental reforms— new institutions of educational governance—was never seriously considered.[29]

Politics, Social Science, and Educational Reform

There are two basic reasons why institutional issues have consistently been ignored. The first is political. When it comes to educational decisionmaking, particularly at the state and local levels where effective authority resides, the most powerful political groups by far are those with vested interests in the current institutional system:

teachers' unions and myriad associations of principals, school boards, superintendents, administrators, and professionals—not to mention education schools, book publishers, testing services, and many other beneficiaries of the institutional status quo.

These groups are opposed to institutional change, or at least any such change that is truly fundamental. Current arrangements put them in charge of the system, and their jobs, revenues, and economic security depend on keeping the basic governance structure pretty much as it is. They do struggle among themselves for power. Most obviously, teachers, as the perennial bureaucratic underlings, are constantly striving to enhance their authority and status. Yet these are intrasystem squabbles among the established players, none of whom ever seriously suggests that, to promote more effective schooling, the system as a whole might possibly require an overhaul. They have a common interest in institutional stability. The vast majority of politicians—in state legislatures and on school boards, especially— therefore have no incentive to take up the cause of institutional reform. Indeed, there would be heavy political costs to pay for even giving the issue serious public consideration. The practical effect is that it never really comes up at all. It is a nonissue.[30]

The educational system is hardly unusual in this regard. All social institutions are protected and stabilized in much the same way. Through their structures and the normal course of their operations, they generate all manner of benefits—for their leaders and members, the recipients of their services, and the suppliers of their inputs, among others—and these beneficiaries naturally resist any fundamental change in the structural arrangements that are the source of their benefits. There is nothing sinister or conspiratorial about this, nor is it something peculiar to politics. It is a normal and unavoidable by-product of social organization.[31]

Something would be strangely amiss, then, if educational administrators, school board members, professionals, teachers, and other established players in the educational system did not strongly oppose institutional reform. If anything is especially interesting about the politics of all this, it is that these defenders of the status quo have faced so little in the way of concerted opposition over the years. Despite all the grumbling, no powerful political groups with a stake in public education—business groups, civil rights groups, civic groups, religious groups—have dedicated themselves to reforming the institutions of educational governance.

Things are different and potentially much more threatening to established interests, however, now that the business community is demanding action on the problem of school quality. So far, though, business's ideas about the problem's causes and possible solutions have had little to do with the basic structure of the system.[32] Its ideas, in fact, have been virtually indistinguishable from the assessments and policy proposals of the established players themselves.

Why has this happened? Why are the potential revolutionaries so hopelessly mainstream? Business, after all, has a genuine interest in discovering the true causes of poor educational performance and in identifying whatever changes in structure and practice might promise significant improvement. Unlike the established players, the business community has strong incentives to take a coldly analytical approach to the problem, and thus to acquire the best possible knowledge about why the problem exists and what can be done about it—and to evaluate, in the process, the full range of policy and institutional options, however unsettling they may be to defenders of the status quo.

There is, however, a division of labor in society when it comes to this sort of thing. Business does not really do its own research on issues of educational performance and reform, but relies instead, as the rest of society does, on the community of social scientists who specialize in educational research.[33] How business and other reformers come to think about causes and solutions, then, depends on how these issues are framed and ultimately answered by social scientists.

This brings us to the second basic reason why institutional issues have been left out of the public debate: the ideas for educational reform are profoundly shaped by the work of social scientists, and social scientists have in fact paid little attention to institutions in their collective attempts over the years to study and explain school performance. The pool of what we might call "scientifically legitimate" ideas—those that, in the view of acknowledged experts, are supported by empirical research and consistent with accepted theories—is thus a highly selective one with almost nothing to say about institutional problems or reforms. When political activists want to know why the schools are so bad and what can be done to turn matters around, the answers they get from social scientists are mainstream answers that fit comfortably with the educational status quo.

Again, this is not the product of some conspiracy against the public interest. The fact is that institutions are difficult targets for social scientific analysis. Most scholars would doubtless be quick to recognize, in the abstract anyway, that different institutional forms are likely to have different consequences for school performance. But the brute reality of American educational practice is that there is just one institutional form by which the public schools are governed, the "one best system." A comparative analysis of alternative institutional forms is generally not possible, therefore, unless attention is restricted to relatively minor institutional details—whether the superintendent is elected or appointed, for example, or whether school board members are elected at large or by district. These sorts of questions have in fact been studied.[34] Larger questions, which involve the consequences of shifting away from the "one best system" altogether, have not. There is essentially nothing out there to study.[35]

The social science of school performance has actually followed a fairly reasonable trajectory under the circumstances. From the beginning, the focus has been on the schools—on their organization, personnel, and funding. In the early years, before much research of any kind had been carried out, the assumption all around was that schools "made a difference" for how much students learned, and that more money, better teachers, better facilities, better leadership, and the like were crucial determinants of performance. This assumption was strongly challenged in a landmark study, *Equality of Educational Opportunity*, carried out by James Coleman and a team of social scientists in the mid-1960s for the U.S. Office of Education under a congressional mandate to explore the issues surrounding desegregation.[36] Because of the impact of this study, the issue of whether schools make a difference was to be the center of controversy for years to come.

Coleman and his associates argued on the basis of extensive empirical data—a rarity in those days—that academic performance was determined almost entirely by background characteristics of students and their peers and hardly at all by characteristics of the schools. The policy implication was grim, particularly for those wanting to engineer better educational opportunities for blacks and other disadvantaged groups: changing school organizations and pumping in more resources—the kinds of things government might actually deliver through new policies—would not significantly affect the educational achievement of students.

The Coleman Report touched off a storm of political controversy. It also raised genuinely provocative intellectual issues about the underlying causes of academic performance, issues that went to the heart of how education scholars had long understood their subject matter. Social scientists responded with a spate of new studies, which, as test scores began their steady decline and public dissatisfaction grew, gave way to a veritable growth industry in educational research on school performance, one that is still booming as we enter the 1990s.

For a while, this line of work largely corroborated the unconventional argument that schools did not count for much.[37] Like the Coleman Report, however, this research generally relied on quantitative measures of educational "inputs"—funding levels, teacher salaries, teacher credentials, numbers of books in the school library—that, as critics complained, did a wholly inadequate job of tapping those aspects of school organization that were most likely to prove important, such as leadership or the quality of teaching. Reliable data on these scores were admittedly costly to collect—which is why, of course, Coleman and the others had been forced to go without them. Yet the methodological point was inescapably correct: the deck would be stacked against finding a significant causal role for school organization until adequate measures for it were somehow obtained.

An alternative approach was to forgo large-scale data sets in favor of intensive case studies of small numbers of schools. This was a low-cost, manageable way for researchers to acquire detailed substantive knowledge about particular organizations. Although researchers were aware that it exacted a price in generality and rigor, they argued that, by selecting their cases judiciously—studying schools commonly regarded as highly effective, for instance, or comparing such schools to those regarded as ineffective—they could still gain considerable insight into the general determinants of performance within the larger population of schools, particularly as the findings of various studies cumulated over time.

This methodology came to dominate social science research on school performance. In increasing numbers, education scholars immersed themselves in the facts of their cases and arrived at the same basic conclusion: school organization does indeed have a significant impact on how much students learn. Doubts about this observation were further reduced by the appearance, in the late 1970s and early 1980s, of a number of highly respected, broadly based studies documenting this same, basic point.[38]

In an ironic twist, one of the strongest arguments for the importance of schools came from James Coleman himself. In *High School Achievement*, Coleman and his coauthors, Thomas Hoffer and Sally Kilgore, used the massive High School and Beyond data set—then newly collected and by far the largest storehouse of information ever gathered on schools—to carry out a comparative study of public and private schools.[39] They concluded that private schools do a better job of educating the typical student than public schools do, and that their superior performance arises from important differences in school organization across sectors. This book stimulated intense controversy over its finding that private schools are better than public schools. Few in the educational community believed it or wanted to hear it.[40] But the underlying theoretical point was never seriously at issue and in fact had become conventional wisdom. Schools matter.

As the research on school performance came into its own over the years, it did more than defuse the troubling claims of the original Coleman Report and put gleams back in the eyes of reformers. It also heightened the intellectual appeal of a broader research agenda. For if school organization mattered, then there were clearly better and worse ways of organizing, and it should be possible through intensive research to identify those aspects or modes of organization that promote effective performance.

By the early 1980s, the findings of all these studies—known collectively as "effective schools research"—were inevitably diverse enough to leave ample room for debate and uncertainty.[41] Yet they were also consistent enough to yield a reasonably clear view of the organizational foundations of effective performance. This view turned out to be roughly what the more traditional strain of conventional wisdom had suggested it ought to be all along, emphasizing, among other things: clear school goals, rigorous academic standards, order and discipline, homework, strong leadership by the principal, teacher participation in decisionmaking, parental support and cooperation, and high expectations for student performance.[42]

Politically, the timing could not have been more perfect. Business pressure and generalized public dissatisfaction had pushed academic excellence and educational reform to the front burners of national and state politics. Reform was about to happen. What all the various players needed—including those whose institutional interests drove them to resist true reform—was the best evidence and knowledge society had to offer about how effective schools might be achieved. Social science was now in a position, however, to provide more than just available evidence and knowledge. It could offer a coherent perspective on effective schools. And so, as hundreds of reform and study commissions were set up by governments and private foundations around the country, there was a striking uniformity to what they learned about problems and solutions. Governments everywhere began moving in roughly the same directions.

Throughout this rush to reform, there remained a yawning gap in social science research that no one paid much attention to or cared much about. Mountains of research had helped identify those aspects of organization that distinguish effective from ineffective schools, but there had been no comparably compelling body of scientific work on the question of how these desirable characteristics could actually be developed and nurtured within existing schools. It is one thing to know what kind of organization promotes effective education. It is quite another to know how to use public policy to engineer that kind of organization. Social science seemed to know a lot about the organizational end to be achieved and almost nothing about how to get there.

What might otherwise have been an important intellectual mystery prompted little consternation among policymakers or reformers. It was another nonissue. Political power and social science research had combined to ensure that the reform movement would see the problem of academic performance entirely in terms of the schools, leaving the traditional system of public education firmly in place as the institutional vehicle through which reform would be channeled and pursued. The engineering question, therefore, was automatically answered by the routine ways in which the system had always gone about its business of direct democratic control: "effective school" characteristics would be imposed on the local schools from above, by political and administrative superiors, through new rules and regulations mandating the changes desired.

For many objectives—tougher academic requirements, more rigorous curricula, better paid teachers—reform simply called for new

legislative or district policies, administered by the educational bureaucracy. Not coincidentally, these have been among the more popular
reforms, adopted amidst great expectations in state after state. Other
aspects of effective organization—cooperative relations with the school,
for instance—were recognized as inherently less amenable to formal
imposition. But these were subject to direct control too, through the
professional side of the democratic control structure. They were
matters of good management and training, matters that could be
taught, learned, and practiced in the interests of better organization.
Whether the means were formal or professional, then, the rationale
of democratic governance in the nation's public education system was,
as it has always been, to "make" schools better by imposing desirable
characteristics on them.

Institutions and Effective Organization

We think these reforms are likely to fail. The reasons take a bit of
explaining, a task that will occupy us throughout this book. Generally
speaking, our pessimism arises from the fact that the last decade's
"revolution" in school reform has been restricted to the domain of
policy, leaving the institutions of educational governance unchanged.
In our view, these institutions are more than simply the democratic
means by which policy solutions are formulated and administered.
They are also fundamental causes of the very problems they are
supposed to be solving.

It is easy enough to see why this view is distinctly unpopular among
politicians and the established interests. It is also easy to understand
why social scientists have shied away from broader institutional issues
in carrying out their research on effective schools, and thus why
problems and solutions have tended to be framed in noninstitutional
terms. Yet the explanations for these developments have nothing to
do with the true relationship, whatever it might be, between schools
and their institutional contexts. And they have nothing to do, in
particular, with the merits of the specific institutional argument we
are making here.

While our perspective on the culpability of prevailing institutions
cannot help being politically radical, it is not intellectually or scientifically radical at all. In fact, its essential features are entirely consistent
with broader social science thinking on the nature of organizations.

On analytical terrain that is familiar to and accepted by education scholars, this institutional perspective simply makes good sense, so much so that we would find it rather odd and implausible to argue the contrary.

Consider the dominant line of theoretical ideas within education. From its earliest years, the social science of education has turned to organization theory as its foundation for understanding schools; and among organization theorists, it is received doctrine that schools are "open systems"—they rely on, interact with, and adapt to their environments in order to survive and prosper as organizations.[43] Almost any textbook on the American education system routinely adopts the open systems perspective and goes on at great length about the vast array of social, economic, and political forces that shape the organization of schools and the workaday lives of principals and teachers.[44]

Understood as open systems, schools are largely explained by the types of environments that surround them. Different types of environments produce different types of schools. The perspective is so deeply ingrained in the discipline that these sorts of aphorisms are reiterated and accepted without question in scholarly work. But if its logic were explored more seriously than it usually is, it would also say something quite obvious, extremely important, and much more substantive about the problem of school effectiveness: when schools turn out to have undesirable characteristics—those conducive to ineffective performance—the most logical culprit ought to be the environment, not the schools themselves. If one really believes that schools are open systems, bad organizational properties must be understood as symptoms rather than causes. The fundamental causes are probably in the environment, and it is there that theory and research on school effectiveness ought to focus.

In practice, however, they have not. The effective schools literature has focused on variables inside and immediately outside the school. It seems to us that its profile of ineffective schools is quite reasonable, as far as it goes, and that it contributes an important and necessary piece of the puzzle to be solved if better schools are ever to be achieved. But so far the wrong puzzle is being solved. The standard view among education scholars (and the reformers who listen to them) is that these profile variables are the causes of ineffective performance and thus are the quantities that need to be manipulated in the interests of school effectiveness. Their automatic presumption is that our institutions of democratic control can be counted on to bring about these changes through new rules and regulations and enlightened management.

None of this comports with the open systems perspective that everyone supposedly accepts. Not only are the alleged causes of poor performance located in the schools rather than their environments, but, ironically, the solution is entrusted to the traditional system—which is the heart and soul of the very same environment that, by open systems logic, is most likely responsible for having generated and nurtured these bad organizations in the first place. If ineffective schools are truly products of their environments, it hardly makes sense to view the "one best system" as a savior. It ought to be the prime suspect.

Theory and Data

At its most abstract, our own theoretical perspective might be stated as follows. All schools—past, present, and future, public and private—develop organizations that reflect and are compatible with their institutional environments, whatever those environments might be. Different environments and, in particular, different systems of institutional control, inherently provide conditions that promote certain kinds of organizations and inhibit others. The result is that different systems tend to give rise over time to different syndromes of educational organization—to schools with distinctive patterns of characteristics. The schools in one institutional environment will tend to be organized differently from the schools in another.

Stated in such general terms, this sounds a lot like the open systems perspective. And it is certainly consistent with it. But, as the ensuing chapters will bear out, our line of reasoning is quite different. We do not, for instance, think of schools as "seeking to survive" or as entering into "exchanges" with their environments. Nor do we build on currently popular descendants of open systems reasoning—which argue, among other things, that schools are "loosely coupled" and acquire organizational features "legitimized" by the larger system.[45] We are not comfortable with a level of abstraction that encourages macroscopic—and usually mysterious—talk about schools and their environments.

Our own perspective is about the choices of people. It is about

students, parents, teachers, principals, school board members, superintendents, politicians, interest group leaders, and others who have
important roles to play in education. We are interested in how these
people make their educational choices, what consequences these choices
have—collectively—for the organization and performance of schools,
and how all this is distinctively shaped by the institutional context.
As we will show, different institutions constrain and aggregate
individual choices in very different ways, and this, in the end, is why
different kinds of organizations emerge, prosper, or fail within them. [46]

In the chapters to follow, then, we will do more than simply assert
that schools are destined to reflect their institutional settings. We will
explain in concrete terms and at some length why this should be the
case, paying special attention to the prevailing system of public
education, to the kinds of decisions people are constrained to make
within it, and to the consequences their decisions jointly have for the
organization of schools.

Our analysis shows that the system's familiar arrangements for
direct democratic control do indeed impose a distinctive structure on
the educational choices of all the various participants—and that this
structure tends to promote organizational characteristics that are ill-
suited to the effective performance of American public schools. This
social outcome is the product of countless individual decisions, but it
is not an outcome that any of the major players would want or intend
if acting alone. It is truly a product of the system as a whole, an
unintended consequence of the way the system works.

Our perspective also suggests that, absent new institutions, the
problem of ineffective performance is likely to continue, however
earnestly reformers may try to engineer effective school characteristics. These desirable properties of organization turn out to be largely
incompatible with the way the system works, and they are unlikely
to take root except under rather special circumstances. This is why,
in addressing the problem of school performance, we place so much
emphasis on institutional reform. If Americans want effective schools,
it appears they must first create new institutions that, in their effects
on the choices of individuals, naturally function to promote rather
than inhibit the right kinds of organizations.

We cannot, of course, marshal all the evidence that might be
necessary to resolve every issue that our theory touches on. But we
do have some important new data to present that sheds light on many

of them. These data derive from an augmentation of the High School and Beyond (HSB) survey, described briefly in appendix A of this book. First administered in 1980 and added to several times since then, HSB is the largest comprehensive data set yet collected on American high schools and their students. The initial survey included some 60,000 students in more than 1,000 public and private high schools, and provided a rich source of information about student achievement, attitudes, activities, and family background. This, as we noted, was the empirical foundation for Coleman, Hoffer, and Kilgore's *High School Achievement*, which touched off a firestorm with its conclusion that private schools are academically more effective than public schools.[47] The Coleman team was unable to go very far in studying the organizational foundations for these performance differences, however, because important aspects of school organization and environment were not part of the original survey.

In 1983–84, we participated in a research consortium created to augment the HSB data base. The result was the Administrator and Teacher Survey (ATS), which went back to about half of the original HSB schools and administered questionnaires to the principal, a sample of thirty teachers, and selected staff members in each. Their responses tell us a good deal more about the schools as organizations—about their relationships with external authorities, their structure and goals, their leadership, their patterns of influence and interaction, their educational practices, and lots of other things. These new data are also described in appendix A. In conjunction with the storehouse of information already supplied by HSB on these same schools and students, they represent the best empirical foundation currently available for exploring the environment, organization, and performance of schools.

The combined ATS-HSB data set presents us with exciting opportunities, but also with daunting challenges. Precisely because it is so massive, so complex, and the product of so many different designers, it is a rather difficult and unwieldy data set for researchers to use, especially when the questions to be investigated are genuinely comprehensive in scope. It threatens to be overwhelming, to bury erstwhile investigators in an avalanche of "facts." We have done our best, through laborious and painstaking efforts over a period of several years, to impose order on all this. We sifted through hundreds of variables, keeping some (220 to be exact) and excluding others, combining many of them into indexes. (The variables and indexes used in our analysis are described in appendix B.) We examined the validity and reliability of all sorts of possible measures. We also pursued a host of methodologies, both for creating new measures and for modeling cause and effect.

This was a complicated process. When all was said and done, however, we came to believe that what the enormous ATS-HSB data set has to say about the environment, organization, and performance of schools is not really all that complicated. In fact, it provides the foundation for an empirical analysis, which we develop sequentially in chapters 3 through 5, that is very simple and straightforward—and quite consistent with the existing empirical research on schools. Three general findings stand out.

One, schools do indeed perform better to the extent that they possess the effective school syndrome of organizational characteristics—to the extent, in other words, that they have such general qualities as clear goals, an ambitious academic program, strong educational leadership, and high levels of teacher professionalism.

Two, the most important prerequisite for the emergence of effective school characteristics is school autonomy, especially from external bureaucratic influence.

Three, America's existing system of public education inhibits the emergence of effective organizations. This occurs, most fundamentally, because its institutions of democratic control function naturally to limit and undermine school autonomy.

Throughout, this book is an attempt to say something about schools in general and why they look and perform as they do. Most of the analysis is therefore carried out on a representative sample of the entire population of American high schools, private as well as public. For all schools in the sample, we have various measures of environment and organization; and these measures, if we have done our job properly, should capture the essential determinants of school performance, regardless of sector. While most education research treats public and private schools separately—indeed, private schools are usually excluded altogether—we have tried to get away from this by understanding all schools in basically the same way.

In two parts of our analysis, however, we do gain additional leverage by comparing across sectors. One is in chapter 2's theoretical discussion, where we set out our institutional perspective on schools.

Our theme that institutions have pervasive consequences for schools is simply much easier to develop and clarify when we are able to contrast how two very different institutional systems work to condition the schools within them. This is especially important given the monopoly that the traditional institutions of direct democratic control have established within the public sector. Were we to restrict our attention to public schools, there would be substantially less institutional variation to explore—and less of a basis for appreciating how seriously constraining the traditional system of public education is.

The second use of sectoral comparison is in chapter 5, which puts the finishing touches on our empirical analysis. There, after demonstrating the importance of autonomy for effective organization in all schools, we show that private schools are organized more effectively than public schools are and that this is a reflection of their far greater autonomy from external (bureaucratic) control. Some public schools are able to achieve comparable levels of autonomy and organizational effectiveness—but these are the lucky ones (in relatively problem-free suburbs) whose unusually "nice" environments happen to be conducive to weak bureaucratic control. The more typical public schools cannot count on such good fortune. The institutional deck is heavily stacked against them, putting them at a serious disadvantage.

We do not offer these sectoral comparisons to glorify private schools or to disparage public schools. Our overriding purpose is simply to try to understand schools, all schools, as best we can. More specifically, we want to try to build a theoretically coherent, well-documented foundation of real use in addressing issues currently salient in both politics and social science—issues having to do, for the most part, with America's public schools and what might be done to improve them.

Private schools are important to this exercise, but not because they seem to be better performers. They would be just as important if they turned out to be poorer performers. From an analytical standpoint, the crucial feature of private schools is that they emerge and operate under very different institutional conditions than the public schools do. By incorporating them in our study and taking account of cross-sector differences, we are better able to get a handle on how environment, organization, and performance fit together—and better positioned, in the end, to gain insight into the public schools, their problems, and reforms that might actually work.

Asking the Right Questions

What is the relationship between democratic control and the organization of schools? Is it possible that there is something inherent in America's traditional institutions of democratic governance that systematically creates and nurtures the kinds of schools that no one really wants? Might it be that genuine, well-intended efforts to "make" the schools better through direct democratic control are destined to make them worse instead?

We cannot say that we know the answers to these questions for certain. No one can. We think it is clear, however, that institutions are fundamental to an understanding of schools, and that, to this point, the public debate about school effectiveness and educational reform has paid little serious attention to them.[48] Questions cannot be answered if they are not even raised. This book is an attempt to do something about that. We want to raise what we think are the right kinds of questions and, through a combination of theory and evidence, try our best to provide reasonable answers.

Because our institutional perspective reflects so poorly on the current system, and because it leads us to recommend a wholly different system—one built around school autonomy and parent-student choice rather than direct democratic control—our perspective will doubtless be met with disfavor among those who normally speak with authority on educational matters. Social scientists with more conventional views will soon respond with analyses of their own to argue that various aspects of our argument do not stand up to scrutiny. We have confidence in the analysis we present here, and we think this kind of exchange is healthy and productive. But we also think that who is right and who is wrong about the specifics is less important in the short term than the kinds of ideas people see as worth arguing about. This is what will drive knowledge, debate, and change in the future. Our book is, above all else, an effort to convince our readers that institutions are worth arguing about, that the "one best system" is worth arguing about—and that many of the issues actually debated among politicians, academics, and reformers are probably not worth arguing about at all.

Chapter Two

An Institutional Perspective on Schools

T HE AMERICAN public school system is bureaucratic and political. This is a simple, accurate description that, in itself, carries no value judgment; for, despite the negative connotations so often attached to these characteristics, neither is intrinsically bad or undesirable. Virtually all organizations of any size are in some sense bureaucratic. They rely on hierarchy, division of labor, specialization, formal rules, and the like in order to coordinate and control their members toward common ends, and it is clear enough that some measure of bureaucracy is often quite necessary for effective social action.[1] Similarly, the public schools are no different from other government agencies in being political. All organizations in the public sector are shaped and surrounded by democratic politics, and, in some form at least, this is clearly necessary if democracy is to work.[2]

The institutional perspective we develop in this chapter, however, will suggest that the public school system suffers from very serious problems along both these dimensions. We will argue that it has a bureaucracy problem and a politics problem, and that the two are closely related. Its bureaucracy problem is not that the system is bureaucratic at all, but that it is too heavily bureaucratic—too hierarchical, too rule-bound, too formalistic—to allow for the kind of autonomy and professionalism schools need if they are to perform well. Its political problem is not that it is subject to any sort of democratic politics, but that the specific political institutions by which the schools are governed actively promote and protect this over-bureaucratization.

The bureaucracy problem is the more immediate explanation for the schools' poor academic performance. The politics problem is the

26

more fundamental: it explains the bureaucracy problem. Political institutions are the key to understanding why the public school system is not doing its job.[3]

Politics and Markets

Any effort to develop an institutional perspective on schools runs immediately into a basic problem. In order to show that institutions have important consequences for schools, one needs to show that institutional variation leads to a variation in schools—yet American public schools are all governed through highly uniform institutions of direct democratic control. There is no significant variation in institutions on which to base an enlightening analysis.

Our solution to this problem is to look beyond the public school system and seek out alternative institutional arrangements to which it can be compared. This is why we find the private sector so useful. It helps us compare institutions—and thus, in the process, understand the public schools.

The private sector is not as homogeneous as the public sector, and this complicates matters a bit.[4] About half of all private schools are Catholic, and the rest are a diverse lot of religious schools, college preparatory schools, military academies, schools for children with special problems or talents, and many other types of schools as well. All schools in the private sector, however, have two important institutional features in common: society does not control them directly through democratic politics, and society does control them—indirectly—through the marketplace. This is what makes the private sector distinctively different from the public sector as an institutional setting for schools.

Education is hardly unique in this respect, of course. Throughout American society, democratic control and markets are the two major institutions by which social decisions get made and social resources get allocated, and they rather consistently distinguish the public and private sectors. Governments rely on democratic control almost regardless of what they are attempting to accomplish, while in the private sector virtually all activities of a productive or commercial nature (as well as many other sorts of activities) are heavily structured by markets. Questions about which is more efficient, more just, or somehow better have long been the stuff of classic debates in political and economic theory. And less monumental variants—having to do, for instance, with the privatization of certain governmental services or the extension of democratic controls into new, previously private spheres—are practical issues that find their way into politics every day.[5]

In this chapter, we build our own perspective on schools around a comparison of these preeminent social institutions. As we do so, we will not try to represent all the variety and complexity we know to characterize schools in the public and private sectors. Our aim is to get beyond much of the detail of schooling in the two sectors and to focus attention on what is theoretically most important about them— their distinctive institutions. In this way, we hope to clarify the major differences that these institutions seem to make for the schools within them.

Authority and Decisionmaking

The place to begin in comparing democratic control and markets is with the distinctive ways in which they allocate authority and prescribe rules for exercising it. These properties set the foundation for educational decisionmaking, determining who has the right to make what kinds of educational decisions in what ways.

The public sector is built around public authority. Democratic institutions allocate decisionmaking rights by attaching public authority to elected and appointed positions of government—for example, school board seats and superintendencies—and by setting out rules that specify who can occupy these positions and how the authority attached to them must be exercised. The "winners" under these rules—including, implicitly, individuals and groups whose interests the officeholders represent—have the legal right to make public policies and to devise governmental structures that are binding on everyone in the polity. The "losers" have the obligation to accept and help finance these policies and structures, however much they may be opposed to them.

In this sense, democracy is essentially coercive. The winners get to use public authority to impose their policies on the losers. Teachers' unions, for example, might prevail over the opposition of administrators or parents on some issues. On others, business groups might succeed in imposing reforms fought by the unions. What makes this peculiar form of coercion broadly acceptable is that public authority does not belong to any individual or group. It is up for grabs. Anyone who plays by the rules and gains sufficient popular support has the same right as anyone else to take control of public authority and to specify the legitimate means and ends of public policy for everyone.

These properties supply the motive force behind democratic politics. Because public authority is enormously valuable and widely available, individuals and groups representing a diverse range of social interests have strong incentives to try to capture it, to exercise it toward ends they deem appropriate, and to prevent their opponents from doing the same. The result is a perpetual struggle for the control of public authority. During elections, the various interests struggle to place their partisans in public offices. Between elections, they struggle to influence how officials actually exercise their authority. Through it all, public authority remains a blank check on which everyone wants to write.

Public authority is also important for market institutions, but its role is far less central to decisionmaking. For markets to operate, governments must create a legal framework that specifies and enforces property rights. They must use their public authority, in other words, to impose a system of rules for determining who owns what property and for assigning to owners the authority to make certain choices about its disposition. Once such a framework is created, individuals are free to enter into exchanges with one another as they see fit, and markets take over.

Effective authority within market settings, then, is radically decentralized. In private sector education, the people who run each school decide what they will teach, how they will teach it, who will do the teaching, how much to charge for their services, and virtually everything else about how education will be organized and supplied.[6] Students and parents assess the offerings, reputations, and costs of the various schools and make their own choices about which to attend. No one makes decisions for society. All participants make decisions for themselves.

The kind of authority that market participants exercise, while public in origin, is extremely limited in scope. The owners of a school have the legal authority to create whatever kind of school they please, but they cannot require anyone to attend or finance it. They have authority over their own property, not over the property of others. Similarly, parents and students have the right to seek out whatever kinds of schools they like. But they cannot force schools to adopt specific courses, hire certain teachers, or pursue certain values. Nor can they force schools to grant them admission. They make decisions for themselves, not for the schools.

The key elements that supply the motivational foundation of democratic politics—the tremendous value, wide availability, and coercive power of public authority—are essentially absent from the marketplace. Individuals and groups do not struggle to capture something that is not there. In markets, their focus is much more myopic. They try to achieve their ends through voluntary exchange with others, and the benefits they receive arise from these transactions. The key to success—for schools, parents, and students alike—is having something to offer that other people want.

Constituents and Consumers

Almost everyone's first impulse is to think that the purpose of schools is to provide children with academic training, with essential information about society and the world, with an understanding of citizenship in a democracy, or something of the sort. On reflection, however, it should be apparent that schools have no immutable or transcendent purpose. What they are supposed to be doing depends on who controls them and what those controllers want them to do.

In the public sector, schools are controlled by whoever controls public authority. Popular myth, of course, lauds the role of local citizens and their elected school boards, but this is misleading. The public schools are not really "locally controlled" and are not supposed to be. The authority exercised by local governments is delegated to them by the states and can be modified or revoked at the states' pleasure. More generally, public authority over schools is legally vested in democratic institutions at all levels. State and federal governments—and thus their constituents—have legitimate roles to play in financing schools, setting standards, and otherwise making and imposing their own educational policies and organizational structures. This means that citizens everywhere, whether or not they have children in school and whether or not they live in the local school district or even the state, have a legitimate hand in governing each and every local school. They are all controllers.

The heterogeneous interests of all these constituents do not automatically find faithful reflection in the policies and structures of government. Democracy, like all other institutions, works imperfectly. Political resources are unequally distributed. The interest group system is biased in favor of some interests over others (the organized over the unorganized, especially). Politicians and administrators sometimes pursue their own interests at the expense of citizens' interests. And so on. As a result, who wins and who loses in politics is not necessarily representative of what ordinary citizens actually want.[7]

These are well-known problems that plague all democracies in one way or another, and they are the sorts of things that attract attention from many critics of American public education. They think the education system would be vastly improved if democracy's imperfections could somehow be overcome. Even if this were possible, however, the fact remains that democratic politics would still be a competitive struggle for the control of public authority. It would still be a game of winners and losers. On any given issue, the winners might include various combinations of interests: those of teachers' unions, associations of professionals, book publishers, ideological groups, or factions among the citizenry at large. But everyone cannot win, and the losers have to take what the winners dish out. This is the single most important thing to know about how interests get represented in a democracy. It is not an imperfection. It is what democratic control is all about.

Notice that we have said nothing so far about parents and students. The myth that parents and students are uniquely special in all this—that the schools are somehow supposed to be what parents and students want them to be—goes hand-in-hand with the myth of local control, and it is equally misleading. The proper constituency of even a single public school is a huge and heterogeneous one whose interests are variously represented by politicians, administrators, and groups at all levels of government. Parents and students are but a small part of this constituency.

A frequent complaint is that parents and students are not well enough organized to be very powerful. In the struggle to control public authority, they tend to be far outweighed by teachers' unions, professional organizations, and other entrenched interests that, in practice, have traditionally dominated the politics of education. This is true enough. But what it implies is that parents and students would get the kind of schools they wanted if they could somehow gain "appropriate" clout—if democracy, in other words, were less imperfect and did a better job of reflecting their interests. This is simply not the case.

The fundamental point to be made about parents and students is not that they are politically weak, but that, even in a perfectly functioning democratic system, the public schools are *not meant* to be theirs to control and are literally *not supposed* to provide them with the kind of education they might want. The schools are agencies of society as a whole, and everyone has a right to participate in their governance. Parents and students have a right to participate too. But they have no right to win. In the end, they have to take what society gives them.

In the private sector, the situation of parents and students would appear to be worse still. There they have no legal right to control the schools at all. The authority to control each private school is vested in the school's owner—which may be an individual, a partnership, a church, a corporation, a nonprofit agency, or some other form of organization—and the owner has the legal right to make all the decisions about policy and structure that, in the public sector, are matters for "the people" and their representatives to struggle over. Despite the formal dominance of owners, however, markets work to ensure that parents and students play a much more central and influential role in private sector education than they do when democracy gives them formal rights to govern. There are three basic reasons for this.

The first is that those who own and run the schools have a strong incentive to please a clientele of parents and students through the decisions they make.[8] This sort of responsiveness is perhaps the most obvious path by which markets promote a match between what parents and students want and the kind of education their schools provide. It is not necessarily the most important, however.

The second arises from a basic prerequisite of market choice: people have the freedom to switch from one alternative to another when they think it would be beneficial to do so. If parents and students do not like the services they are being provided at any given school, they can exit and find another school whose offerings better meet their needs.[9] Even if schools were entirely unresponsive to their clienteles, then, this process of selection and sorting would tend to encourage a match between what parents and students want and the kind of education they receive.

The third arises from a basic property of markets that operates on the population of schools as a whole: natural selection.[10] Schools that fail to satisfy a sufficiently large clientele will go out of business (or, if subsidized, become an increasing burden to their patron organizations, generating pressures that work in the same direction). Of the schools that survive, those that do a better job of satisfying consumers will be more likely to prosper and proliferate. They may be joined or challenged at any time, moreover, by new schools that enter the marketplace to offer similar services in a better way, or perhaps to appeal to specialized segments of consumer demand that are not being met adequately. The dynamics of entry, success, and failure, driven by the requisites of parent-student support, all tend to promote the emergence of a population of schools that matches the population of parents and students.

A standard claim about public schools is that there are strong forces, including quasi-market forces, that tend to promote this kind of matching in them as well.[11] For instance, although the local public school is usually a monopoly, in the sense that all children living in a designated geographical area are typically assigned to a particular school, parents and students can still exercise exit and choice by taking account of school quality in deciding where to live. If they like the schools, they can move into the area. If they do not like them, they can move out.

It is true that residential mobility does tend to promote the kind of matching that occurs in markets; but it is a very rough and inadequate approximation to the real thing, even for those citizens affluent enough to move where they want when they want. In general, residential decisions involve many factors in addition to education—proximity to work, quality of housing, availability of public services—and, once they are made, the financial costs and personal adjustments entailed by moving are quite high. Low or declining educational quality need not keep parents from moving into an area, and it is even less likely to prompt existing residents to pick up and leave.

It might prompt them to consider a private school—another exit option that would help drain off the disgruntled and improve the average satisfaction of those who are left in the public sector. But here parents confront a major disincentive: public schools are free, private schools are not. Because of this cost differential, the perceived value of private schools must far outweigh that of public schools if they are to win students. To put it the other way around: public schools, because they are relatively inexpensive, can attract and hold students without being particularly good at educating them.

Lacking feasible exit options, then, whether through residential mobility or escape into the private sector, many parents and students will "choose" a public school despite dissatisfaction with its goals, methods, personnel, and performance. Having done so, they have a right to try to remedy the situation through the democratic control structure. But everyone else has the same right, and the determinants of political power are stacked against them. Democracy cannot remedy the mismatch between what parents and students want and what the public schools provide. Conflict and disharmony are built into the system.

While this is an inherent feature of democratic control, we do not mean to imply that markets are somehow capable of perfectly satisfying parents and students. Obviously, they are not. Markets are inevitably subject to all sorts of real-world imperfections, just as democratic institutions are. Monopolizing, price-fixing, territorial agreements, and other restrictive practices by producers may limit the choices available to consumers. Consumers may be too poorly informed to make choices that are truly in their best interests. Transportation costs may eliminate many options. The unequal distribution of income in society may bias certain markets in favor of the rich and against the poor. To the extent that these and other imperfections are serious, markets are less likely to generate the diversity, quality, and levels of services that consumers want, and prices are likely to be higher than they otherwise would be.

These imperfections cannot be eliminated. They can be (and in fact are) substantially reduced by various means—antitrust laws, consumer information services, publicly assisted transportation, progressive taxation, and direct subsidies (for example, food stamps, housing vouchers), among others. These are governmental actions that, like the rules specifying and enforcing property rights, help create a framework more conducive to the beneficial operation of markets.[12]

It is a mistake, however, to place too much emphasis on these sorts of imperfections, just as it is a mistake to be obsessed with the imperfections of democratic control. Both systems are inherently imperfect. Both are easily criticized when compared with an ideal social state—the perfect market, the perfect democracy—that does not exist and never will. It is much more instructive to compare real-world institutions in terms of their basic, distinguishing properties and essential features. The crucial thing is not that they are imperfect, but that they are different.

When it comes to the basic issue of whose interests find reflection in society's schools, these two systems clearly function under real-world conditions to promote very different social outcomes. Under a system of democratic control, the public schools are governed by an enormous, far-flung constituency in which the interests of parents and students carry no special status or weight. When markets prevail, parents and students are thrust onto center stage, along with the owners and staff of schools; most of the rest of society plays a distinctly secondary role, limited for the most part to setting the framework within which educational choices get made. These differences are absolutely fundamental to the two systems, however imperfectly each may work in practice.

Bureaucracy and Autonomy

So far, we have discussed how democratic control and markets allocate authority and attach weight to social interests. These are rather abstract concerns that may seem to have very little to do with something so concrete as the organization of schools. But in fact they have a great deal to do with it. To see why, let's turn to what many educators view as the most fundamental organizational issue facing the schools today: the issue of bureaucracy versus autonomy.

Markets: Decentralization and Discretion

While markets decentralize effective decisionmaking authority to the suppliers and consumers of services, they do not automatically give rise to organizational structures that are themselves decentralized. The economic system obviously boasts all sorts of organizational forms, some of them highly centralized bureaucracies in which subordinate levels of organization have little discretion. Presumably, an educational market system might do the same if centralized organization were an efficient way to supply educational services that satisfy parents and students.

As a rule, however, this is unlikely to be so. One very basic reason has to do with the technical requirements of producing educational services. Because education is based on personal relationships and interactions, on continual feedback, and on the knowledge, skills, and experience of teachers, most of the necessary technology and resources are inherently present in the school itself, and thus are at the bottom of the organizational hierarchy (if there is one). Higher-level administrative units have little to contribute that is not already there.[13]

It is no accident, for example, that so much attention in both the academic literature and the policymaking process has focused on teacher professionalism. True professionalism requires not simply that teachers be experts in their subject matters and the methodology of learning, but also that they have the autonomy to exercise discretion in applying it to the infinitely varying individuals and circumstances that make up their jobs. The widely accepted notion that education would be better if teachers were treated as professionals is but another way of saying that the schools already have (or should already have) what it takes to provide quality education—they just have to be allowed to use it.[14]

A second basic reason has to do with the purely administrative requirements of controlling education from above. Effective bureaucracy is commonly built around rules that specify appropriate behavior, rewards and sanctions that encourage such behavior, and monitoring to ascertain whether goals are being met, whether rules are being followed, when rewards and sanctions are called for, and whether rules and incentive systems need to be adjusted. All are rendered highly problematic in education, because good education and the behaviors conducive to it are inherently difficult to measure in an objective, quantifiable, formal manner.[15] The measurement problem makes it difficult or impossible for education administrators to know what they are doing—and their controls, as a result, threaten to be ill suited to the ends they want to achieve.

While virtually everyone in a given school typically knows who the good teachers are, for instance, their assessments arise from actual experience and judgment, not from formal tests of teaching competence. As teachers are quick to point out, there are no formal tests that can adequately tap the intangible qualities that make someone good or bad at the job, it is impossible to hand down a set of rules from on high that will somehow transform bad teachers into good ones—and it is organizationally counterproductive to reward and sanction teachers on these grounds.[16] For the most part, the people at the bottom of the hierarchy do not have a serious measurement problem. They essentially solve it without really trying, just by taking part in the everyday life of the school. The people at the top are the ones with the measurement problem. The organization as a whole has a serious measurement problem only to the extent that there are people at the top who try to control the people at the bottom.

A third reason why centralized organization is unlikely to prove efficient arises from the market constraint that schools must, above all else, please their clients. The school staff members who interact with students and parents day in and day out are in a far better position than administrators to sense whether their clients are happy with the services they are getting. They are also better able to devise and implement whatever adjustments might be necessary to enhance the school's appeal. Again, they know what administrators cannot because it is a natural, integral part of their work in the schools.

A common demand on the part of parents and students is that students need to be treated and understood as individuals if they are to make the most of their educational experience. Given the variety of human personalities and family environments, this happens to make good scientific sense as well.[17] Principals and teachers can get to know their students, gain a sense for their special needs and talents, and respond accordingly. Administrators cannot. Administrators know students in terms of numbers, categories, rules, summary statistics, theories, and methods, all of which lead to precisely the kind of treatment that parents and students do not want: treatment that is insensitive to what is different or special or unique about them. Bureaucracy inherently requires equal treatment for people who are in fact very different. Schools can recognize and respond to those differences—as long as they are unconstrained by bureaucracy.

In a market setting, then, there are strong forces at work—arising from the technical, administrative, and consumer-satisfaction requirements of organizational success—that promote school autonomy. Organizations that want to build and nurture successful schools will have incentives to decentralize authority to the school level. Similarly, schools that exist on their own, as well as individuals and groups that

want to start schools from scratch, will tend to find that the requirements of success do not entail highly bureaucratic organization and
indeed militate against it.

The advantages of autonomy are weakened when school leaders
have agendas of their own that schools are intended to further,
regardless of what parents and students might want. In some organizations—churches, for instance—those in charge may prefer "pure"
schools to growing, prosperous ones, and the obvious way to see that
their schools toe the line is through bureaucratic subordination. In
private sector education, however, just as in other market settings,
the hierarchical imposition of such an agenda on schools involves a
painful trade-off: if schools are constrained in their efforts to please
clients, dissatisfied clients can leave. Superiors seeking purity in their
schools may consider this an acceptable price to pay, but it is still a
price—one that threatens organizational well-being, can be fatal if
unchecked, and can be countered by granting the schools a greater
measure of autonomy. Thus, even if there are higher-order values to
be pursued, market forces still discourage tight hierarchical control
in favor of more autonomy. They also tend to weed out, through
natural selection, organizations that ignore these market signals.

Politics: Bureaucracy and Hierarchical Control

In the public sector, the institutional forces work in the opposite
direction. The raison d'être of democratic control is to impose higher-
order values on schools, and thus to limit their autonomy. The schools
are not in the business of pleasing parents and students, and they
cannot be allowed to set their own agendas. Their agendas are set by
politicians, administrators, and the various democratic constituencies
that hold the keys to political power. The public system is built to see
to it that the schools do what their governors want them to do—that
they conform to the higher-order values their governors seek to
impose.

Bureaucracy arises naturally and inevitably out of these efforts at
democratic control. While most everyone seems to complain that the
public schools are overly bureaucratized, American political institutions
give all the major players strong incentives to pressure for more
bureaucracy, not less, when official decisions get made about what
the schools ought to be doing, who should be doing it, and how. The

same people who complain about bureaucracy find that it is their dominant political strategy.

To see why, we must first recognize that public authorities do not have the luxury of creating an organization de novo. The Constitution and countless federal, state, and local laws made pursuant to it already set out a structure of democratic authority—a massive, fragmented, multilevel "organization" blanketing the entire country—in which various offices have certain rights to impose decisions on the local schools.[18] There is no analogue to the private sector owner who exercises concentrated authority in designing an organization. Instead, there are multiple "owners"—authorities at the federal, state, and local levels—who all have legitimate roles to play within the existing "organization." They all have some authority to shape and control the schools, and they all inevitably come under pressure from organized groups and constituents to put their authority to use. The question is not whether they will use their authority, but how.

Consider the situation from the standpoint of those who exercise authority at the federal level. They are in a position to impose higher-order values on the schools through policies of their own choosing. For federal authorities to succeed, however, they must somehow ensure that their policies—which many people in local communities may flatly disagree with—get implemented as they want. They do not have any choice but to exercise hierarchical control. In doing so, they face some of the same technical problems—the bottom-heavy nature of education technology and the difficulty of measuring school performance—that private owners face. But they also face, as all government authorities do, two other kinds of problems that are especially severe because of the democratic "organization" in which their control efforts must take place.[19]

First, they cannot assume that principals and teachers will expertly harness their energies, talents, and resources toward federally imposed policies. If federal policymakers had the authority, they could act like private owners and choose their own principals and teachers on grounds of philosophy, personal goals, expertise, or even loyalty. But they do not have that authority, and they are unable to do much of anything to guarantee that their policies do not end up in the hands of school personnel who disagree with their goals, who find the prerequisites of effective implementation to be burdensome or objectionable, or who are simply not competent enough to be effective.[20] The misuse of federally granted discretion, therefore, can easily be serious and widespread. To make matters worse, federal authorities are far removed and cannot directly observe what is going on in each and every local school around the country. Thus they cannot easily tell where or when their grants of discretion are being put to bad use.

Second, these dangers of noncompliance and ineffectiveness are rendered far more threatening by the presence of multiple authorities within the democratic "organization." Any discretion left in the hands of school personnel is subject to legitimate influence and control by other democratic authorities at the state and local levels. These authorities have their own groups and constituencies to look out for and their own political interests to pursue. Given the opportunity, they can be expected to turn discretionary programs and federally supplied resources toward ends that may be at odds with federal intentions.

Given the widespread incentives and opportunities for noncompliance, the most attractive solution is simply to bureaucratize the implementation of policy. Through bureaucracy, federal officials can strategically reduce the discretion of school personnel by specifying the kinds of behavior they want—and requiring them by law. They can insist on the adoption of specific practices, procedures, and decision criteria they think are most conducive to federal policy goals; they can impose information-collecting, reporting, and monitoring requirements as means of holding schools accountable for their performance; and they can impose sanctions for noncompliance. It is no surprise that federal education programs, which now number nearly one hundred, are constantly criticized by lower-level authorities for being excessively bureaucratized.[21]

The incentives to bureaucratize the schools are somewhat different for different levels of government. Those who exercise authority at the federal (especially) and the state levels, for instance, are farther away from what actually happens within the schools, have much larger and more diverse populations of schools (and personnel and competing authorities) to worry about, and are probably more prone to extensive formal controls than districts and other local governments are. But even at the local level, where consolidated city and county school systems serve large populations—sixty-two different school districts now serve at least 50,000 students each—there will still be strong incentives to pursue school-level compliance through an array of bureaucratic controls.[22]

The general point is the important one. All public authorities, in seeking to impose higher-order values on schools—values that many in society, including many in the schools, may not embrace—face serious control problems that are endemic to the larger democratic "organization" in which they are forced to operate. They cannot solve these problems by granting the schools lots of discretion. Discretion is the very source of their problems. The best means of ensuring that their values get implemented is to engineer the schools' behavior through formal constraints—to bureaucratize.

From a technical standpoint, of course, this is far from ideal. Given the bottom-heavy technology of education and the measurement problems inherent in trying to control it, bureaucracy is a clumsy and ineffective way of providing people with educational services. Within the context of American democratic institutions, however, those who seek to impose higher-order values through public authority have no better options. Discretion and autonomy are out of the question. Bureaucratizing the schools is their best strategy.

Politics: Bureaucracy and Political Uncertainty

The problem of hierarchical control is perhaps the most straightforward reason why those who exercise political authority would actively impose bureaucratic forms of organization on the schools. But the pressures favoring bureaucracy in the American system are much greater than this suggests. There is something inherent in democratic politics, in the ongoing struggle to capture and exercise public authority, that adds significantly to its strategic appeal. This has little to do, at least directly, with recalcitrant subordinates or multiple levels of authority. It is about the *right* to govern, and the political uncertainty of gaining and holding onto it in the future.[23]

Perhaps the best way to illustrate this is to consider how interest groups are motivated to play the game of democratic politics. Groups advocating all sorts of social interests regularly engage in competitive struggles to exercise public authority, and those that succeed have legal rights (in effect) to impose their values on the schools. What should they do to see that their values are pursued as effectively as possible? In part, for all the reasons we just discussed, their solution is to use bureaucracy as a means of controlling schools from above. But this is not the whole of it. For, owing to the political uncertainty inherent in democratic politics, hierarchical control turns out to be a two-edged sword.

Unlike school owners in the private sector, those groups that gain access to public authority do not have property rights that guarantee them continuing authority over the schools. Their rights are temporary and can be taken away as new elections, new appointments, changes in political alignments, and all the usual dynamics of democratic politics give other groups heightened access to public authority. Groups fortunate enough to exercise public authority, therefore, know that whatever policies they put in place today threaten to fall under the legitimate democratic control of other groups tomorrow—groups that may act to subvert what proponents have labored so hard to achieve. If proponents want their new policies to flourish, these policies must somehow be insulated from legitimate democratic control by other groups in the future. This means that they must be insulated, so far as possible, from politics and public authority.

How can this be done? The answer is conditioned by the extensive fragmentation of political power that causes American political institutions to be heavily biased in favor of the legal status quo. Separation of powers and federalism, along with myriad checks and balances routinely built into governing institutions at all levels, work to ensure that significant legal change tends to be extremely difficult for proponents to achieve and correspondingly easy for opponents to block. A crucial corollary is that, if proponents succeed in imposing new laws, these laws are then very difficult for other interests to overturn later. The new laws become part of the political landscape, part of the status quo that the system inherently works to protect.

As proponents seek to insulate their favored policies from subversion by future power-holders, then, the most immediate threat is not that their opponents will be able to destroy programs and agencies wholesale. Institutions are structured to discourage this. The real and continuing danger is that opponents will use their authority to influence how existing laws are implemented and how existing structures do their jobs. Their greatest threat is to whatever is left discretionary, and thus to whatever is not clearly, specifically embedded in law.

The best way for groups to protect their achievements from the uncertainties of future politics, therefore, is through formalization: the formal reduction or elimination of discretion, and the formal insulation of any remaining discretion from future political influence. The latter can be pursued through a range of structural devices that imperfectly buffer public organizations. Agency "independence"— defined by rules restricting appointments and removal, how agency budgets are handled, and the like—introduces such buffers. So do aspects of professionalism, since professionals are highly sensitive to the norms of their professional communities and are notoriously difficult for superiors to control. And so does civil service, whose rules (tenure, for instance) insulate public personnel matters from political influence. Groups that want to protect their new policies from subversion will tend to favor these kinds of structures. The great problem, however, is that the people to whom discretion is granted can be counted on to have interests of their own, and they may use their insulation to move in directions that proponents do not want.

The other prong of the formalization strategy addresses this problem as well as the general problem of political uncertainty. It is simple, direct, and leaves as little as possible to the vagaries of the political future: policy proponents can specify precisely what they want the schools to do and build these specifications explicitly into legislative mandates and administrative regulations. In this way they can formally enshrine not only the goals schools are required to pursue, but also the criteria and standards they are to employ, the procedures and methods they are to follow, the types of personnel they are to hire, and virtually anything else of relevance to the implementation of policy. The dangers of political subversion are therefore vastly reduced, because there is little or no discretion left to subvert. This is the ultimate in insulation.

While the technology of education may argue that schools be granted substantial discretion in carrying out a given policy, then, political uncertainty drives the policy's supporters to see school discretion (and thus school autonomy) as politically dangerous and irrational. Supporters want their policies to be well implemented; but, more fundamentally, they have to ensure that their policies survive and are not diverted to other ends when competing interests take hold of public authority later on. So they have little choice but to make trade-offs, and, because of politics, they push for bureaucratic solutions that they know full well are technically inappropriate.

These uncertainty-induced pressures for bureaucracy are compounded by a related feature of the American political system: the need for compromise. While we have discussed how a policy's supporters tend to approach issues of educational structure, the fact is they will usually be unable to get what they want without compromising—thanks, once again, to the institutional fragmentation of power that makes political success so difficult and opposition so easy. How do groups approach compromise? What kinds of arrangements do they demand and find acceptable?

Compromises are agreements among contending, often mutually suspicious, sides that can easily come apart over time if they are informal and subject to discretion. This is true of most contractual arrangements among private parties, but it is especially serious in politics—for, as political power ebbs and flows, what one side gains today might be taken from it tomorrow as the other side assumes control of public authority. The forms compromise can take, therefore, are fundamentally shaped by the political uncertainty that pervades politics more generally. The way groups on both sides can secure themselves against its risks and dangers is, accordingly, to put everything in writing, down to the last detail, and make it legally enforceable—to formalize the agreement. For example, largely as a result of years of compromise among contending political groups, the federal government's largest education program, Chapter 1, has generated 174 pages of statutory amendments and new legislative authority since it began as a 9-page statute providing aid to disadvantaged students in 1965.[24]

In sum, the politics of democratic control promotes the piece-by-piece construction of a peculiar set of organizational arrangements that are highly bureaucratic. As we will see, the precise nature of these arrangements can vary with their context: some contexts promote more bureaucracy than others. In general, though, democratic authorities (and their group supporters) are driven to bureaucratize the schools in response to two basic problems that plague their efforts to impose higher-order values on the schools: hierarchical control and political uncertainty. The former is a problem experienced in all large organizations. The people at the top cannot assume that the people at the bottom will do what they want them to do, so they resort to various bureaucratic means of engineering compliance. The political uncertainty problem, on the other hand, is a trademark of democratic politics. It arises because those in authority have uncertain future rights to govern, and therefore must take steps to protect their favored policies from hierarchical control by opponents who may govern in the future.

These problems jointly determine how bureaucracy is put to use. Those in positions of authority have strong incentives to use bureaucracy as a means of exercising hierarchical control—but, because any control mechanisms they set up might fall into the wrong hands, they also have strong incentives to use bureaucracy as a means of protecting *against* hierarchical control. Bureaucracy is both a means of control and a means of protection.

All this promotes an admixture of organizational properties that lend distinctive structural form to American public education—a form that, were it not for politics, would be perplexing indeed. To put it most generally: schools and their personnel are granted a measure of discretion by technical necessity, but detailed formal specifications in legislative mandates and administrative regulations are voluminously imposed on all concerned, so that the schools' scope for discretionary action is sharply narrowed—and the discretion that remains is then insulated from political control through extensive reliance on civil service, tenure, (nominal) professionalism, and other structural means. Schools are thus subject to democratic control, but they are purposely made difficult to control. Schools are filled with "professionals," but their personnel are systematically and intentionally denied the discretion they need to act as professionals. Schools give the appearance of substantial autonomy, but what they have is insulation without discretion—which is really not autonomy at all.

Politics: Bureaucracy and Bureaucrats

It is all too common for academics and reformers to blame the overbureaucratization of America's public schools on the bureaucrats themselves—and thus, implicitly, to explain bureaucracy as the product of bureaucratic power. We think this is a mistake.

It is true enough that bureaucrats like bureaucracy. The imposition of formal constraints on those below them in the public hierarchy enhances their status, power, and opportunities. This is the essence of their job, it is what they are empowered to do, and it is what they are rewarded for doing. True autonomy for the schools—real discretion in important matters of policy—is the antithesis of the bureaucratic job and the ultimate threat to bureaucratic security. A world of autonomous schools would be a world without educational bureaucrats.

In politics, moreover, bureaucrats routinely take action to advance their pro-bureaucracy interests. As public officials, they have incentives to expand their budgets, programmatic authority, and administrative controls. These are the basics of bureaucratic well-being, and their pursuit is an integral part of the job. Bureaucrats also belong to important interest groups—of administrators, of education "professionals"—that lobby government from the outside (ostensibly) as well. Although traditionally they have tried to portray themselves as nonpolitical experts pursuing the greater good, they are in fact a powerful constellation of special interests dedicated to hierarchical control and the formalization of education.[25]

This said, it is still a mistake to blame bureaucracy on the bureaucrats. America's system of public education emerged and took root not because turn-of-the-century educators and administrators were massively powerful in their own right, but because, over a period of many years, Progressive politicians and interest groups gained increasing control of public authority and used it to support and impose a bureaucratic educational system. By bureaucratizing education, they insulated the schools from the insidious influences of their political enemies: the party machines, the lower classes, ethnic groups, immigrants. By bureaucratizing education, they reduced the discretion of schools and their personnel to ensure that America's children would be "properly" educated, socialized, and disciplined. In a political environment permeated by diverse, threatening interests and powerful opponents, bureaucratization was the key to the Progressives' strategy of imposing their own values and protecting them from future subversion.

Now, as then, bureaucrats are best understood not as political prime movers, but as the creations of those who exercise superior public authority and make the more fundamental decisions about what the structure and personnel of government—including the schools—ought to look like. It is true that bureaucrats benefit from more bureaucracy. They hardly have to be dragged along when groups and politicians insist on creating highly formalized structures that entangle the schools in bureaucratic constraints. But bureaucrats are not the cause of bureaucratization.

The real cause is the public education system as a whole. Its institutions of democratic control are inherently destructive of school autonomy and inherently conducive to bureaucracy. This happens because of the way all the major participants—politicians, interest groups, bureaucrats—are motivated and empowered by their institutional setting to play the game of structural politics. Whatever the technological and intellectual arguments against bureaucracy may be, and however frustrated people from all walks of life may be with the unworkable constraints under which schools are forced to operate, virtually all are driven to pursue their own goals by adding to the bureaucracy problem.[26]

Were the same people picked up and placed in a different system, they would behave differently. Were they placed in a market system, in particular, they would find that decisions about the structure of education were no longer the province of public authority, no longer the product of a struggle to gain legitimate governing status, no longer built around the imposition of higher-order values, and no longer driven by the need for protection against the political uncertainties of the democratic process. Emancipated from the hierarchical imperatives of the democratic "organization," and with property rights—and therefore governing rights—guaranteed, they would be free to adopt structures well suited to the goals they want schools to pursue: structures that, given the technology of education, the difficulties of hierarchical control, and the market requirement of pleasing clients, would tend to grant substantial autonomy to schools and their personnel.

The Organization of Schools

Now let us move from the general to the particular by considering what all this means for the specific features of school organization. To simplify matters, we will take a look at four dimensions that are obviously quite basic and important to the performance of schools: personnel, goals, leadership, and practice.[27] These dimensions, like almost any others we might have employed here, are bound up together and cannot be understood in isolation from one another. Nonetheless, we purposely begin our discussion with personnel, for it raises a fundamental distinction between political and market institutions—the role of teachers' unions—that we have yet to deal with explicitly, and, for reasons that will become apparent, it has a special role to play in promoting strikingly different syndromes of organization across sectors.

Personnel

In the public sector, principals are likely to find that their control over who works at their school and how staff incentives are structured is significantly limited. The reason is that personnel decisions are constrained, if not dictated, by formal rules designed and imposed by higher levels of government.

For the most part, these rules have two concrete sources. First, they arise from tenure laws, certification requirements, and other civil-service-like protections enacted by public officials over the years to insulate teachers from political influence. These reforms—which, for reasons inherent in the democratic struggle, have long been widely endorsed by groups, politicians, and bureaucrats of all political stripes— put an end to the early use of schools for political patronage. They also ensured that principals would have limited discretion in choosing or motivating school personnel.

The second source of formalization is teachers' unions. When party machines reigned supreme in politics, teachers' unions were resisted by politicians wedded to spoils. But as the old arrangements of power broke down over time and party politics gave way to interest group politics, unions found powerful allies—and success. Organized teachers could offer money, manpower, publicity, and votes to politicians eager for electoral support; and, especially in state and local elections, where turnout is typically very low, these proved to be attractive inducements indeed. The transformation took decades, but eventually the vast majority of public school teachers came to be unionized, and unions came to be an established power in the politics of education.[28]

Most personnel matters are now subject to collective bargaining between the unions and the relevant public authorities, usually those representing the school district. Through collective bargaining, unions make demands for more pay, fringe benefits, and vacations. But they also demand that economic rewards be governed by formal rules that specify who gets what and when, and that remove as many employee incentives as possible from the discretionary choice of "management." The notion that rewards might somehow be linked to merit is anathema, since merit cannot be measured objectively and any subjective assessment of merit threatens to put discretion in the hands of principals and other superiors.

Unions also make demands about the structure of teachers' jobs, right down to the number of minutes of preparation time, assignments to lunch or hall duty, tutoring students, participating in extracurricular activities, and anything else teachers might be asked to do (or want to avoid doing). And more generally still, unions make demands about the structure of the school as a whole, intended to carve out larger spheres of influence for teachers in the making of school policy—and intended, in particular, to ensure that teachers are protected from discretionary acts of authority by the principal.

Collective bargaining leads to formal contracts that specify, usually in excruciating detail and at spectacular length (a recent Philadelphia agreement ran 133 pages), the formal rights and obligations of both parties and the formal machinery by which these rights are to be implemented and enforced.[29] This translates directly into bureaucracy: rules governing organizational incentives, rules governing what teachers do, and rules governing how basic educational decisions must get made and who gets to make them. Unions use their power in collective bargaining to formalize public education and to eliminate managerial discretion.

We should point out that unions are important not only in collective bargaining, but also as interest groups that participate in the broader political struggle to control public authority. In this role, they represent an apparent exception to the general logic we outlined in the last section: unlike the typical group, which favors the formal reduction of discretion in order to impose and protect its favored policies, unions actively pressure for laws that grant substantial discretion to subordinates—namely, to teachers. In the world of power politics, then, unions might be regarded as the champions of school "autonomy." Everyone else fights to limit school autonomy; unions fight to promote it.

Whether in politics or collective bargaining, however, unions do not really favor school autonomy. They favor teacher autonomy, which is very different indeed. They want teachers to be free from control by organizational superiors, including the principals who are charged with running the schools. Their pursuit of autonomy thus leads them to wage a war of formalization against principals—restricting their discretion, stripping them of managerial and policymaking power, forcing them to share power with teachers, and imposing new structures and processes by which decisions are to be made. For unions, the path to teacher autonomy is the bureaucratization of the schools.

The formalization of personnel has consequences for school organization that are so pervasive that their importance would be difficult to exaggerate. The alleged leader of the school, the principal, is purposely prevented from staffing the organization and arranging incentives according to his best judgment. The principal may value expertise, enthusiasm, collegiality, communication skills, creativity, facility in dealing with parents, special sensitivity to student problems, or any number of qualifications related to the school's goals—but he is prevented from taking effective action to obtain teachers who possess these qualifications and to eliminate those who do not. For the most part, the principal is stuck with the teachers the system gives him. They are stuck with him. And the teachers are stuck with one another.

Serious disabilities are easy to anticipate. Aside from ham-fisted attempts by administrators to measure expertise, the qualifications crucial to good teaching may have little to do with the formal criteria that determine who ends up teaching in a given school. And even if public officials and unions were moved to try to include these qualifications, they would find them impossible to formalize anyway. People at the school level know collegiality, enthusiasm, and sensitivity when they see them, but there is no way to devise a formal test that would take such assessments out of the domain of discretionary judgment. In a bureaucratic system dedicated to the elimination of discretion, especially on matters of personnel, all of the intangible properties so necessary for effective performance are "ruled out" and cannot be recruited or mobilized for the pursuit of school goals. The bureaucratization of personnel tends to ensure that public schools will lack the proper mix and balance of talents on which effective education inherently depends.

It also tends to leave the school organization vulnerable to disunity and disarray. Teachers may reject the principal's leadership, dissent from school goals and policies, get along poorly with their colleagues, or fail to perform acceptably in the classroom—but they nonetheless have formal rights to their positions. Because personnel is likely to be heavily bureaucratized, there is no systematic way to screen out people who are bad fits, nor is there is a systematic way to recruit and retain the kinds of people who would fit and function well together as a team. To make matters worse, principals are unlikely to be granted the formal tools of leadership that might allow them to create a team out of the motley crews the bureaucracy may give them.

This promotes conflict and discontent, as people who disagree with one another and have little in common struggle to have their own ways—or simply to be left alone. It also inhibits the development of social relations—of collegiality, cooperation, and mutual respect—that are conducive to jointly productive behavior. In the process, the bureaucratization of personnel drives a wedge between the principal and his teachers and virtually ensures that principals will not voluntarily share their powers and prerogatives. It also ensures that principals will resist treating teachers as professionals by allowing them to run their own school. Principals and teachers are not really on the same team at all. Nor are teachers a team in their own right. There is no team. All these people just happen to work at the same school.

In a market setting, things are likely to be very different. The most general reason is that market forces give the owners of schools strong incentives not to organize bureaucratically but to grant their schools substantial autonomy instead. Now that we have considered in more explicit terms just how serious and far-reaching the consequences of bureaucratization may be, it is easier to appreciate why these incentives are as strong as they are. In the marketplace, where other schools compete for support and clients are free to go where they want, the bureaucratization of personnel is a good way to create an organization fraught with disabling problems, incapable of effective performance, and destined to fail.

Consider how different the organization of schooling is likely to be when personnel decisions are decentralized to the school and left to the discretion of the principal. Under these conditions, the principal can systematically recruit the kinds of teachers he wants and weed out those he does not, giving weight to whatever qualifications have a direct bearing on organizational performance, regardless of how intangible or resistant to formalization they might be. Through this selection process, principals are in a position to create and maintain what can meaningfully be called a team—a group of teachers whose values, talents, backgrounds, and personalities mesh well together and promote the cooperative pursuit of organizational objectives.

All this can be systematically reinforced through the incentive structure: when the principal is able to make jobs, job assignments, and the rewards associated with them contingent on performance (in all its aspects, however intangible), teachers have strong incentives to be "good team players" on a continuing basis. This applies to all teachers, whatever their true qualifications. Teachers who initially lack expertise, finesse, or sensitivity in the classroom will be motivated to improve. Their motivation, moreover, will focus on actual performance and its determinants—not on "paper qualifications" such as formal degrees and tests. These will tend to be seen for what they are: largely meaningless.

It might seem that teachers are destined to be the classic subordinates in this arrangement and principals the classic bosses, but this is unlikely to be so. In the first place, owing largely to the technology of education, principals have incentives to grant teachers discretion in their work: the effectiveness and success of the organization are heavily dependent on their expertise and professional judgment. In the second place, and perhaps ironically, it is the principal's concentrated authority that frees him to do this aggressively and on a grand scale. Precisely because the principal is able to build a hand-picked team of "right-thinking" teachers whom he respects and trusts, teachers are not a threat to his leadership. They are on his side. And knowing that they are, he has every reason to take full advantage of what they have to offer by granting them substantial autonomy in their own spheres of expertise, encouraging their participation in decisionmaking about important matters of school policy, and promoting a context of interaction, exchange of ideas, and mutual respect. The principal has every reason, in other words, to treat teachers as true professionals—and, indeed, to build the school around their professionalism.

The bureaucratization of personnel tends to rule out this distinctive form of organization and all its tremendous advantages, substituting a very different form plagued by debilitating problems. The basic paths to formalization in the public sector—civil service protections and unions—should therefore have little appeal to decisionmakers in the private sector. As a market strategy to attract good teachers, private schools could choose to offer tenure and other civil-service-like protections, particularly given that public schools already offer these benefits. But if private schools can offer true professionalism and other attractive educational benefits—and there is every reason to believe that they can—they can attract good teachers without relying extensively on tenure or other formal protections.[30]

Similarly, teachers are free to join unions if they want to, and unions are free to try to organize them for collective bargaining. But unions operate at a serious disadvantage in a market setting. Teachers who are team players, who have lots of autonomy in their work, who routinely play integral roles in school decisionmaking, and who are treated as professionals are hardly good candidates for union membership. They are likely to be happy with their situations. On those occasions when a union does succeed in organizing a school, moreover, its achievements threaten to translate into higher labor costs and the bureaucratization of personnel, both of which take their tolls on the school and put it at a competitive disadvantage in the educational market. Unions do best in noncompetitive, protected, regulated settings—like government—where costs can simply be passed on and ineffectiveness has almost nothing to do with organizational survival.[31]

The extent to which personnel decisions are bureaucratized, then, is largely a reflection of the institutional settings in which schools find themselves. Because institutions of democratic control prevail in the public sector, personnel decisions for the public schools should tend to be heavily bureaucratized. Because market forces are so important in the private sector, personnel decisions for private schools should tend to be more informal and discretionary. These institutional differences, in turn, have enormous consequences for schools—consequences that shape and pervade almost every important aspect of their organizations and combine to generate distinctly different organizational forms across sectors.

Goals

Although we will still use the terminology, it is a bit misleading to say that the public schools have goals. They are public agencies, and, as the word "agency" implies, their role is to take action on behalf of others: the citizens, organized groups, politicians, and bureaucrats who have the authority to specify what the schools should be trying to accomplish and how. The schools do not really set their own goals, especially in an institutional system dedicated to reducing their discretion on all matters that really count. Their goals are largely contained in the laws and regulations by which the higher-order values of their democratic authorities are formally imposed on them.

What can we say, then, about the nature of these goals? First, they are almost countless in number. Schools are legally bound to honor and be constrained by all laws and regulations on the books—local, state, and federal. Many of these explicitly deal with educational policies and practices. But many have nothing directly to do with education at all—those dealing with due process rights, for instance. In sheer magnitude, the set of goals that public schools are expected to pursue is overwhelming.[32]

Second, there is no necessary coherence to the overall structure of school goals. In politics, whoever gains public authority can impose almost anything they want on the schools, regardless of what has been imposed by others in the past or might be imposed in the future. Schools can therefore be asked to move in every direction at once, from sex education to psychological counseling to the socialization of immigrants to vocational training to desegregation to mainstreaming of the handicapped to bilingual education. Somewhere in all this, they are also expected to provide students with "academic excellence."

Third, school goals will tend to be weak and watered down, owing to the huge, heterogeneous constituency of public education and the necessity for political compromise. Thus schools will be directed to pursue academic excellence, but without making courses too difficult; they will be directed to teach history, but without making any value judgments; they will be directed to teach sex education, but without taking a stand on contraception or abortion. They must make everyone happy by being all things to all people—just as politicians try to do.

None of this has anything to do with public school principals and teachers lacking standards or somehow having no sense of what good education is all about. It is an institutional matter, a matter of authority and constituency. Principals and teachers do not have the authority to set basic school goals—far-flung, diverse constituencies do. School goals are therefore likely to be piled on until they are so numerous, incoherent, and diluted that they can provide teachers and principals with no clear sense of mission and no foundation for working together as a team. When schools lack mission, when there is no meaningful way of saying what it is they are supposed to accomplish—how is it possible, even in principle, to design an effective organization? Effective for what?

In the private sector, schools do not have to be all things to all people. To be successful, they need to find their niche—a specialized segment of the market to which they can appeal and attract support. The obvious way to do this is through the strategic design of their curriculum. They might offer a broadly based liberal arts education, for instance, or they might specialize in math and science, in the dramatic arts, in the humanities, in vocational education, or in almost anything else that a clientele of parents and students might value. They are also free to target their appeals to other value dimensions: discipline, religion, theories of learning, the socioeconomic and ethnic make-up of the student body, school or class size, athletics and other extracurricular activities, perspectives on personal growth, sensitivity to particular cultures and languages—the list could go on until it exhausts the educational concerns of parents and students.

As a population, schools in a market setting should tend to reflect a full, heterogeneous range of educational concerns. The goals of individual schools, however, are likely to be far simpler, clearer, and more homogeneous than those of the typical public school. They are intended to appeal only to a portion of the market, and perhaps a very small and highly specialized portion. Their goals are also more likely to have true intellectual coherence—for they are not ad hoc collections of value-impositions, but packages that are consciously designed to constitute an integrated whole. The market allows and encourages its schools to have distinctive, well-defined "missions."

This vastly simplifies the job of organizing an effective school. Schools know what they want to accomplish, and they can consciously design their organizations in ways that appear best suited to accomplishing it. They can match organizational means to organizational ends. They may make mistakes in the process, but they have strong incentives to try to correct these over time by moving toward structures better suited to their goals—and if they falter, the marketplace will penalize them and ultimately put them out of business.

Leadership

Much of what we need to know about leadership is already implicit in our discussions of personnel and goals. Private school principals are likely to be in a position to lead their organizations. They may not succeed, but they should have the tools and the flexibility to do what leaders need to do. Public school principals, on the other hand, are systematically denied much of what it takes to lead.

It may be better to think of the public school principal as a lower-level manager than as a leader. In the public sector, the principal is a bureaucrat with supervisory responsibility for a public agency. Most of the important decisions about policy have been taken by higher authorities: they set the goals and the principal is expected to administer them. Many of the important structural decisions are also taken by higher authorities: the principal is bound by all sorts of formal rules and regulations that dictate aspects of internal structure. And many of the important personnel decisions are imposed from above as well: the principal is unlikely to have much control over the choice of teachers or the incentives that motivate them. The real leaders of the public school are the authorities, not the principal.

Most of the high-level rhetoric about the importance of the principal's leadership role is essentially just that. The fact is that those who succeed in exercising public authority want principals to behave more like bureaucrats than leaders. Authorities want principals to ensure that formal hierarchical directives are put into effect; they do not want principals to exercise real discretion. The public system is set up accordingly. The position of principal is a bureaucratic office in a recognized hierarchy of offices. People who desire advancement within the educational system begin as teachers—the lowliest of bureaucrats—then advance up the ladder to assistant principal, then principal, then into the district office as assistant superintendent, and so on. They are on a career track, and the principalship is one step along the way. Doing a good job as principal qualifies one for advancement.

The nature of the job and its career path inevitably generate a process of selective attraction. People who like administrative work and who desire advancement in an administrative hierarchy tend to be attracted to the job, while people who want to be genuine leaders tend to be turned off. Once in the job, moreover, the incentives promote behavior that is classically bureaucratic. Doing a good job, and thus doing what is necessary to get ahead, requires playing by the rules, implementing them as faithfully and effectively as possible— and staying out of trouble. The easiest way to get into trouble is to launch bold, aggressive, innovative moves: discretionary acts of leadership that are bound to be threatening to the interests of someone, somewhere, in a position of political power.

In a market setting, the basic forces run the other way. For all the reasons that bureaucracy in general is discouraged, the role of principal should tend not to be a bureaucratic one. While important policy decisions may still be taken by owners or governing boards, they have incentives to decentralize and thus to grant principals the discretion and resources necessary for leadership. What successful leadership calls for, in terms of specific behaviors, will vary with the circumstances. A school that occupies a stable, supportive niche in the parent-student environment may call for a conservative emphasis on continuing the package of offerings, structures, and personnel that have worked in the past. A school whose niche is in flux, however, or that has attractive opportunities to move into new niches, may require more dynamic, innovative leadership.

While the hallmarks of effective leadership can be expected to vary, the technology of education and its market setting should tend to impose an important uniformity. Principals, like their own superiors, will have incentives to exercise leadership by decentralizing—which means, as we have discussed, building a team based on professionalism, high interaction, and shared influence. Another way of putting this is that effective leadership in a market setting should be heavily oriented toward teaching. Team-building requires that principals know their teachers well, know what happens in the classrooms, understand what good teaching is all about, and employ the substantial—but largely intangible—human capital of teachers to the school's best advantage. Success does not call for a power struggle. Nor does it call for a supreme administrator. It calls for effective leadership—which, in turn, calls for a firm anchoring in the profession, culture, and everyday experience of teaching.

Certain kinds of people are more likely than others to find this sort of job attractive and succeed at it. It is not a stepping stone along a recognized career path, but is likely to be regarded—as the job of teaching is by most teachers—as a stopping point. People who aspire to the job are likely to do so not because they have their eyes on other, more attractive, probably very different jobs, but because this particular job is what they want to do with their professional lives. Accordingly, they are likely to be the types of people who want to be leaders, not rule-followers or managers, when it comes to important matters of school policy and structure. They are also likely, given the requirements of effective leadership, to be people whose approach to schooling is deeply rooted in teaching.

Practice

"Practice" refers to what principals and teachers, especially the latter, do in the performance of their jobs. It refers to the various behaviors by which programs are carried out, services provided, and children taught. It therefore includes most of the activities within a school that are directly related to education, and is the most immediate determinant of a school's effectiveness. From the standpoint of the people involved, not surprisingly, it tends to be regarded as the crucial difference between success and failure: "practice" is what education is all about. Given the bottom-heavy technology of education, we can only agree. But we must add a caveat: the form that educational practice takes in any given school is not simply a matter of what seems to work best, but is largely a reflection of the other aspects of organization we have already discussed—personnel, goals, and leadership—and the institutional setting that shapes them all.

In the public sector, the whole thrust of democratic politics is to formalize and constrain educational practice. As public authority is captured and put to use by various interests over time, the discretionary exercise of professional judgment is systematically curtailed, and the practice of education is transformed into an exercise in administration. Because technical concerns remain important to those who make political decisions, all discretion is not eliminated. Moreover, because so much technical and operational knowledge is concentrated at the lower reaches of the organization in people whose professional sensibilities are violated by formal constraint, hierarchical control is inevitably imperfect: teachers will subtly be able to evade some of the rules without detection or punishment.

Nonetheless, the public world of educational practice is a world of rules imposed on the schools by local, state, and federal authorities. Some of these specify what teachers are to do and how they are to do it—rules about curriculum, about instructional methods, about the design of special programs, about textbooks, about time spent on various activities, about what can and cannot be discussed. In addition, there are all sorts of rules—monitoring and reporting rules—designed to ensure that teachers are doing these things and not evading hierarchical control. Thus teachers are doubly constrained in their efforts to perform their educational tasks as they see fit. First, they are required to follow rules that cause them to depart from what they might otherwise do, and thus to behave in ways that contradict or fail to take advantage of their professional expertise and judgment. Second, they are required to spend time and effort documenting, usually through formal paperwork, that they have in fact followed these rules. The combination may leave little room for them to do the kind of teaching they think they ought to be doing.

Some of the most formal aspects of educational practice are imposed by federal and state authorities, who are far from the scene and thus particularly vulnerable to discretionary departures from the objectives they want schools to pursue. But local politics is an important source of formalization as well—collective bargaining agreements, for instance, may specify in detail who is to do what, when, and how. Even in the absence of formalization, moreover, local politics still puts an indelible stamp on how education gets carried out.

Consider, for instance, local practices having to do with such things as homework, academic tracking, or discipline. Districts may abstain from imposing formal rules on these scores, but this does not mean schools are truly free to adopt practices that, on professional grounds, seem most conducive to effective education. The fact is that school practices can easily become politicized when one or more groups become disgruntled and pressure the authorities for action. Were teachers to decide that most students should be academically tracked, assigned significantly more homework, and held to strict academic standards in order to pass, the size and heterogeneity of the democratic constituency threatens a fearsome political response. Similarly, were schools unable to control violence and drugs on their campuses, the political authorities would inevitably come under pressure to "do something" by imposing disciplinary policies from without.

If schools do not anticipate and defuse these political problems through their choice of practices, then, the district is likely to exercise its authority to adopt formal rules on homework, tracking, discipline, and any other school practices that excite constituents—the result of which is still more bureaucracy and still less discretion for schools. Conversely, the absence of formal rules does not mean the schools are using their apparent discretion to adopt practices that are considered best on professional grounds. It may mean that they have settled on practices that are politically acceptable, and thus safe from formal reprisal by the authorities.

In a market setting, principals and teachers are likely to have a great deal of discretion in determining school practices. In putting that discretion to use, they need not be driven to adopt practices whose major justification is that they avoid offending anyone. Schools can be clear, bold, and controversial in the practices they adopt as long as they attract a specialized clientele that values what they do. They are free, in particular, to adopt whatever practices they consider most suitable to the effective pursuit of the school's mission—and they have strong incentives, as we have seen, to do just that by building an organizational team that enables a school to take advantage of the expertise and judgment of its teachers.

Given the segmentation of market demand and the diversity of views among professionals, the population of private schools is likely to reflect a rich heterogeneity of educational missions and practices. Some schools may base their appeal on academic rigor, but others may put their emphasis elsewhere—on personal growth, say, or artistic expression—and their practices may vary quite dramatically as a result. Similarly, schools that pursue academic rigor may choose to approach it in different ways—some through a highly structured curriculum and lots of homework and discipline, others through more fluid, open-ended processes encouraging discovery and creativity. Amidst all this organizational diversity in the marketplace, however, the hallmark of the individual school is likely to be organizational coherence: a coherent mission, a coherent set of practices, a close and productive fit between the two—and a professional dynamic that continuously seeks to maintain their intellectual integrity.

Central Tendency and Variance

This comparison of politics and markets is an attempt to set out, as simply and clearly as possible, the logical foundations of behavior within each system and their consequences for the organization of schools. Along the way, we have tried to highlight institutional differences by emphasizing the general thrust of the various forces at work. Democratic control tends to promote bureaucracy, markets tend to promote autonomy, and the basic dimensions of school organization—personnel, goals, leadership, and practice—tend to differ in ways that reflect (and support) each sector's disposition toward bureaucracy or autonomy.

Obviously, we do not mean to say that all public schools look and perform alike or that all private schools do. While the most dramatic and theoretically instructive contrasts, in our view, are those that can be drawn across systems by comparing their central tendencies, we are able to draw these contrasts only after arriving at a basic understanding of school organization within each system. The same theory that allows us to understand why organization varies across systems, then, might also be employed to understand why organization varies within them.

The fact is that the central tendencies of each system can be expected to hide a fair measure of organizational variation. Markets tend to promote autonomy, but the population of private schools will not be entirely uniform. If we were to place these schools on a continuum ranging from highly bureaucratic to highly autonomous, we would expect their distribution to be skewed toward the autonomy end of the continuum—but there would still be a distribution, with some schools laboring under many of the bureaucratic constraints we have associated with democratic control. Similarly, were public schools placed along the same continuum, we would expect their distribution to be skewed toward the bureaucratic end—but, again, there would still be a distribution, and some public schools would prove to have many of the "effective school" characteristics we have associated with markets.

Some of the most interesting questions about within-sector variation have to do with these atypical schools, and thus with why some schools in one sector may turn out to look like those typical of the other. While we save most of our examination of these matters for our data analysis, we have already suggested perhaps the most fundamental reason for bureaucratization in the private sector: the imposition of higher-order values. When organizations have fixed values that they seek to pursue—values that are unresponsive to what parents and students want and may be quite inconsistent with the best professional judgment of teachers—they will tend to bureaucratize as a means of constraining behavior toward these ends. The most obvious candidates are churches. Even for churches, however, only some values—having to do with religion, morality, and perhaps discipline—are likely to be fixed; the rest, including those bearing on academics, are not, and thus are unlikely to be pursued through formal constraints.

It is no accident that the imposition of higher-order values should cause some private schools to look like public schools in their organization. The imposition of higher-order values is what democratic control in the public sector is all about, and this, in the final analysis, is why the public schools themselves are so heavily bureaucratic. There are strong forces at work, however, that prevent private schools from going too far in the bureaucratic direction. These are explained by the market and its incentives (backed by sanctions) to please clients and perform effectively. But they are also explained by the absence of bureaucracy-producing factors that are present in the public sector with a vengeance: the struggle to control public authority, the dangers of political uncertainty, the multiple levels of government.

Atypical private schools do not raise the most important questions about school organization, however. Given the crisis atmosphere that currently surrounds public education, the question of most obvious importance is why some public schools develop the kinds of organizations typical of markets. The answer is not that they are somehow able to escape the imposition of higher-order values. As long as public schools are governed by institutions of democratic control, everything about them is subject to the imposition of higher-order values through public authority. This is an institutional fact of life. The key to an answer rests with how public authority actually gets put to use—and why its impositions are different for some schools than for others.

While a comprehensive answer will occupy us throughout this book, it seems to us that two general conditions—which turn out, in fact, to be largely overlapping in American society—are especially important in this regard, and go a long way toward accounting for organizational variety within the public sector. The first is social homogeneity. The second, for lack of a better phrase, is the absence of serious problems.

Social homogeneity is important because of its relation to political uncertainty. When there are no serious conflicts of interest about important educational issues that set one faction off against another, the threats and costs of political uncertainty are low. This can happen when one group firmly dominates politics, but, more commonly, it should happen when there is simply broad agreement throughout the community about basic matters of educational policy (if not their details). In these settings, groups that succeed in gaining public authority for a time are not driven to formalize in order to protect their achievements from subversion by their enemies; there really are no enemies. Homogeneous polities should tend to have less bureaucratic schools.[33]

Bureaucracy is also inhibited by the absence of serious problems that schools appear incapable of solving on their own. When schools are plagued by problems—poor academic performance, drugs, violence, absenteeism, high drop-out rates—public officials come under intense pressure to take corrective action in the form of new policies. Much the same happens when the schools' problems are seen to be anchored in more fundamental problems that beset their student populations— economic hardship, broken families, poor nutrition, physical handicaps, language difficulties. Here there is pressure for governmental programs that address the educational symptoms of these problems, usually by requiring schools to provide certain kinds of services.

Part of the reason problem-infested environments promote bureaucracy is that they undermine whatever homogeneity may exist. When problems are numerous and truly serious, the political process is hardly a cooperative exercise in analytics. It is a fractious struggle to control public authority—a struggle to determine which problems get addressed, which of many proposed "solutions" will be adopted, how scarce public resources will be allocated, which constituencies will receive money and services, and which constituencies will pay the bill. Interests are in conflict, the stakes are high—and so are political uncertainty and its corresponding incentives to formalize.

Even in the absence of substantial conflict and political uncertainty, however, those who exercise public authority would still be under strident demands from all sides to "do something" concrete, and they would still have strong incentives to formalize—to create new administrative rules and monitoring requirements—to ensure that schools behave in ways consistent with programmatic and budgetary intentions. This is especially true when state and federal governments are drawn into problem solving, since their at-a-distance control problems are especially severe and the threat of noncompliance especially great. But it is also true for those who exercise authority at the local level, since the predominant view in problem-infested environments is likely to be that the schools are failures that cannot be relied on or entrusted with substantial discretion. Why set them loose so they can fail again? Better to constrain them so they will behave differently—and then hold them formally accountable.

All this is compounded by the more specific effects that problem-plagued schools and environments have on the bureaucratization of personnel. Unions are likely to be stronger and more militant the worse the conditions in which teachers work. They are likely to seek more changes, more protections—and more formalization, since this is the means by which unions get what they want. In addition, the most problem-plagued schools are precisely the ones in the greatest danger of losing their best, most experienced teachers, who tend to use their formal rights within the public system to transfer to more desirable jobs at better schools in more problem-free environments. The consequences are felt throughout the school organization, as problem-plagued schools become more rule-bound in their practices, more difficult for principals to manage, more prone to internal conflict, increasingly drained of the talent they so desperately need—and thus even less capable of solving the severe problems that face them.

Clearly, then, we do not expect all public schools to have the same kinds of organizations. In the abstract, we might simply say that the extent to which individual public schools are bureaucratized depends on how public authority gets used to structure them, which in turn varies according to how homogeneous and problem free their environments are. Schools with homogeneous, problem-free environments should tend to be the least bureaucratic, while schools with highly heterogeneous, problem-filled environments should tend to be the most bureaucratic.

This abstract way of framing our expectations can usefully be restated in much more practical terms, reflecting familiar features of the American social landscape. The nation's large cities are teeming with diverse, conflicting interests of political salience—class, race, ethnicity, language, religion—and their schools are plagued by problems so severe, wide-ranging, and deeply rooted in the urban socioeconomic structure that the situation appears out of control and perhaps even beyond hope. Urban environments are heterogeneous and problem filled in the extreme.[34]

America's suburbs are not free from all this, of course. Suburban schools have also been faced by problems—drugs, especially—that are difficult to conquer. Nonetheless, the contrast between urban and suburban settings as environments for schools is striking. The contrast between urban and rural is perhaps less striking, since some rural areas are more burdened by problems (due to poverty, for instance) than suburban areas. But in general, rural areas should stand in clear contrast to the cities too.

A more concrete and illustrative way of saying how the organization of schools ought to vary within the public sector, then, is that urban schools should be far more bureaucratized than nonurban schools. It is among the latter, and especially among suburban schools, that we should expect to find instances of "effective school" organizations most similar to those associated with markets and private schools.

It is important to stress that the capacity of some public schools to develop reasonably healthy, effective organizations does not imply that all public schools can somehow do so. The fact is, suburban schools are lucky. They are more likely to be blessed with relatively homogeneous, problem-free environments, and, when they are, their organizations should tend to benefit in all sorts of ways as a result. Urban schools do not look like suburban schools because urban environments do not—and in the foreseeable future, obviously will not—look like suburban environments.

Moreover, the fundamental obstacle to effective organization among urban public schools is not their conflictual, problem-filled environments. It is the way democratic control tends to manage and respond to such environments. And this may well prove more troubling than we have indicated thus far. For democratic control threatens to generate a vicious circle of problems and ineffectiveness.[35] Precisely where the problems are the greatest—in poor urban areas—and thus where strong leadership, professionalism, clear missions, and other aspects of effective organization are most desperately needed, public authority will be exercised to ensure that schools are highly bureaucratized. There will be little discretion to allow for strong leadership. Teachers will be unable to participate as professionals. Talent will be drained off. Unions will insist on myriad formal protections. Principals will be hamstrung in their efforts to build a cooperative team. And so on.

The institutions of democratic control are thus likely to respond to serious educational problems by adding to the schools' already disabling bureaucracy—rendering them even less capable of solving the problems that face them. The more poorly the schools perform, the more the authorities are pressured to respond with new bureaucratic constraints, which in turn make the schools still less effective. Hence the vicious circle.

It is worth noting, finally, that even the lucky public schools, the ones with nice environments, do not escape entirely from the bureaucratizing tendencies of democratic control. They are still creatures of public authority, and, for this very fundamental reason, can never really be "like" private schools. Their relative autonomy is tenuous: it can be chipped away or simply destroyed should problems arise that propel the authorities to respond. And even as they enjoy autonomy, they tend to have less real discretion than a market setting would grant them—for their personnel, goals, leadership, and practices are all constrained by formal rules, protections, and requirements that, although less restrictive and troublesome than those for urban schools, are still likely to go beyond what the typical school must endure in a market setting.

This is why it is so important to understand the central tendencies of the two systems and their institutional foundations. The most basic causes of ineffective performance among the nation's public schools are only partially reflected in the differences between urban and nonurban schools, and it is a bit misleading, as a result, to think that we can learn what we need to know by restricting ourselves to an analysis of public schools. In our view, it is really what these public schools have in common—their subordination to public authority— that is at the root of the system's problems, and that inexorably skews the entire distribution of public schools toward the bureaucracy end of the continuum. Only when we take the public system as a whole and compare it with something else—to a market system, in our case— do these fundamentals and their wide-ranging consequences strikingly stand out.[36]

Conclusion

The theoretical road we have traveled in this chapter has been rather long and complicated, taking us from the institutional foundations of politics and markets to their general implications for bureaucracy and autonomy to their more specific implications for personnel, goals, leadership, and practice. The purpose of all this, however, has been to say something quite simple and general about how schools can be better understood—and how, on that basis, they might be made more effective.

Schools, we believe, are products of their institutional settings. America's public schools are governed by institutions of direct democratic control, and their organizations should be expected to bear the indelible stamp of those institutions. They should tend to be highly bureaucratic and systematically lacking in the requisites of effective performance. Private schools, on the other hand, operate in a very different institutional setting distinguished by the basic features of markets—decentralization, competition, and choice—and their organizations should be expected to bear a very different stamp as a result. They should tend to possess the autonomy, clarity of mission, strong leadership, teacher professionalism, and team cooperation that public schools want but (except under very fortunate circumstances) are unlikely to have.

The primary lesson to be drawn from this comparison is not that private schools are inherently better than public schools. For—as we will go on to argue in some detail in chapter 6—there is every reason to believe that, with the right governing institutions, the public schools could be disposed to develop these same effective school organizations. The differences between schools in the two sectors do not arise from immutable public-private differences. They arise from institutional differences. And this is the primary lesson. It is a lesson about the pervasive ways in which institutions shape the organization and performance of *all* schools, about the value of understanding schools from an institutional perspective—and about the crucial role that institutions and institutional reform ought to play in the thinking of those who want to improve America's schools.

This lesson is an important foundation for understanding schools. But it is only a beginning. In our effort to make a clear, simple case for the role of institutions, we purposely avoided trying to juggle and make sense out of the welter of influences—student aptitude, social class, peer groups, economic resources, and all sorts of other things—that also seem to have a role in determining how schools are organized, how well they perform, and thus how much students actually learn. We think it is clear that institutions are profoundly important for schools. But how important are they relative to these other influences?

And how do they all seem to fit together in producing the kind of education America's children will receive?

In the next three chapters, we will address these questions through the analysis of a large, representative sample of public and private high schools. In chapter 3, we will profile the organizations of effective and ineffective schools, describing how they differ in their goals, leadership, personnel, and practices. In chapter 4, we will tackle the more complicated issue of the causes of student achievement—focusing, most centrally, on whether school organization does in fact have an important influence on student achievement when all other relevant factors are taken into account. These two chapters set the stage for chapter 5, where we will turn to the two causal issues that have the most bearing on our own theoretical claims: how consequential is school autonomy—freedom from external (bureaucratic) control—for effective school organization, and to what extent is autonomy (or constraints on it) a product of the institutional setting? The result of all this is a more coherent and more firmly grounded perspective on how the various pieces of the puzzle fit together: on how performance is linked to organization, how organization is linked to autonomy and bureaucracy, and how autonomy and bureaucracy are linked to institutions.

Given this augmented foundation, we will go on in chapter 6 to argue that America's institutions of democratic control are indeed significant obstacles to the improvement of its schools—and that, if the nation wants better schools, it will need to govern them through very different institutions than it has in the past.

Chapter Three

The Organization of Effective Schools

THE GENERAL purpose of the analysis that will occupy us in this and the next two chapters is to clarify the rather hazy relationships among the institutional environment of the school, the school organization, and school performance. In so doing we also hope to provide a firmer foundation for thinking about the structural reform of schools.

Despite the long history and substantial influence of research into school organization—from studies of scientific management that helped establish the "one best system" to research on "effective schools" that guided much of the reform of the 1980s—there is little about the causes of school organization or even its consequences that is definitely settled.[1] We therefore want to begin our empirical analysis by reexamining the issue that effective schools research has addressed, and that logically must be the first issue resolved before any organizational reform should proceed: does the organization of schools really make a difference for school performance—specifically, for the achievement of students? With the benefit of data on some 20,000 students, teachers, and principals in a nationwide sample of schools, it is possible to address this issue with some precision and confidence.[2]

This chapter, an organizational comparison of high and low performance schools, is concerned mainly with description. It details how the goals, leadership, personnel, and practices of schools are associated with the achievement of students. It also discusses why these elements of school organization may be important causes of school performance. The next chapter takes up the issue of causality directly. There we will try to estimate just how much the organizational properties introduced in this chapter really matter.

69

Measuring School Performance

Across this diverse country, schools attempt to accomplish many things. They try to equip all students with basic literacy and computational skills. They strive to help many students master traditional bodies of knowledge and to reach higher cognitive planes. They aim to provide other students with the training and discipline that they will need for gainful employment. Public schools hope to socialize students of disparate backgrounds into the nation's civic culture. Private schools often work to inculcate specific systems of moral and religious values.

Since at least the middle of the nineteenth century, when schooling began to be universally provided, these and other school objectives have been a major source of political and professional contention.[3] Parents and educators, business and labor, religious organizations and other interest groups have never been able to agree, at least for long, on such important matters as how much emphasis should be given to classical academic subjects as opposed to more relevant topics, or how basic moral training should be provided. Today the public seems to believe that if the nation is to prosper in a world of increasing technological sophistication, schools must make "academic excellence" a higher priority. But agreements on educational objectives tend to be fleeting—recall the brief commitments to science and mathematics education in the late 1950s, and the intense but passing concern with alternative education in the late 1960s. New priorities may well replace academic excellence in the 1990s.

The measurement of school performance is complicated by this unending debate. No single indicator can capture all that schools are trying to accomplish. No one criterion of performance will be completely fair to all schools. Nevertheless, it is highly impractical to evaluate schools along a number of dimensions. As will soon become clear, a proper analysis of even one dimension is a major undertaking. We will therefore direct our attention to one indicator of school performance, student academic achievement, throughout our analysis.[4]

We think this focus is most appropriate for an analysis of school performance. All schools take the academic development of their students to be one of their main orders of business. Circumstances may force schools, or free them, to pursue other student objectives—self-discipline, personal growth, moral development, occupational readiness. But academic achievement, at least in the basic subject and skill areas that we will examine, is an indicator of the kind of cognitive development that every American high school tries to promote. In addition, academic achievement is the most common indicator of school performance in education research; it is a pretty fair predictor of the future economic productivity of students; and it is the measure of effectiveness that school reformers now rely on most.[5]

To measure student achievement, we began with five of the six standardized tests that were administered as part of the High School and Beyond (HSB) survey.[6] The tests—in reading comprehension, vocabulary, writing, mathematics, and science—were taken by a cohort of sophomores in the spring of 1980 and retaken by the same students at the end of their senior year in 1982. (We excluded from this study a civics test that the cohort also took, because the test was relatively unreliable.) The HSB tests were designed to measure basic skills ordinarily acquired before high school as well as the knowledge and abilities usually associated with a high school curriculum.[7] Although the tests are somewhat short—together the five tests include 116 items to be answered in sixty-three minutes—each test is a reliable measure of the academic achievement it was intended to gauge.[8] In addition, the scores on the five tests are all highly correlated with one another. This indicates that the tests are all tapping a student's general academic ability, and that they can be combined into more reliable, comprehensive indexes of total student achievement for sophomores and for seniors.[9]

Our analysis will focus on total student achievement, but our index of achievement will not be based on the sophomore or senior test scores alone. It will be based on the differences between them. We created our primary measure of student achievement by calculating the gains that students registered between the sophomore and senior years on each test. We then aggregated those gains into an index. We did this because gain scores are more valid measures of high school achievement than either sophomore or senior scores. Gain scores measure only the learning that takes place during high school whereas scores for the sophomore and senior years alone are contaminated by many years of prior learning. Since our main purpose is to account for the effectiveness of high schools in promoting student achievement, it is especially important to factor out of the analysis those influences— school, family, peer groups—that precede the high school years.

The Achievement Test Results

To appreciate the size of the contribution that schools might make to student achievement, it is useful to consider how widely student achievement varies across American high schools and their students. A representative picture of this variation is provided by the random samples of roughly 400 schools and 9,000 students in the final Administrator and Teacher Survey (ATS)-HSB data set.[10] Here at the outset we offer a more detailed picture of academic achievement than we will ultimately analyze. We report the scores of students and schools for three indexes of achievement gains—an index of verbal achievement employing the reading, writing, and vocabulary tests, an index of quantitative achievement employing the mathematics and science tests, and an index of total achievement employing all five tests.[11] The verbal and quantitative indexes are each based on 58 test questions. On the verbal composite, sophomores and seniors each posted scores ranging from a low of 4 questions correct to a high of 57 correct. On the quantitative composite, the range was from 5 to 57 for sophomores and 3 to 58 for seniors. The spreads for the index of total achievement were 15 to 114 for sophomores and 11 to 115 for seniors. Plainly, the levels of academic achievement of American high school students range widely.

But what about the changes that occur in these levels over the last two years of high school? Those changes, our main interest, are described in tables 3-1 and 3-2. In each table, the first for students and the second for schools, the far left columns report achievement gains in terms of the raw test scores. Thus the average number of items gained by high school students (table 3-1) was 4.26 on the verbal battery and 2.35 on the quantitative battery. On the five tests taken together, the total achievement index, seniors gained an average of 6.64 items over their sophomore scores.

In a sense, these gains are rather small. The average test scores of sophomores left considerable room for improvement by the senior year. Sophomores averaged only about 31 items correct on each battery of tests. Typical sophomores therefore had 27 questions left to answer correctly on the verbal tests and 27 on the quantitative tests the second time around—54 missed questions to reflect their learning overall. Yet the gain scores indicate that high school students mastered only fractions of what they might have learned—16 percent

TABLE 3-1. Student Means for Sophomore-to-Senior Changes
in Achievement Test Scores[a]

Test battery and population	Number of items gained	Gains measured in years	Log gain score	Gains measured in years
Verbal[b]				
All students	4.26	2.00	.231	2.00
Lowest quartile	− 2.39	− 1.12	− .119	− 1.03
Highest quartile	11.97	5.62	.632	5.48
Quantitative[c]				
All students	2.35	2.00	.119	2.00
Lowest quartile	− 4.28	− 3.64	− .177	− 2.97
Highest quartile	9.97	8.49	.462	7.76
Total[d]				
All students	6.64	2.00	.186	2.00
Lowest quartile	− 4.66	− 1.40	− .088	− 0.95
Highest quartile	18.13	5.46	.500	5.38

a. Sample weighted to achieve a nationally representative sample of public and private high school seniors.
b. The verbal battery consists of tests in reading, vocabulary, and writing, with a total of 58 questions. The number of verbal items gained is the sum of the sophomore-to-senior differences in the number correct on each of the three tests. The verbal log gain score is the sum of the log gain scores on each of the tests.
c. The quantitative battery consists of tests in mathematics and science, with a total of 58 questions. The number of quantitative items gained is the sum of the sophomore-to-senior differences in the number correct on each of the two tests. The quantitative log gain score is the sum of the log gain scores on each of the tests.
d. The total battery consists of the five tests comprising the verbal and quantitative batteries, with a total of 116 questions. The total number of items gained is the sum of the sophomore-to-senior differences in the number correct on each of the five tests. The total log gain score is the sum of the log gain scores on each of the tests.

of the remaining verbal material, 9 percent of the remaining quantitative material, and only 12 percent of all the material that remained for them to learn. This is not to say that students all should have scored 100 percent by their senior year; the tests were designed to distinguish high from low achievers in the senior year too. It must also be said that some students may have mastered considerable amounts of new material, yet forgotten old material, and consequently posted only modest net gains. But the fact remains that the standardized tests left ample room for students to demonstrate cognitive growth, and the average American high school student used little of it.[12]

Not all students made such modest progress, however. And this is very important to note: the variations in student gains and school performance, and not their average levels, hold the key to understanding academic achievement. Thus we see in table 3-1 that while the gain scores of high school seniors were generally low, senior gain scores also varied rather remarkably. The students who gained the most, those in the highest quartile, improved their overall scores by

TABLE 3-2. School Means for Sophomore-to-Senior Changes
in Achievement Test Scores[a]

Test battery and population	Number of items gained	Gains measured in years	Log gain score	Gains measured in years
Verbal				
All schools	4.26	2.00	.230	2.00
Lowest quartile	1.97	0.92	.117	1.02
Highest quartile	6.46	3.03	.358	3.11
Quantitative				
All schools	2.22	2.00	.108	2.00
Lowest quartile	0.02	0.02	.012	0.22
Highest quartile	4.25	3.83	.217	3.98
Total				
All schools	6.50	2.00	.181	2.00
Lowest quartile	2.71	0.83	.091	1.01
Highest quartile	10.10	3.11	.279	3.08

a. Sample weighted to achieve a nationally representative sample of public and private schools. National school means are based on means of student achievement scores (calculated as described in table 3-1) for each school.

nearly 23 items more than the students in the lowest quartile did. In part this occurred because the best students learned nearly three times as much as the average student learned. But the wide range of student achievement also occurred because the worst students performed so badly. On average they scored nearly 5 items worse in their senior year than in their sophomore year. Indeed, while many students mastered impressive portions of the test material that remained to be learned after the sophomore administration, 18.3 percent of all students failed to learn any additional portion at all.

At the school level the variation in student achievement gains is somewhat less. As we see in table 3-2, the process of averaging the scores of students within each school tends to wipe out the highest and lowest student gain scores. Accordingly, the spread between the schools whose students gained the most, the top quartile, and the schools whose students gained the least, the bottom quartile, is about seven and a half items. Yet, even when student gains are averaged for each school, the variations across American high schools are substantial.

To appreciate this interpretation, let us assume that the average changes in verbal, quantitative, and total achievement for all schools are measures of the typical amounts of learning that occur in these areas during the final two years of high school. If these two-year averages are reduced by half, they can then be thought of as indicators of the average amounts of verbal, quantitative, and total achievement that take place in a representative American high school each year. These one-year averages can also be used as straightforward standards— measures of grade equivalents of achievement—for interpreting changes in test scores. From the end of the sophomore year to the end of the senior year, the period spanned by this analysis, the average school, by definition, registers an improvement in achievement of two grade equivalents or years.

By this standard, students in schools in the highest quartile (see table 3-2) gained 3.03 grade equivalents or years in verbal skills, 3.83 years in quantitative skills, and 3.11 years overall. Students in the schools in the lowest quartile improved less than one year in every area, and scarcely improved at all in the quantitative area. The difference in total achievement between the most successful schools and the least successful ones, then, was about two and a quarter grade equivalents. The fact that this difference emerges during only two years of high school makes the difference a large one indeed.

In the analyses that follow, achievement gains will frequently be interpreted in years or grade equivalents. Our measures of achievement gains and grade equivalents will differ from the ones just discussed in an important respect, however. To this point we have been gauging student achievement in terms of the raw test and gain scores. This was useful for introducing our basic measuring instruments and methods. But there are better ways of gauging student achievement than by simply comparing the number of items answered correctly in the sophomore year with the number answered correctly in the senior year. Measurement should take into account such factors as the varied usefulness of individual test items and the different potential for improvement of students with different initial scores. We take account of these factors by making two adjustments to the raw gain scores.

In the analyses that follow, the raw scores on each of the five tests were first replaced with "IRT scores" (item response theory scores). These revised measures of the number of correct answers allow for item differences in difficulty level, discriminatory power, and the likelihood of being guessed correctly.[13] The sophomore and senior IRT scores were then used to construct "log gain scores" that adjust improvements for the level at which improvements begin. All things being equal, improvements are more likely for students who score poorly in their sophomore year than for students who score well. Students who score poorly as sophomores have many more items available to reflect their learning. They are also more likely, because of the chance of "regressing to the mean," to improve their scores even if they learn nothing. By gauging change scores on the individual tests against a logarithmic scale, the gains of below-average sophomores are deflated a bit and those of above-average sophomores inflated.[14] For example, if two students each improved their IRT scores on a 20-item test by 5 items, but one scored 10 as a sophomore and the other scored 15, the one who began with only 5 items left to learn would register a log gain score (1.79) nearly three times that (0.61) of the student who had half the items still to master.

In the aggregate these measurement procedures scarcely alter the picture of student achievement just sketched. As table 3-1 shows, the adjusted student gains (the far right columns of the table) are only slightly less than the gains in raw scores. The total difference in grade equivalents between students who gained the most and those who gained the least is reduced from 6.86 years to 6.33 years. As table 3-2 shows, the changes in the school-level picture are more minor still. Between schools in the lowest quartile of gainers and those in the highest, improvements in verbal achievement continue to differ by about two years, in quantitative achievement by around four years, and in total achievement by roughly two years. Assuming for the sake of illustration that all high schools begin with students at the same tenth grade level of achievement, the better schools in our sample graduated their students at an achievement level equivalent to grade 13 while the worst schools graduated their students at a level comparable to only grade 11. Although this gap is also evident in the raw test results, our search for the correlates and causes of the gap will nevertheless employ the more valid IRT log gain scores.

An Exploratory Analysis

We begin our search for the causes of student achievement with a comparison of the organization of "high performance" and "low performance" schools. Schools falling into the top quartile of the school-level distribution of total achievement log gain scores are classified high performance. Schools falling into the bottom quartile are labeled low performance. We compare the two types of schools on the four basic dimensions of school organization introduced in the last chapter. In exploring each dimension we consider a range of specific school characteristics that effective schools research has often found to be associated with student achievement.

We make these initial comparisons without any allowance for the host of circumstances or conditions that might cause school organization to differ. For example, we ask whether teachers in high performance schools have a greater sense of efficacy—a stronger belief in their ability to boost student achievement—than teachers in low performance schools do. We also ask whether students in the top schools take more academic courses than students in schools that perform at the bottom. But we do not ask whether teacher attitudes or student course-taking are associated with school performance when the schools being compared all have students of roughly the same academic ability or who come from families with about the same interest in education. In other words, we do not make "controlled" comparisons. We do not make such comparisons because our purpose at this point is not to determine what causes student achievement.

Our purpose here is exploratory. For that reason we also do not subject our comparisons to tests of statistical significance. We do not ask, for example, whether we can be 95 percent confident that high and low performance schools differ in their leadership. There is little point in knowing the answer to this question if it turns out that leadership has no independent effect on student achievement—if it turns out, in other words, that the relationship between leadership and student achievement disappears when other relevant factors, such as student aptitude or family background, are taken into account through statistical controls. By the same token, there is little point in knowing that high and low performance schools do not differ signifi-cantly in their leadership when leadership could easily turn out to have a significant effect on achievement once other factors are taken into account. In the next chapter we will consider such factors and conduct a proper causal analysis. In this chapter we want to explore organizational variables that deserve to be included in it.

Goals

In recent years researchers and reformers have become quite concerned with the goals and objectives of American high schools. Today, schools have many more purposes than they had decades ago. With the consolidation of schools and school districts, the increase in high school attendance by the poor and the working class, and the development of the comprehensive high school, America's schools grew larger. In addition, these larger schools began providing different programs of study and different kinds of courses—including a plethora of elective courses—to different kinds of students.[15] During the 1960s and 1970s these trends were reinforced by a proliferation of federal and state programs—for compensatory, vocational, and bilingual education, for example—that caused schools to provide services that were more specialized still.[16]

To many observers the growth and internal differentiation of school purposes is a positive development. It permits schools to meet the varied needs of a heterogeneous population of students more effectively.[17] But to other observers, especially those who have contributed to the literature on effective schools, the proliferation of school objectives is a serious problem. It has robbed schools of any clear sense of purpose and caused schools to lower their academic expectations for most students. Schools are no longer leading students—or teachers—to do their best, or to do anything in particular at all.[18]

In the early 1980s this line of criticism became the centerpiece of many of the national reports on America's education crisis.[19] It also led to a very concrete proposal for reform. The states, which had allowed their high school graduation requirements to slip over the preceding two decades, should raise their requirements forthwith. In the coming years virtually every state did so.[20] Higher graduation requirements proved to be the kind of reform that state politicians and educational administrators could adopt easily. All they required were new state laws and simple new rules and regulations.

But observers of effective schools have a good deal more in mind when they argue that schools have become unfocused and undemanding. What they are talking about is not very well reflected in formal requirements. After all, there is little evidence that the decline in student achievement during the 1960s and 1970s was caused directly by declining graduation requirements.[21] Research suggests that while

TABLE 3-3. 1982 Graduation Requirements for All Students in High and Low Performance Schools, in Years[a]

Subject area[b]	Low performance schools	High performance schools
English	3.56	3.75
Foreign language	0.04	0.52
History	2.48	2.72
Mathematics	1.58	1.89
Science	1.45	1.59

a. Sample weighted to achieve a nationally representative sample of public and private high schools.
b. Requirements for all subjects are based on a four-year high school experience.

requirements may be a useful indicator of what a school is trying to accomplish, the best measures of a school's true goals are the priorities articulated—or not articulated—by the principal, and the objectives perceived and internalized by the teachers. Goals that are written down in an organization manual or posted on a bulletin board—however lofty and thoughtful those goals may be—will not have the impact on the day-to-day effectiveness of a school that goals shared and acted on by the school staff will have. Unfortunately for America's public schools, a clear and ambitious sense of collective purpose is not something that politicians can require or that administrators can easily encourage principals and teachers to develop.

The objectives and priorities of the ATS schools are basically consistent with the broadly critical view of school goals in the effective schools literature. That is, there is some evidence that formal requirements may account for differences in school performance. But there is more evidence that informal aspects of school goals are what matter most for student achievement.

The principals in the ATS schools were asked to report the number of years of instruction in five subjects that every student needed to complete in order to receive a diploma.[22] As would be expected for the early 1980s, the averages for high and for low performance schools, reported in table 3-3, are indeed undemanding. Four years of English is not a universal requirement. Foreign language has been virtually eliminated as a prerequisite for high school graduation. Neither mathematics nor science need occupy a student in a typical school for even half of the high school years.

Requirements are not quite as abysmal in high performance schools as in low performance ones, however. Students in high performance

TABLE 3-4. Mean Priorities Assigned to Major School Objectives in High and Low Performance Schools[a]

Objective	Low performance schools		High performance schools		Difference in rank
	Average ranking	Rank order	Average ranking	Rank order	
Basic literacy skills	1.57	1	2.47	1	0.90
Good work habits	3.30	2	3.37	3	0.07
Academic excellence	3.56	3	2.62	2	−0.94
Personal growth and fulfillment	4.16	4	3.51	4	−0.65
Citizenship	4.37	5	4.63	6	0.26
Human relations skills	4.50	6	4.26	5	−0.24
Specific occupational skills	5.78	7	6.53	7	0.75

a. Sample weighted to achieve a nationally representative sample of public and private high schools. Based on responses of principals.

schools must take more of every subject than students in low performance schools in order to graduate. The average difference, though, is only .272 years per subject. That amounts to a difference of a little more than one additional year of one subject overall. When other factors that influence student achievement are taken into consideration, small differences in graduation requirements may make significant differences for achievement. But for now, it appears that formal requirements are less important than their popularity among reformers suggests they ought to be.

More important for student achievement may be informal manifestations of what schools expect students to accomplish. To begin with, principals in high performance schools express different priorities than principals in low performance schools. Principals were asked to rank order a number of general objectives that their schools could be expected to pursue. The rankings, averaged for high and low performance schools in table 3-4, suggest that principals in academically successful schools are leading their students and teachers in a distinctly different direction than principals in unsuccessful schools are leading theirs. The direction in low performance schools is plainly pragmatic. The principals in those schools rank basic literacy, good work habits, citizenship, and occupational skills above where principals in high performance schools rank them. These are important goals, but they do not match the aspirations of principals in successful schools, who give relatively greater priority to higher-order individual needs: academic excellence, personal growth and fulfillment, and human relations skills.

To be sure, there is considerable similarity in the goals of successful and unsuccessful schools too. All but two goals have the same rank order in high performance schools as in low performance ones. On average, good schools as well as bad schools rate basic literacy their number one priority. But, especially among the highest priorities of successful and unsuccessful schools, there are unambiguous differences. Principals in low performance schools say that their second most important objective is to instill good work habits. Principals in high performance schools say that academic excellence is second for them—and a very close second at that. In low performance schools academic excellence is a poor third: it is nearly a full rank lower in average importance than its position in high performance schools.

Not surprisingly, successful schools are also more likely than

TABLE 3-5. Summary Characteristics of School Goals in High and Low Performance Schools[a]

Percent

School characteristic	Low performance schools	High performance schools
Academic excellence is top priority	12.0	28.7
Goal clarity, above average[b]	54.0	63.0

a. Sample weighted to achieve a nationally representative sample of public and private high schools.
b. This measure is also part of the more general index of the principal's vision.

unsuccessful ones to make academic excellence their number one objective. As we report in table 3-5, nearly 30 percent of all high performance schools rate academic excellence their top priority. Only 12 percent of all low performance schools do the same. This is potentially quite important because observers of effective schools repeatedly stress the great impact that high expectations can have. Of course, it only stands to reason that a school will be more likely to find academic success if it makes academic excellence its major goal.

Naturally, schools with bright students may find it easier than schools without such students to focus on academic excellence. Principals whose schools are filled with educationally disadvantaged students may believe it is necessary for them to emphasize basic literacy skills and good work habits.[23] Or, they may just be taking the easy way out. High expectations are tough to meet. But whatever the reason, if the kinds of students in a school are a big influence on the kinds of goals a school sets for itself, the differences that we have observed in the goals of high and low performance schools may have somewhat different implications than we have proposed they have. School objectives may not be quite as important for student achievement as they now appear to be.

Not all of the differences that we observed in school goals can be so easily traced to differences in student bodies, however. The prime example of this is goal clarity (as measured by teacher perception), which we report in table 3-5. Principals in high performance schools not only articulate goals that are more academically ambitious, they also articulate goals that are clearer. About 10 percent more of the high performance schools than of the low performance schools are above average in goal clarity.[24] This is hardly a difference of day and night. Many schools with unclear goals succeed and many schools with clear goals fail. But the tendency for successful schools to have relatively clear goals may have real significance for student achievement. There is little reason to believe that as schools try to establish a coherent sense of purpose they are either helped or hindered by the academic ability of their students. There is every reason to believe that once schools have a coherent sense of purpose they are better able to promote student achievement.

Observers of effective schools, especially schools serving the educationally disadvantaged, have often said that good schools succeed because they have a "mission." From what we can tell with the ATS-HSB data, high performance schools seem to have missions too. Their goals tend to be academically ambitious and their purposes better focused.

Leadership

If successful schools are in fact schools that have strong academic missions and other characteristics of effective organization, they may owe much of their success to their principals. Schools work in complex environments that impose all sorts of demands. Parents have countless ideas about what schools should do, and all schools must take parents into account. All schools have governing boards whose demands schools are obligated to meet. Most schools, and certainly all public schools, are surrounded by some sort of administrative apparatus that sees to it that the demands of local, and increasingly, federal and state authorities, are carried out. The problem for schools, and for the principals who must run them, is that there is no guarantee that this welter of demands will be consistent in any way, shape, or form with effective school organization. Indeed, as we argued earlier, the demands on public schools, the accumulated products of several levels of political decisionmaking, are likely to be inconsistent with effective organization.

Whether schools are public or private, however, principals are likely to shape their organizations. Principals must decide how schools should respond to the barrage of demands from authorities and interests on the outside. They must decide which demands to deflect and which ones to accommodate. Research has shown that it is often difficult for principals to manage these demands very effectively: the external pressures on today's principals are sometimes simply over-whelming.[25] But research has also shown that successful schools are more strongly led. Effective schools seem to be headed by principals who have a clear vision of where they are going, who are knowledgeable enough about teaching and education to help teachers and students work toward desired ends, and who are able to protect schools from the kinds of demands that make it difficult for schools to operate on a professional basis.[26]

We have already seen from the ATS-HSB data that principals in high performance schools articulate a different set of priorities than principals in low performance schools do. In the view of teachers, priorities are clearer in high performance schools too. Now we shall see that the principals of successful and unsuccessful schools differ in many other ways. These differences suggest, moreover, that the leadership of principals is likely to have a great deal to do with whether schools get organized effectively.

The principals of high and low performance schools differ in the basic motivations they bring to their jobs. Principals were asked to rank order a variety of possible reasons for assuming their current positions. Some reasons, such as the "desire to take on the challenges of being a principal" did not distinguish principals in high and low performance schools. But four reasons clearly did. Principals in academically successful schools gave higher priority to gaining control over their school's curriculum, gaining control over their school's personnel, and gaining control over their school's policies. Principals in low performance schools expressed a relatively greater desire to advance their careers.

We used these responses to create a composite measure of the principal's motivation. Principals who were more interested in gaining control over their schools—in one way or another—were less interested in advancing their careers. Accordingly, we decided to gauge a principal's motivation by taking the difference between the two (where motivation for control is measured by the highest ranked of the three control dimensions). Principals who score high on this composite measure are motivated more by concerns for career than by desires for control. In table 3-6 we report on the negative of this measure, the propensity of principals to be motivated by control. A clear majority of the principals in high performance schools are highly

TABLE 3-6. Leadership Characteristics of High and Low
Performance Schools[a]
Percent

School characteristic	Low performance schools	High performance schools
Principal's motivation (to control), above average[b]	18.9	61.9
Principal's dedication to teaching, above average	42.5	59.7
Principal's vision, above average	55.6	61.3

a. Sample weighted to achieve a nationally representative sample of public and private high schools.
b. These percentages are based on the negative of the principal's motivation index, which is coded such that stronger control motivations (lower rank orders) reduce the value of the index.

motivated by control, whereas only a fifth of the principals in low
performance schools are so highly motivated.

A similar difference in job orientation is suggested by an index of
what we call the principal's dedication to teaching. We measure this
quality with two closely related indicators on the ATS principal's
questionnaire, the principal's teaching experience and the principal's
desire to move up to a higher administrative post. Principals with
more years of teaching experience tend to be less interested in
administrative promotions. We assume that principals with more
teaching experience and weaker administrative aspirations are more
dedicated to the pedagogical and instructional parts of their jobs than
to the managerial parts. If effective schools research is correct,
moreover, the ability of a principal to provide educational and instructional leadership may be important for school success. As it turns out
(see table 3-6), principals in high performance schools are indeed more
likely to exhibit an above average level of dedication to teaching.

Principals in better schools, then, not only come to their positions
with a greater interest in the educational missions of their schools,
they also seem to maintain that interest while they are there. At some
risk of overinterpretation, America's low performance schools appear
to be headed by principals who perceive their role to be more that of
a middle manager while its high performance schools seem to be run
by ones who view themselves more as educational leaders.

This interpretation is reinforced by a final measure of leadership also reported in table 3-6. According to the teachers, the principals in high performance schools tend to show a greater propensity to know what kind of school they want, to value innovation and new ideas, and to keep the school apprised of where it should be going. Because these traits are also closely related to the perceived clarity of the school's goals, we combined our measure of goal clarity with our measures of these other qualities in a comprehensive index that we call vision. High performance schools are more likely than low performance schools to be led by principals who are above average in vision. The difference in likelihood is by no means great, but when taken together with the other differences in leadership, it reinforces the impression that better schools are headed by stronger educational leaders.

There are many indications, moreover, that this strength is an important source of superior academic performance. The qualities that distinguish the leadership of the high performance ATS schools—high expectations, clear goals, dedication to teaching, motivation to control, and strength of vision—also characterize the behavior of principals in many of the effective schools studied by others.

Personnel

Not surprisingly, research on effective and ineffective schools has more to say about teachers than about any other topic. Teachers, after all, do the teaching that determines whether students learn. What is surprising, however, is that research has found little to say about many of the qualities of teachers and teaching that reformers have long thought important. In particular, relatively little is said about the educational credentials of teachers, about how teachers score on competency tests, or about how much teachers are paid. Formal qualities such as these do not seem to make a significant difference for academic performance.[27]

What seems to matter is a set of informal characteristics that encourage and support effective teaching. From one study to another these characteristics are labeled and listed somewhat differently. But all studies that find these characteristics to be important are talking about essentially the same thing. They are talking about teachers who operate as a true community of professionals.[28] They are talking about teachers who are not organized as bureaucratic underlings in a hierarchical administrative system.[29]

In a community of professionals, educational values are widely shared. Teachers, perhaps associated with the same school for many years, know what other teachers in the school are doing. Schoolwide decisions are reached by discussion and consensus. Principals in effective schools are strong educational leaders—but their teachers are also influential. Principals encourage teachers to participate in planning and policymaking outside of the classroom. Principals and administrators also respect the professional knowledge, skills, and judgment of teachers and grant them ample latitude to run their classrooms.

Together these qualities are thought by many observers to be perhaps the most important source of school effectiveness. Schools with these qualities tend to buoy teachers' feelings, helping them to overcome the isolation, loneliness, and even victimization—by students, parents, and administrators—that they often experience in the classroom. Schools with these qualities also tend to nurture the development of genuine professionalism in their teachers. Students tend to benefit from all of this. Their instruction is provided by teachers who feel more efficacious and satisfied, and who are better able to respond to differing student needs. The total school experience of students is also more integrated and driven more by a common educational purpose.

The Administrator and Teacher Survey was designed to capture the various qualities of what it may be like to teach in a school that operates as a professional community. Our interest in these qualities is driven by more than their potential importance for school performance, however. To us they are doubly important because they stand to be greatly influenced by the bureaucratization of school administration and to be rooted in institutions of school control. We therefore want to take a very close look at the role that professional communities play in high and low performance schools.

We begin, in table 3-7, by looking at the experience of teachers. It turns out that the key to effective teaching is evidently not years of teacher service to a single school. Only a fraction more of the teachers in the best schools than in the worst schools have worked in their current institutions for at least ten years. This suggests not only that an unusual degree of staff stability is not crucial to the development of professional communities, but also that the sheer experience of a school's teaching staff may be unrelated to the achievement of its

TABLE 3-7. Staff Characteristics of High and Low Performance Schools[a]

Percent

School characteristic	Low performance schools	High performance schools
Teachers at school for		
at least ten years	35.9	37.4
Teaching esteem, above average[b]	39.7	57.8
Teachers judged excellent		
by principals	23.3	31.7
Teacher professionalism,		
above average	27.7	59.3
Teacher influence, above average	44.5	52.5
Teacher efficacy, above average	32.7	60.1
Teacher absenteeism problem,		
below average	39.5	63.8
Staff harmony, above average[c]	42.7	61.4
Teacher cooperation, above average	33.8	62.0
Teacher collegiality, above average	49.2	65.9

a. Sample weighted to achieve a nationally representative sample of public and private high schools.
b. This index also includes the principal's dedication to teaching.
c. This index also includes the principal's vision.

students. Successful schools and unsuccessful ones are equally well staffed by veteran teachers. This is not totally surprising. Teachers who remain in their schools for long periods of time may improve with each year of experience, or they may simply reach a performance plateau and remain there. Especially given the personnel rules of most public schools, which reward seniority more than performance, it is quite plausible that teacher experience and student achievement are unrelated.

The differences in the teaching staffs of high and low performance schools appear to have much more to do with the quality of teacher service than with its quantity. To begin with, a larger proportion of the teachers in successful schools than in unsuccessful ones—one-third versus one-quarter (see table 3-7)—were judged by their principals to be excellent. This may mean that better schools have teachers who are objectively better—teachers with, perhaps, superior training or greater competence. Or it may mean that better schools have teachers who are subjectively better—that is, who are held in higher esteem by their principals. Either way, students should benefit. Teachers who are held in high esteem by their principals, and who feel that their work is highly valued, should teach with greater dedication and enthusiasm, performing objectively better too.

Interestingly, schools in which principals rate their teachers highly are also schools that tend to be headed by principals who are more dedicated to teaching, as identified in table 3-6. Moreover, schools that are led by principals with either of these characteristics tend to have a host of other organizational characteristics in common. These relationships suggest (and various factor analyses confirmed this) that a principal's evaluation of teachers and a principal's dedication to teaching are probably alternative indicators of one more general school characteristic. We therefore combined these indicators in a new, broader index of school organization that we labeled teaching esteem. The values of this index for high and low performance schools are given in table 3-7. As gauged by the index, teaching is more highly regarded in good schools than in bad.

It is consistent with this high regard that teachers in the best academic schools are also entrusted with relatively greater responsibility and discretion. As we also report in table 3-7, teachers in high performance schools tend to enjoy above-average levels of influence while teachers in low performance schools tend to have levels of influence below the national average. This is potentially quite important for the development of professional communities because the matters over which teachers exert greater influence in effective schools—determining behavior codes, establishing the school curriculum, assigning students to classes, shaping teacher development programs, and disciplining students—are matters that are usually settled outside of the classroom, often at the discretion of principals and higher administrative authorities.[30]

We also found (see table 3-7) that teachers in high performance schools have more efficacy than teachers in low performance schools. Of course, it only stands to reason that teachers with more influence over matters affecting their teaching would feel more efficacious, all things being equal. Thus teachers in the successful schools are less likely than teachers in the unsuccessful ones to believe, in the words of the survey, that their success or failure is beyond their control, or that it is a waste of time to try to do their best. Evidently, such feelings of frustration also influence teacher behavior: we found (see table 3-7) that teachers in low performance schools present much more of a problem of absenteeism for their principals than teachers in high performance schools present for theirs.

This is not to say that high levels of efficacy and low levels of absenteeism are products of teacher influence alone. They are almost certainly conditioned by the kinds of students being taught—as teacher influence may be also. But all three of these traits—influence, efficacy, and absenteeism—are likely to represent a force of some independent importance in the educational process. Together they describe what is usually meant by teacher professionalism. Truly professional teachers are ones who are sufficiently knowledgeable, wise, and dedicated that they can be trusted to work effectively without extensive direction and supervision and to contribute constructively to the overall operation of an effective school. Truly professional teachers are also the kinds of teachers that reformers now strongly believe schools must recruit and develop.[31] Because several of the teacher qualities that we measured—influence, efficacy, and absenteeism—are dimensions of professionalism, it is no surprise that they are correlated with one another and can be combined in an index of teacher professionalism. That index, employed in table 3-7, reveals that low performance schools strongly tend to be staffed by teachers who are below average in professionalism while high performance schools tend to be staffed by teachers who are above average.

This difference in professionalism also seems to be evident in the relationships among teachers in the two types of schools. By establishing a basis for mutual respect among teachers, professionalism tends to encourage cooperation and collegiality. Teachers who share a commitment to a school and who are collectively entrusted with significant responsibility for a school's success have good reason to work closely with one another as a community of equals. As we shall see, forces other than professionalism may also encourage this. But however bonds of community are created, cooperation and collegiality distinguish high performance schools from low performance ones.

The differences, as the indexes in table 3-7 show, are also rather large. In the better schools, teachers spend more time meeting with one another to coordinate instruction and matters related to it; they regard one another as more helpful with their classroom problems;

they work more assiduously to align their courses; and they are more knowledgeable about one another's classes. These are the components of our index of cooperation, on which high performance schools tend to be well above average and low performance schools far below average. High performance schools also tend to be much above average on our index of teacher collegiality. Concretely, this means that teachers in the best schools are especially likely to agree that their fellow teachers "can be counted on anytime, anywhere"; that they all "share beliefs in the central school mission"; and, among other things, that the school is "like a big family."

The coherence that characterizes the teaching staffs of high performance schools is consistent with other outstanding qualities of top schools, especially one of the qualities of good school leadership. The best schools tend to be led by principals who provide a clear vision of where their schools are going and who know how to get teachers moving in one direction. This kind of leadership would seem to encourage the sort of cooperation and collegiality that we found in the top schools, and to foster the kind of community feeling and esprit de corps that observers of effective schools argue are so important. It turns out, in fact, that our index of the vision of school leadership is correlated with our indexes of cooperation and collegiality. And the relationships among the three are sufficient to justify the creation of a more comprehensive index of a school's organizational coherence, an index we label staff harmony. Not surprisingly, as we report in table 3-7, high performance schools tend to have above average levels of staff harmony; low performance schools tend to have below average levels.

Overall, then, the organizations of academically successful schools and academically unsuccessful ones are rather different. The former tend to have goals that are more focused and ambitious, to be headed by purposeful educational leaders, and to be staffed by teachers who work with one another and with the principal as a community of professionals—as a close-knit team. Unsuccessful schools are organized rather differently. They tend to hold lower and more ambiguous expectations of their students, to be managed rather than led, and to be staffed by teachers who are lacking in the requisites of professionalism and effective interaction. Low performance schools look less like professional teams and more like bureaucratic agencies.

Practice

There are many reasons to believe that schools that are organized as teams of professionals will outperform schools that are not. Students will achieve more if more is expected of them and if their achievement is reinforced by similar expectations for all students in a school. Teachers will work more effectively as a group, and complement each other more in their teaching, if they have a clear idea of where the school is heading. Teachers will bring more enthusiasm and pride to their work if they have more control over it and understand that it is vital to the success of the school as a whole. The list goes on and on. But ultimately students learn in their classes. It is therefore important to ask whether there are differences in the courses that students take and in the way classes are conducted in successful and unsuccessful schools.

Course Work

Research has shown, to no great surprise, that course work is a key to student achievement. Students who take more academic courses and more courses that are academically rigorous tend to achieve more than students who do not.[32] This is important because schools have considerable control over course work. They influence the amount and difficulty of the material being taught. And they influence what courses students take. We have no way of measuring course content directly, but we do have measures of what students take. We saw earlier that high schools do not require students to take very many academic courses in order to graduate, and that successful schools do not require much more work than unsuccessful ones. Nevertheless, there is pretty strong evidence that successful schools somehow get their students to take more academic courses and also more demanding ones.

The first evidence of this has to do with tracking. With the postwar proliferation of comprehensive high schools, students have increasingly been "tracked" into programs of study—typically, academic, general, or vocational—that organize course work according to student interest and ability. Courses in these programs differ in number, kind, and difficulty. Students in academic or college preparatory programs typically take more academic courses than students in general or vocational programs who are not being expressly prepared for college.

TABLE 3-8. Percentage Distribution of Student Bodies of High
and Low Performance Schools, by Curriculum Program[a]

Program	Low performance schools	High performance schools
Academic	28.3	63.7
General[b]	38.6	12.4
Vocational[c]	33.1	23.9

a. Based on responses of principals to questions about program distribution of tenth grade students. Sample weighted to achieve a nationally representative sample of public and private high schools.

b. This is a residual category that includes only nonvocational general students.

c. This category is the sum of enrollments in the following vocational specialties: agriculture, business, distributive education, health, home economics, technical, and trade.

The courses in English, history, mathematics, and science that make up an academic program are also likely to be more rigorous than the courses in the same subjects that make up the general and vocational programs.[33] To understand student achievement, it may therefore be important to know not only what courses students are taking but what program or track students are in. Schools may be able to promote student achievement by placing more students in academic programs or by encouraging more students to enroll in them.

In table 3-8 we compare the program enrollments of high and low performance schools. In high performance schools nearly two-thirds of the students are taking an academic program of study while only 12.4 percent are enrolled in the general track. In low performance schools the academic track is the least populated of the three major programs of study; students are more likely to be taking either a general or a vocational program. Of course, there is a complicated reciprocal relationship between student achievement and tracking. While enrollment in an academic track may boost student achievement, student achievement affects the track that schools place students in. Nevertheless, it is unlikely that school placement decisions and student program choices are unaffected by the expectations that schools hold of their students or by the encouragement that schools otherwise provide to academic work. The plain fact that high performance schools enroll more than twice the proportion of students that low performance schools enroll in academic programs may therefore be of real consequence for student achievement.

As we have said, this consequence may follow from the greater rigor of academic track courses, or from the greater number of academic courses that academic track students take. We therefore

TABLE 3-9. Mean Semesters of Course Work Completed by Student Bodies of High and Low Performance Schools, Sophomore Year through Senior Year, by Curriculum Program[a]

Subject and program	Low performance schools	High performance schools
English		
Academic	5.95	6.04
General	5.76	5.93
Vocational	5.50	5.70
All students	5.71	5.96
Foreign language		
Academic	2.42	2.96
General	0.70	1.35
Vocational	0.77	1.11
All students	1.14	2.48
History		
Academic	3.97	4.62
General	2.96	3.32
Vocational	2.47	2.89
All students	3.21	4.06
Mathematics		
Academic	4.74	5.19
General	3.68	4.11
Vocational	3.36	3.36
All students	3.91	4.62
Science		
Academic	4.51	5.03
General	4.48	4.83
Vocational	4.20	4.71
All students	4.47	4.97

a. Sample weighted to achieve a nationally representative sample of public and private high schools.

consider in table 3-9 the academic courses that students in high and low performance schools take. As could be expected, students in successful schools take more academic courses than students in unsuccessful schools. Unexpectedly, this is a fact for all students and all programs of study. In both the academic and the general tracks, students take more course work in English, foreign language, history, mathematics, and science in the high performance schools. For students in vocational tracks, greater course-taking is characteristic for all subjects except mathematics, which vocational students in high and low performance schools take in equal amounts. It is also notable that the difference in course work taken per subject is nearly as large for general track students as for students in an academic track. The general track students in the high performance schools finish .396 semesters more course work per subject than their counterparts in the low performance schools while the academic track students in high performance schools top their counterparts by .450 semesters of course work per subject.

To be sure, the differences in course work that separate the best and the worst schools are not large. Once other factors such as student ability are taken into account, they may not explain the substantial differences in student achievement between these schools. But the differences in course work are 60 percent larger than the differences in graduation requirements between high and low performance schools. And the differences in course work reinforce the clear impression provided by the quite sizable differences in program enrollments: the country's best schools seem to succeed in part because they are somehow able to emphasize academic instruction.

Classrooms

When all is said and done, the bulk of formal education takes place in the classroom, and it is there that an effective school must ultimately succeed. Unfortunately, less is known about effective classrooms than about effective schools, especially at the level of secondary education. While instructional methods for elementary education have been the subject of voluminous research with relatively clear implications for practice, approaches to the teaching of high school subjects and skills have not been studied as extensively or yielded such firm conclusions.[34] Still, research does point to certain general qualities that seem to characterize more effective high school classes.[35] These include the common sense observations that effective classrooms are able to maximize learning time, or perhaps more accurately, minimize non-learning time; that they seem to experience fewer disruptions; that they expend less energy on administrative routines; and that they devote less time to student discipline. Effective classrooms also appear to be able to keep their students as focused on academics out of class as in class, getting them to complete more homework.

In table 3-10 we look at a variety of measures of effective classroom practices in high and low performance schools. What we see are basically two things. First, the classrooms of successful and unsuc-

TABLE 3-10. Classroom Characteristics of High and Low
Performance Schools[a]

School characteristic	Low performance schools	High performance schools
Mean minutes of homework assigned per subject daily	22.5	25.0
Mean number of writing assignments per subject annually	24.0	24.2
Amount of time devoted to administrative routines, above average (percent)	59.4	42.6
Amount of classroom disruption, above average (percent)	45.3	33.9
Disciplinary practices, above average in fairness and effectiveness (percent)	42.6	61.8

a. Sample weighted to achieve a nationally representative sample of public and private high schools.

cessful schools often differ very little. There is a remarkable sameness
to the classrooms of America's schools. But what we also see is that
where classrooms differ, the differences seem to be closely related to
the differences that we have observed in effective and ineffective
schools more generally. In other words, schools with effective organizations seem to encourage the operation of classrooms with at least
some of the requisites of successful instruction.

Let us begin with those classroom characteristics that do not seem
to distinguish successful and unsuccessful schools. Research has
provided some evidence that student achievement depends on homework, and reformers, convinced of the relationship between the two,
have been urging schools to assign more of it.[36] As we report in table
3-10, high performance schools ask their students to complete more
homework than low performance schools require. But the average
additional amount required is only two and a half minutes per subject
per night. That adds up to about one additional hour of homework per
week for students in the high performance schools when compared
with those in the low performance ones. It remains to be seen whether
this difference will help explain the variation in achievement across
the ATS schools, but it is certainly a less promising difference than
the recent enthusiasm for homework gives cause to expect.

Homework is not the only measure of classroom requirements to
suggest this kind of conclusion. Teachers in the ATS schools were

also asked to report the number of writing assignments that they gave students each grading period. We used these reports to estimate the number of assignments that students were given each year in a typical class. The estimates, for good schools and for bad, are reported in table 3-10. In high and low performance schools alike, students are required to complete twenty-four written assignments of one page or longer in each class each year. The teachers in successful schools require their students to complete only a fraction more written assignments than the teachers in unsuccessful schools require theirs to complete. As with homework, students in better schools may devote more time and effort to writing than students in other schools. But if students in better schools do this, it is not because of additional requirements imposed in classrooms.

The big differences in the classrooms of high and low performance schools are not in the academic demands made on the time of students but in the nonacademic demands made on the time of teachers. In essence, teaching is subject to measurably less interference in schools that are succeeding than in those that are not. In a variety of ways, summarized by a comprehensive index reported in table 3-10, administrative routines are less burdensome in the top schools. In particular, this implies that in high performance schools the staff is less likely to complain that teaching is obstructed by "routines and paperwork," and teachers estimate spending less time on such things.[37] The difference in the index of administrative routines also implies differences in classroom administration: teachers in the better schools report spending less class time reviewing major examinations and quizzes, and are less likely to correct, grade, record, and return every homework assignment. This is not to say that teachers in the more successful schools are less effective in providing students with feedback—a practice that research strongly suggests is vital—only that they do not provide it in a manner that is quite so routinized, time consuming, and, by association with other indicators of administrative tasks, burdensome.

The classrooms of high performance schools are also subject to less disruption. In part this is an indication of the behavior of students who, teachers in the better schools report, spend less time "fooling around" or otherwise avoiding assigned tasks. But the difference in disruptions is also an indication of schoolwide organization. The index of classroom disruptions that we report in table 3-10 is based on a measure of the attentiveness of students plus measures of the interruption of instruction by "messengers from the office," "announcements," "noise in the hallways," and other forms of intrusion. These seemingly disparate sorts of disruptions are closely related to one another in the ATS schools. We therefore use them in an index. Like the burdens of administrative routines, the frustrations of classroom disruptions may also stem from school organization. Schools that are organized along classic bureaucratic lines are more prone to formalism, routinization, and central interference than schools that are organized along more cooperative and decentralized lines, as professional teams.

To be sure, the intrusions on teaching in the low performance schools are not only the result of organization. Students are almost certainly an additional cause. They may be a source of routinization. For example, weak students may lack the self-discipline to be trusted to complete ungraded assignments or to review tests on their own. And students are almost certainly a source of disruption themselves. For reasons beyond the control of schools, the students of some schools will have a greater propensity to misbehave than the students of other schools. This implies not only different levels of prominent schoolwide problems such as fighting, vandalism, and alcohol or drug abuse but also different incidences of various disruptive behaviors in class.

Nevertheless, schools must attempt to maintain order, and their success in doing so is widely thought to exert an independent influence on student achievement. The ATS schools reinforce this line of thinking. The disciplinary climates of high and low performance schools appear to be substantially different. As the index in table 3-10 implies, students in the schools at the top of the distribution of achievement regard the discipline in their schools as fairer and more effective than the students in the schools at the bottom of the distribution view the discipline in theirs.

Again, differences in discipline may have as much to do with the problems presented by students as with the responses to them by schools. But apportioning responsibility, a difficult analytical task, is not appropriate or necessary at this juncture. The important observation is that teaching in high performance schools apparently takes place in a more disciplined atmosphere requiring less effort by teachers to maintain order. How this discipline is maintained—whether it benefits from the teamlike organization of successful schools or relies on tough sanctions—is not clear.[38] But what is clear is that the classes of high performance schools are subject to fewer intrusions and disruptions of all kinds. Much of this is to be expected given the less hierarchical organization of high performance schools. Yet, whatever the source, the product is more class time for the educational activities deemed by teachers to be most appropriate.

Conclusion

Although this exploratory analysis is but a first cut at the data, it appears that school organization and performance are indeed related. High performance schools differ in goals, leadership, personnel, and educational practices from low performance schools. Their goals are clearer and more academically ambitious, their principals are stronger educational leaders, their teachers are more professional and harmonious, their course work is more academically rigorous, and their classrooms are more orderly and less bureaucratic. On any given indicator the differences between high and low performance schools are not always great; the organizational similarities across America's schools are quite impressive. But what is also very impressive is the consistency of the differences across so many dimensions of school organization.

Whether these differences account for the variation in performance across America's schools is, of course, another question. Prior research suggests that these are precisely the kinds of organizational differences that we should expect between effective and ineffective schools. But the differences in school organization that we have observed may well be artifacts of other, perhaps more fundamental, factors that we have yet to take into account—differences between schools, such as student abilities, for instance, or family values.

Even if the differences in schools that we have observed are not artifacts of other relationships, some of them may prove much more significant for academic performance than others. In particular, informal organizational differences may be far more important than formal ones. High and low performance schools appear to be distinguished more by their leadership, professionalism, and teamwork, for example, than by their graduation requirements, or homework and writing assignments. This has potentially important implications for school improvement. If school success really depends on the development of a professional, teamlike organization, improvement will be harder to bring about than if it hinges on the imposition of rigorous requirements. In particular, for all of the reasons that we explained in chapter 2, improvement will be harder to achieve through the bureaucratized systems of democratic control that have governed public education for such a long time. Still, it is one thing for teamwork, professionalism, and the like to be associated with high performance; it is quite another for them to be its cause. Distinguishing between the two is the task to which we now turn.

Chapter Four

The Causes of Student Achievement

THE STRONGEST and most consistent finding in research on student achievement is that family background is a major influence, perhaps even a decisive one.[1] It is a major influence in the home, where parents establish basic educational values and scholastic work habits. It may be a significant influence on inherited intelligence. It is also an influence at school, where children bring their values and habits and spread them among other children. By comparison, the influence that schools have on student achievement has often appeared weak. Indeed, researchers have generally been unable to establish a statistically significant relationship between student achievement and any of the school characteristics that are often thought important: teacher-pupil ratios, teacher education, teacher salaries, and per pupil expenditures.[2] This should come as no great surprise. Over the last two decades, as school performance has deteriorated and stagnated, per pupil spending on schools has increased nearly 100 percent after inflation, class sizes have shrunk more than 20 percent, and most teachers have acquired master's degrees.[3] The influence of family background appears to have overwhelmed everything else.

Despite all this, we found in the last chapter that successful and unsuccessful schools do seem to differ. We found, much as effective schools research has found, that high performance schools differ from low performance schools in their goals, leadership, personnel, and practices. Yet effective schools research has been less than convincing in its efforts to attribute student achievement to these differences. Small samples, limited measures of student achievement, and most of all, inadequate allowances for family background have left doubts about how strong the influence of school organization is.[4] School organizations may differ primarily because they are serving different kinds of students. School organizations may have relatively little influence on student achievement above and beyond the well-known influences of families and friends.

Our findings thus far are subject to similar doubts, but the ATS-HSB data provide a solid foundation for addressing them. In this chapter we begin to do so. Using statistical models of student achievement gains, we will compare the influence of family background, school financial resources, and other possible causes of student achievement with one another and to the organizational influences described in the last chapter. The models, quite similar to those that in other research have confirmed the influence of family background, will occupy us throughout most of the chapter. First, though, we want to introduce the alternative causes we will consider. As in the last chapter, we explore these alternatives by looking at them in high and low performance schools. We do so, again, not to draw conclusions about cause and effect but only to consider what should be included in a proper causal analysis.

Economic Resources

Although countless studies have concluded that economic resources of various kinds are unrelated to school performance, economic resources should nevertheless be part of any well-balanced analysis of how schools perform. It makes sense to think that schools ought to operate more successfully the more resources they have to work with. Schools that offer higher salaries and smaller classes—both of which require more financial resources—should attract more talented teachers, who in turn should do a better job of teaching. Similarly, schools with superior facilities, equipment, and supplies—for example, bright, clean buildings and classrooms, state-of-the-art laboratories and computers, current and innovative instructional materials—should be more successful than schools that are physically antiquated or dilapidated.

We therefore present in table 4-1 some preliminary evidence of the potential importance of economic resources for school performance. As in chapter 3, we report the average characteristics of schools in the lowest and in the highest quartiles of the distribution of school-level achievement gains. By these measures it appears that resources may matter for school performance. When differences in expenditures at the school level and the district level are averaged, schools in the

TABLE 4-1. Mean Economic Characteristics of High and Low Performance Schools[a]

Dollars unless otherwise indicated

School characteristic	Low performance schools	High performance schools
Annual per pupil expenditure by school	1,470	1,837
Annual per pupil expenditure by district	1,469	1,724
Minimum teacher salary	14,217	14,989
Maximum teacher salary	27,440	26,339
Student-teacher ratio	15.7	13.8
Economic resources, above average (percent)	29.9	50.2

a. Sample weighted to achieve a nationally representative sample of public and private high schools. Per pupil expenditure data are from 1980. All other data are from 1984 except average economic resources, which are from both years.

top quartile of student achievement gains spend about 20 percent more per pupil than schools in the bottom quartile.

Interestingly, these additional funds do not appear to be used to pay commensurately higher teacher salaries. The minimum and maximum salaries in the high performance schools are each within about a thousand dollars of those in the low performance schools. This does not necessarily mean that the top schools do not attract better teachers with their salaries. It is possible that by simply offering the same compensation as schools with low levels of achievement, and other problems—student misbehavior, unsupportive parents—as well, the schools with high levels of achievement may still be quite a bit more attractive.

The main difference that seems to occur as school resources increase is not that teachers are paid more but that more teachers are hired. High performance schools have a lower ratio of students to teachers than low performance schools have—13.8 to 1 compared with 15.7 to 1. This difference, of about two students per teacher, is fairly substantial: if low performance schools wanted to reduce their student-teacher ratios to the level in high performance schools, they would need to hire 14 percent more teachers. Since teacher salaries are roughly half of public school district budgets, low performance schools would need to increase their expenditures per pupil at least 7 percent and probably considerably more—since more teachers require more support staff, instructional materials, and physical space. A conservative estimate is that low performance schools would have to raise their expenditures more than 10 percent to be staffed as intensively as high performance schools. Such an increase would make up more than half of the existing difference between the current expenditures of high and low performance schools.[5]

The key consequence of higher school spending, then, is apparently better staffing ratios and not higher staff salaries. This is further indicated by the correlations among these school qualities in the full sample of ATS schools. School expenditures and staffing ratios are strongly correlated with each other but not with teacher salaries. Because of this, we created an index—which we call economic resources—out of per pupil expenditures and student-teacher ratios. Schools that have high expenditures and low ratios score high on this index.

As table 4-1 reports, schools that differ in achievement also differ on this index. Half of all high performance schools have above-average economic resources; only 30 percent of all low performance schools do. This difference may or may not be an indication that economic resources are important for student achievement. But it is certainly an indication that economic resources warrant further investigation.

School Size

A different but equally basic resource that education researchers have long thought important to school performance is school size. The traditional thinking is that relatively large high schools have advantages over small ones. Schools with many students, say at least several hundred per grade, can take advantage of economies of scale in such things as capital investments (for example, buildings, books, and buses) and administrative costs and thereby operate more efficiently.[6] They can also exploit opportunities for division of labor and specialization, providing each student with a program and a set of instructors closely matched to his or her needs. This virtue, given great weight by proponents of the comprehensive high school, should enhance student achievement.[7]

There is another, more recent, line of thinking, however. A critique of the comprehensive high school, this perspective suggests that high schools have become too large. Modern high schools often find it impractical to monitor individual student needs very sensitively.

Teachers really do not come to understand the problems of the hundreds of students who file in and out of their classes each year. Students are prone to drift through large high schools without attention or direction unless they stray egregiously off course. Many students are also likely to be left to take programs of study that are generally beneath their level of ability. Smaller schools are putatively less vulnerable to these problems. They may also be better able to foster the teamwork, esprit de corps, and focus of effective schools.[8]

The facts, at least as the schools in the Administrator and Teacher Survey (ATS) present them, do not support either view of school size very strongly. As table 4-2 reports, high performance and low performance schools are about the same size on the average. The mean enrollment in successful schools is 729 while that in unsuccessful ones is 695.[9] That amounts to a difference of about eight students per grade. To be sure, this difference provides some support for the "bigger is better" argument. But the distributions of school size suggest that matters may be more complicated. Many (18.4 percent) of the most successful schools are tiny, enrolling fewer than 100 students, while none of the least successful schools is so small. In addition, roughly equal proportions of high performance and low performance schools are very large, enrolling 1,500 students or more. If bigger is indeed better, then, other factors must be obscuring the relationship.

Family Background

However schools may differ in their size, their economic resources, or their overall organization, they may differ much less in their effects on student achievement than those differences might lead us to expect. The primary reason is that student achievement, school organization, and school resources may all be powerfully influenced by one other factor—the family background of students. Families affect school finances through their willingness to pay taxes and tuition. They influence school organization through their support for, or opposition to, various school goals. They affect student achievement through their reinforcement of school work and educational values in the home. To begin to allow for these confounding influences, we take a look here at just how strong and extensive the influences of families may be.

TABLE 4-2. Size Distribution of High and Low Performance
Schools
Percent unless otherwise indicated

Total high school enrollment[a]	Low performance schools	High performance schools
0–99	0.0	18.4
100–299	32.2	13.2
300–499	23.8	11.3
500–999	19.4	28.6
1,000–1,499	9.3	16.6
1,500–1,999	10.4	7.0
2,000–2,999	4.2	4.6
3,000 or more	0.7	0.2
Mean enrollment	695	729

a. Sample weighted to achieve a nationally representative sample of public and private high schools.

We start with family income, which distinguishes high and low performance schools by quite a lot. As we report in table 4-3, the families of students in successful schools annually earn about 35 percent more than the families of students in unsuccessful schools. As we also report in the table, however, bad schools do not just serve the poor, and good schools do not just serve the rich. A third of all low performance schools have families with average income above the national median, which was $21,071 in 1980. Only one high performance school falls below the 1980 poverty level of $8,382 in average family income, but, interestingly, only one low performance school has a student body that on average is in poverty.[10] Moreover, about a fifth of all high performance schools have student bodies with less than average levels of family income.

The same sort of relationship characterizes school performance and parent education. In table 4-4 we see that the fathers and the mothers of students in high performance schools average about a year and a half more formal education than their counterparts in low performance schools. The average parent in an unsuccessful school has barely twelve years of education, the equivalent of a high school diploma. The average parent in a successful school has a year to two years' education beyond high school. Two and one-half times as many fathers and mothers in the top schools have four-year college degrees compared with fathers and mothers in the schools at the bottom. Nevertheless, the overwhelming majority of parents in the high performance schools do not have college degrees, and nearly half of the mothers in those

TABLE 4-3. Distribution of Annual Family Income for Student
Bodies of High and Low Performance Schools[a]
Percent unless otherwise indicated

Mean annual family income	Low performance schools	High performance schools
$ 9,999 or less	1.1	0.2
$10,000–14,999	21.1	0.7
$15,000–19,999	34.8	17.4
$20,000–24,999	32.2	35.0
$25,000–29,999	9.8	24.6
$30,000 or more	1.0	22.1
Mean income (dollars)	18,934	25,874

a. Sample weighted to achieve a nationally representative sample of public and private high schools. Data are from 1980.

schools have no education beyond high school whatsoever. About a third of the parents in low performance schools have been educated beyond high school. Much like family income, then, parent education is directly related to school performance, but it is far from a perfect predictor of it.

Generally speaking, the most dramatic differences between the families of high and low performance schools are in income and education. We can see this in table 4-5 where we look at other family characteristics that are often thought to influence student achievement. For example, two-parent families have certain advantages over one-

TABLE 4-4. Distribution of Parent Education for Student Bodies
of High and Low Performance Schools[a]
Percent unless otherwise indicated

Education completed	Low performance schools		High performance schools	
	Father	Mother	Father	Mother
Less than high school	29.3	25.5	16.1	12.6
High school	40.4	46.6	22.7	34.6
Postsecondary vocational school	9.1	8.0	9.7	8.8
Some college	8.8	9.3	15.8	18.6
Four-year college degree	6.2	6.9	17.2	16.0
Graduate or professional degree	6.2	3.7	18.5	9.4
Mean years of education	12.3	12.2	14.0	13.4

a. Sample weighted to achieve a nationally representative sample of public and private high schools.

TABLE 4-5. Characteristics of Households of Student Bodies of High and Low Performance Schools[a]

Percent

Characteristic	Low performance schools	High performance schools
Two parents in home	74.4	83.1
Mother working while student in high school	67.5	69.1
Number of home learning tools, above average	34.6	76.4
Father closely monitors school work	64.7	71.7
Mother closely monitors school work	84.9	84.8
Student expected to attend college[b]		
By father	65.3	76.4
By mother	67.8	79.4

a. Sample weighted to achieve a nationally representative sample of public and private high schools.
b. Based on 80 percent of sample that reported knowing parental expectations.

parent families in providing a positive home learning environment. All things being equal, parents in two-parent families have more time available for supervising and assisting with schoolwork than parents in one-parent families. Two-parent households are also less likely to burden children with the emotional repercussions of adult problems—divorce, abandonment, unwed motherhood—that may impair concentration on schoolwork. Yet, whatever the advantages of two-parent households, they do not really stand out in the comparisons of high and low performance schools. Nine percent more of the students in high performance schools than in low performance ones come from families with both parents present in the home.

There is also reason to believe that children may benefit educationally from having their mothers in the home rather than in the work place. Among other things, nonworking mothers may have more time than working mothers to meet their children's educational needs. They may have more time to help out at school, to assist with homework and school projects, and to see that assignments are properly done. Nevertheless, there is only a 2 percent difference in the employment rates of mothers in successful and unsuccessful schools. And the difference is not in the commonly expected direction. Mothers in successful schools are slightly more, not less, likely to work.

Other family characteristics reveal somewhat greater differences. For example, students in the best schools (see table 4-5) come from homes where there are more learning tools. Students were asked in the High School and Beyond (HSB) survey to report whether their homes contained a typewriter, a calculator, a set of encyclopedias, and more than fifty books (among other things). The reports of these possessions are highly correlated; homes with calculators also tend to have encyclopedias, and so forth. Consequently, we used an index of home learning tools to gauge the availability of all such tools simultaneously. According to this index, about a third of the households of low performance schools have more than average numbers of home learning tools while three-quarters of the households of high performance schools have above average numbers of them. Clearly, the homes of the best schools are better equipped for learning.

The homes of the best schools also are more likely to have parents who directly encourage their children to learn. Specifically, the families in the top schools monitor their children's schoolwork more attentively and maintain higher expectations for their achievement. Thus about 7 percent more fathers in high performance schools than in low performance schools closely monitor schoolwork. Mothers, the main monitors of schoolwork in both types of schools, do not differ in their vigilance, however. And in both types of schools the majority of students are monitored by their parents. The differences in parental expectations are similar. In both types of schools the majority of parents expect their children to attend college, but the expectation is somewhat more common among parents in high performance schools. About 10 percent more of the parents in the best schools than in the worst ones expect their children to go on to college.[11] These differences, like those for other family characteristics, suggest that while student achievement may be influenced by family background—perhaps even very strongly—achievement is hardly determined by this influence alone.

The influence of family background is felt not only in the home, however. It is also felt in the school. Through their peers, students are influenced by the families of other students in a school. Insofar as the educational values and economic circumstances of the home tell us something about the academic orientations of the students from those homes, family characteristics are therefore doubly meaningful. In the subsequent analysis we will take into account the family

TABLE 4-6. Socioeconomic Characteristics of Student Bodies of High and Low Performance Schools[a]

Percent

Characteristic	Low performance schools	High performance schools
Black	21.2	5.1
Hispanic	4.6	2.8
Economically disadvantaged	23.7	8.0
Socioeconomic status, above average	25.0	70.0

a. Sample weighted to achieve a nationally representative sample of public and private high schools.

background of the individual student whose achievement we are trying to explain as well as the average family background of the students in the school the student attends.

The most prominent differences in student bodies are summarized in table 4-6. High and low performance schools have very different racial makeups. Whereas 21.2 percent of the students in low performance schools are black, only 5.1 percent of the students in high performance schools are black. Hispanics, another large, disadvantaged minority, are only slightly more common in the worst schools than in the best ones, however. In fact, the only racial distinction that is sharply associated with achievement at the school level is the distinction between black and white.

Not surprisingly, there is an important economic distinction associated with school achievement too. High performance schools have far fewer students who are officially classified as economically disadvantaged than low performance schools have. Nearly a quarter of the students in the typical low performance school but less than a tenth of the students in the typical high performance school can be classified economically disadvantaged and declared eligible for federal compensatory education aid.

Overall, the student bodies of the best and the worst schools can be distinguished by what is usually referred to as their socioeconomic status, or SES. We measure SES with an index of parental income, education, occupation, and home learning tools (summarized, by and large, by the indicators in tables 4-3, 4-4, and 4-5) that is provided as part of the HSB data. We use this index primarily because it summarizes what seem to be the largest differences in the families of students in high and low performance schools. We also employ it because it is a standard index used widely in analyses of the HSB data. As we show in table 4-6, it does indeed draw a clear line between the student bodies of high and low performance schools. While 70 percent of the high performance schools have student bodies above average in SES, only 25 percent of the low performance schools have students that are so well-off.

Modeling Student Achievement

We have now seen that student achievement is associated with family background, school resources, and school organization. Our next task is to determine whether any or all of these can be considered causes of student achievement. This is not an easy task. The relationships among students, families, schools, and school systems are extraordinarily complicated. Relationships that appear to have great causal significance can easily turn out to be spurious associations. Some schools that are thought to be excellent, for example, may have little special impact on their students; on analysis, family background may turn out to be the primary cause of high achievement in such schools. Because of this complexity, we want to explain very carefully how we will go about drawing our conclusions.

To begin with, we need to recognize two analytical problems. The first of these is the problem of selection bias. Relationships among schools, families, and students are greatly complicated by the fact that many families select the schools that their children attend. Private schools and many fine public schools have students whose parents place a high value on education and have chosen to pay tuition or hefty mortgages and property taxes to place their children in schools with reputations for effectiveness. Presumably these students will tend to be more motivated to learn than students whose parents have not selected their schools. Students whose parents select their schools will probably also have their educations reinforced more in their homes. There is reason to believe, then, that schools whose students are enrolled by choice will presumably have an easier time producing a given level of achievement than schools whose students are not self-selected. This edge must somehow be taken into account if schools with self-selected students are not to be given undue credit for achievement that is better explained by the special character of their students.

It is difficult to take this edge directly into account, however, because selection cannot be adequately observed. We do not know which families have actively selected schools for their children and which ones have not. We could assume that all private school families actively select their schools and that all public school parents do not. But such an assumption—too often made in comparisons of public and private schools—plainly ignores the selection that occurs into many good public schools. As a consequence, such an assumption would almost certainly introduce additional (pro-public school) bias into an analysis of student achievement. We therefore do not build school selection into our models directly, but try to accommodate its influence in other ways.

One way we try to do this is by allowing student achievement to be influenced by many of the kinds of variables—for example, family SES and student ability—that also ought to predict whether students select their schools. A second way we try to overcome self-selection is by measuring student achievement in terms of gains made only in high school. As we noted in the last chapter, our measure of achievement—a measure limited to achievement gains made during the final two high school years—factors out of the analysis all of the influences that selective families have on the achievement of their children prior to high school. The final way that we allow for school selection is to replicate our analysis of student achievement using only public school students. By dropping from our analysis those students most likely to have selected their schools—private school students—we can determine whether our estimates of the effects of schools on student achievement allow sufficiently for the influence of selection. The details of the replication are reported in appendix D.

There is an additional problem of selection that these allowances do not accommodate, however. That is selection *out* of school. Many students leave their schools prior to their senior years. Some do so as early graduates and still others as transfers to different schools, but most students who leave their schools before the end of their senior years do so as dropouts. This creates a potential problem for the analysis of high school achievement. If the effects of high schools are estimated on the basis of only those students who finish high school, those estimates are likely to be biased. Schools that students frequently select themselves out of (schools with high dropout rates) will tend to look more effective than they really are.

Fortuitously, we can mitigate this form of selection bias directly. Because our sample of students was surveyed twice, we have data on students who remained in school through their senior year as well as data on students who left school prior to their senior year and were therefore excluded from our achievement analysis. This information can be used to estimate the probabilities of each student leaving school early. These probabilities can then be included in the models of student achievement to ensure that other variables are not credited with influences that really stem from a student's propensity to drop out of school. The details of this correction procedure are provided in appendix C.

The other problem that complicates an analysis of student achievement is the problem of reciprocal causality or endogeneity. When two or more variables are both causes and effects of each other—when variables are in reciprocal causal relationships—it can be difficult to estimate causes and effects. The three variables that most interest us—student achievement, school organization, and school control— may present this problem. For example, we believe that schools with effective organizations promote high levels of student achievement. But we also recognize that schools that successfully promote student achievement may also find it easier to develop desirable organizational traits. Organization may be both cause and effect.

The problem may also be present in our system of variables as a whole. In our view, school control is a major determinant of school organization, and in turn, student achievement. But student achievement may also help determine how schools are controlled—schools with few problems, for example, being rewarded with autonomy. Our three key variables, then, may be connected in a causal loop, each influenced to some extent by the other two. Each would then be endogenous—caused by other variables in the system.

The endogeneity problem that we face, however, is not limited to the variables that most interest us. Virtually everything that influences school performance is also influenced *by* performance. For example, family background is a well-known cause of student achievement and school performance, and presumably an important influence on school organization too. But family background is also a consequence of school organization and performance. While most research on school performance ignores this, the fact is families are attracted to schools— public as well as private—by school reputations for effectiveness. The family background of the school clientele may therefore be a product of school organization and performance as well as a cause of them.

Statistical methods cannot really solve the problem of distinguishing cause from effect when the two are so thoroughly intertwined. Standard statistical remedies—simultaneous equation models—will not work because there are simply too few exogenous variables (variables that can be considered causes but not effects) to explain the many variables that are endogenous.[12] It would do little good for us to assume that lots of variables that are really endogenous are exogenous, and then analyze—with simultaneous equations—the three variables of greatest interest to us, as if they were the only ones subject to reciprocal causality. Such an approach would assume a solution where none had been found. By complicating the analysis, we would also find it very difficult to determine whether assumptions about cause and effect were sound.

We do not wish to pretend that we have a solution to the endogeneity problem—for we do not—but we do believe we have a workable method of analysis that keeps the endogeneity problem in clear view. Despite all we have said about the problem of reciprocal causality, we believe that the key influences on student achievement tend to run in one direction. We believe that school control affects school organization more than the other way around, and that school organization is primarily a cause of student achievement and not a result of it. We also believe that this causal chain is firmly anchored at the front end by institutions. Political control and market control may well respond to student achievement and thereby create something of a causal loop, but the strength of direct school control is basically determined by forces rooted in institutions—which, in this whole complicated process, are the variables that come closest to being truly exogenous.

Our analysis therefore centers around three single-equation models— the first of student achievement, the second of school organization, and the third of school control or bureaucratic influence. We specify each equation as best we can to minimize the potential distortions of reciprocal causality. And we interpret the estimates of each equation in light of the effects that reciprocal causality may be having. Throughout our analysis we take a very conservative approach to this statistical problem and to various others. We specify our models first and foremost so that they do not lead us to overestimate the influence of the variables that are of greatest interest to us.

A General Model of Student Achievement

We assume that student achievement can be explained by the simple sum of several influences. The relative importance of each of these influences will be determined by the data. To make this determination we specify student achievement as the dependent variable in a linear regression equation containing a number of independent variables that hypothetically influence and account for the variation in student achievement.

The Dependent Variable

Our measure of student achievement is the measure introduced in the last chapter, the total log gain scores for a representative sample of high school seniors. As we discussed there, the use of this measure of student achievement facilitates the assessment of student progress and school performance in many ways. It also mitigates the two most serious problems of modeling student achievement.

First, the measure weakens the influence of reciprocal causality. To estimate the influence of school organization on student achievement we must somehow distinguish that influence from the influence that runs in the other direction. Using achievement gains to measure student achievement accomplishes this to a great degree. School organization is much more likely to be influenced by the average level of achievement in a school than by the difference in achievement between sophomores and seniors. If a school is enabled by its good students to have a strong academic orientation, for example, it is probably because the students entering that school have a high level of achievement and not because the students, once in the school, post high achievement gains. School organization is far more likely to be a cause of achievement gains than a consequence.

Achievement gains also reduce the potential seriousness of selection bias in our models. Because the gain scores are not contaminated by the academic achievements that students make prior to their sophomore year, the gain scores enable us to exclude from the analysis much of the academic benefit that students in special public schools or private schools derive from their families, and that may be difficult to measure or control directly. True, students in private schools and exclusive public schools may continue to benefit from unusually strong parental support during high school. And these benefits must also be taken into account. But the gain scores eliminate the bulk of such benefits from consideration and thereby provide a more valid measure of what private and exclusive public schools are really accomplishing.

The Independent Variables

We assume that the student gain scores are the sum of a number of influences, some based in the school and some outside of it. As we saw in the last chapter and the beginning of this one, the number of particular influences is potentially very large. This presents a problem, because the more numerous the sources of influence on achievement, the more difficult it becomes to gauge the independent influence of any one source. Statistical models that are built by automatically including every conceivably relevant variable are prone to yield estimates of the effects of these variables that are imprecise and subject to change.[13] We try to avoid this problem by specifying models that are comprehensive yet simple. To accomplish this, we measure the variables in the models in ways that drastically reduce their number. Our general model represents student achievement as a function of five major factors—student ability, family background, peer group influence, school resources, and school organization—each of which subsumes a number of more specific influences.

Student Ability. Perhaps the most obvious influence on the amount of learning that takes place in high school is student ability. All things being equal, students who enter high school with more cognitive aptitude, sharper basic skills, and more academic knowledge should learn more rapidly than students with less of these attributes of student ability. The HSB data offer a suitable measure of student ability in the sophomore achievement test scores. The tests in reading, writing, vocabulary, mathematics, and science attempt to measure raw aptitude, basic skills, and acquired knowledge. Together, the five tests provide a reasonably complete picture of a student's readiness for the final two years of high school.

The sophomore scores on the five tests are also strongly associated with achievement gains. Students in high performance schools (that is, students posting the largest gains) averaged 69.2 correct answers on the five tests in their sophomore year. Students in low performance schools averaged only 56.8 correct answers. We include student ability in our general model of achievement gains, measuring ability with a standardized index of IRT scores on the five tests.[14]

Including the index in our model of student achievement has a very important implication for our analysis. It helps to ensure that our estimates of the effects of schools on student achievement will be conservative ones. In analyses of student achievement where achievement has been measured at two points in time, it is standard to use the first measure of achievement to control for the learning that occurs prior to the time period being studied. This is typically done in one of two ways. One way is for the first scores to be subtracted from the second scores. The other way is for the second scores to be modeled as functions of the first scores. For example, the HSB sophomore scores could be subtracted from the senior scores and the resulting gain scores then explained in an analysis, or the senior scores could become the focus of the analysis and the sophomore scores used as part of the explanation.

These approaches are essentially equivalent. They use the initial scores to control once for the subsequent scores.[15] Our approach is different. We use the initial scores as controls *twice*. First, we subtract the sophomore scores from the senior scores to create a measure of achievement gains, a measure of the amount of learning that takes place only during the final years of high school. Then, we use the sophomore scores as an independent variable in a model of achievement gains, in order to allow for the possibility that academic readiness influences academic performance.

We employ this double control in part because it makes good theoretical sense: gain scores, perhaps as much as final scores (that is, senior scores), are likely to be influenced by student ability, as measured by sophomore scores. But we also employ the double control because it provides a more conservative estimate of the effects of schooling, where conservatism is clearly needed. Even though the problems of reciprocal causality and selection bias are substantially mitigated by our use of gain scores as a dependent variable, what remains of these problems may still lead school organization to appear to be more important than it actually is. By using sophomore scores as both a benchmark for measuring achievement and as a control for student ability, however, the model goes a long way toward ensuring that the academically important qualities students bring to school will not be erroneously credited to high schools in the statistical explanation of achievement. This is a more cautious approach to the estimation of school effects than has been employed in other analyses of the HSB data.[16]

Family Background. In keeping with our cautious approach, the next independent variable in our model of achievement gains is the family background of the student. In the first half of this chapter we saw that the family backgrounds of the student bodies of high and low performance schools differ markedly in a number of basic respects. The families of students in the top schools have measurably more income, education, and learning tools in the home. They are also about 10 percent more likely to expect their children to attend college. To a less impressive degree the families in the high performance schools also have more two-parent households, more mothers working, and more fathers monitoring school work. Many aspects of family background may have an influence, then, on student achievement.

We, however, are not interested in the details of how family influence operates. We are concerned mainly that the influence of families on student achievement be measured to the fullest extent compatible with measuring other kinds of influences on achievement. If we were to include in the model separate indicators of every conceivable aspect of family influence, and of other major influences too, the estimates of the effects of the individual influences would be imprecise and unstable. We are consequently building our model from a small number of comprehensive measures of each major kind of influence. To gauge the influence of family background, we use the index of family SES that, as reported in table 4-6, distinguishes high and low performance schools most sharply.

Little is lost by employing a single comprehensive indicator. The only individual indicators of family background that our model omits are ones that have relatively weak bivariate relationships with achievement.[17] The comprehensive index also has many virtues. It is a more reliable measure than the individual indicators. It simplifies the structure of the model and the task of distinguishing alternative causes. It also makes our explanation of achievement easier to compare with explanations from other research, which typically measures family background with an SES index too.

Peer Groups. The comprehensive measure of family influence serves one other important purpose in our analysis. The influence of families works not only directly on family members but indirectly through the interaction of students from different families. Indeed, since the work of James Coleman and his associates appeared in the 1960s, this indirect influence has generally been considered to be of crucial importance. Researchers have found that student achievement is influenced by the attitudes and behavior of other students in a school— by the pressures from student peer groups.[18] These pressures tend to vary with the kinds of families that students throughout the school come from. Because the ATS-HSB data set contains information on a sample of students within each school, we have the opportunity to gauge the influence that students from different families have on the achievement of their fellow students.

To take advantage of this opportunity, we conduct our analysis of student achievement at the student level. That is, we use the test scores, individual characteristics, and school characteristics of approximately 9,000 students to explain the nationwide variation, from student to student, in achievement. For each student, then, we have thus far described an achievement gain score, a score to measure initial ability, and an SES index to indicate the student's own family background. Now we add to the model a measure of the family background of the other students in each student's school. This measure is the average of the SES index scores for each student in a given school. It provides the best available proxy for the general kind of student influence that the average student in each school is likely to experience. Because the index is primarily economic in orientation, however, we will include in our analysis (at least provisionally) a separate indicator of the racial composition of the student body—the percentage of students in a school who are black. As we saw earlier, this indicator of race distinguishes the student bodies of high and low performance schools quite clearly.

These schoolwide measures of family background serve useful purposes in our analysis. First and foremost, they enable us to gauge peer group influences, which research has shown to be of considerable importance for student achievement. Second, they enable us to overcome a criticism that has been leveled at other research on the HSB data: that research has typically looked only at the individual-level influence of families and not at their schoolwide or contextual influence.[19] Third, by introducing yet another factor to compete with school organization, the schoolwide measure of family background ensures further that the effect of school organization on student achievement will not be overestimated.

School Resources. To assess school effects, we begin by employing two general measures of school quality, representing two distinct types of school influence. The first measure is our index of a school's economic resources. We saw earlier in this chapter that high performance schools spend roughly 20 percent more per pupil than low performance schools and have lower ratios of students to teachers. We also saw that high and low performance schools have about the same amounts of other resources. High and low performance schools pay their teachers approximately the same salaries and enroll essentially the same numbers of students.[20] Based on these observations (as well as factor analyses of various resource measures), we constructed an index of economic resources using expenditure levels and staffing ratios. As we saw in table 4-1, this index distinguishes high and low performance schools unambiguously. We therefore include the index in our model of student achievement. It will represent the influence of those economic inputs to schooling that reformers have long considered vital to school improvement, and that common sense suggests should matter. If the other factors that influence student achievement are also adequately represented in the model, the data should show that, all things being equal, students achieve more in schools that are better endowed financially.

School Organization. The second measure of school quality in the model is the key measure in this part of our study. It is a comprehensive index of school organization, constructed to represent each of the major components of school organization and effectiveness: goals, leadership, personnel, and practice. In chapter 3 we saw that many school characteristics representative of these components are associated with academic achievement.[21] We also saw that many of these characteristics are closely associated with one another and can be combined to index more general components of school organization. Whenever possible, we used these broad indexes to construct our comprehensive measure of school organization. Our objective was to obtain a single, well-rounded measure of school organization using a minimum number of multiple indicators.

Why we wanted to do this requires some justification. It might seem that since we have reliable indexes of major organizational variables, such as goals, leadership, and professionalism, that we ought to estimate the separate effects on student achievement of each of them. It seems to us, however, that that would be the wrong approach. Certainly it is the wrong way to begin.

One of the most important lessons of effective schools research is that effective schooling does not appear to depend primarily on any one element of school organization. There is no single key—a strong principal or ambitious academic goals, for example—to higher student achievement. Rather, school effectiveness seems to depend, as John Goodlad has said, on the school "as a total entity."[22] Two of the most important and certainly most rigorous studies of school effectiveness come to similar conclusions. In their study of British secondary schools, Rutter and his associates stress that school performance depends on an overall school "ethos" that has an impact greater than the sum of its parts.[23] In their analysis of Michigan schools, Brookover and his colleagues reach much the same conclusion: effective schools differ from ineffective ones in their general "climates."[24]

The most thoughtful recommendations for reform to emerge from effective schools research have also taught this lesson. For example, the late Ron Edmonds, once perhaps the most influential proponent of organizational reform, emphasized "five factors" that must be changed *simultaneously* if schools are to improve their performance.[25] Most research indicates that the full impact of school organization is not likely to be well represented by any set of *independent* organizational influences.

It is not just research on school effectiveness that leads us to measure school organization comprehensively. Research aside, we believe that the internal components of a school are inevitably interdependent to a great degree. The leadership of principals is contingent on the quality of teachers, and the behavior of teachers is contingent on the behavior of principals. The rigor of school goals depends on the strength of principals, who must articulate them, and on the competence of teachers, who must implement them. Every element of school organization is bound up with every other element. Modeling elements as if they are in principle independent is therefore not the most sensible analytical direction in which to go.[26] Organizational interdependence implies instead that organizational effectiveness should be thought of as a syndrome of related influences and gauged with a measure that represents them all.[27]

Our comprehensive measure of school organization is a standardized index of ten indicators that were selected to represent as parsimoniously as possible our four major dimensions of school organization: goals, leadership, personnel, and practice. To represent the first dimension, the index includes two indicators of the academic emphasis of school goals: an index of high school graduation requirements in the five major academic fields, as described in table 3-3, and a measure of the priority that the school attaches to academic excellence, as reported in table 3-5.

The index then includes two indicators of leadership: the principal's motivation (see table 3-6), and the esteem in which principals hold their teachers—an indicator that incorporates the principal's dedication to teaching (see tables 3-6 and 3-7). The third component of the index is composed of two indicators of personnel: teacher professionalism (which subsumes teacher influence, efficacy, and absenteeism), and staff harmony (which subsumes teacher cooperation, teacher collegiality, and the principal's vision), all of which are described in tables 3-6 and 3-7.

The fourth and final part of the comprehensive index gauges the educational practices of the school—in particular, how students are assigned to classes and what takes place in those classes. This part of the index includes an indicator of the aggressiveness of academic tracking: the percentage of sophomores in an academic program (see table 3-8). It also includes all of the most promising indicators of effective classrooms: the amount of homework assigned daily, the amount of time devoted to administrative routines, and the fairness and effectiveness of disciplinary practices (see table 3-10). In sum, our comprehensive index includes indicators of every element of school organization that the descriptive analysis indicated might be of importance and excludes nothing of obvious significance.[28]

Selection Bias Correction. As we just explained, student self-selection poses a problem for our analysis. It threatens to bias our estimates of school influence by causing schools to receive credit for effects on student achievement that are really due to students and their families. As we also explained, this bias can enter our analysis in two ways: as students select themselves into schools and as students select themselves out of schools. We try to manage the first of these potential sources of bias through our measurement of achievement and the use of control variables in our achievement models. We also replicate our analysis of achievement (in appendix D) using just public schools. The second of the potential sources of selection bias—selection out of schools—we manage more directly.

The dropout rate is 7 percentage points higher in our low performance schools than in our high performance ones. Because a school's worst students are the ones most likely to drop out, our low performance schools will tend to be represented in the achievement analysis by samples of students that are relatively more select than the samples of students representing high performance schools. To allow for the varying selectivity of the samples of seniors, we build a measure of selectivity directly into our model of achievement. The construction of that measure is explained in appendix C. In essence, we estimated the probability that a student would leave school between the sophomore and senior years, and then we used a measure based on that probability in the model. The measure, an indicator of the likelihood of a student leaving school before taking the HSB tests in the senior year, should be negatively associated with achievement. It should also purge the other variables in the model of erroneous influences that occur because of student selection out of the analysis.

Summary

In table 4-7 the structure and measurement of our complete model of student achievement is summarized. For all the complexity of the model's measures, its structure is really quite simple. Student achievement gains are expressed as a function of five factors (and a correction for selection bias) that research suggests are likely to be the most important elements of any complete explanation. Each factor (with the temporary exception of the student body) is represented by one comprehensive index constructed to give the factor its best opportunity to account for variations in achievement gains. Overall the model gives a truly substantial opportunity to nonschool factors to dominate the accounting. The student's own capability is represented directly by his or her initial test performance and indirectly by the influence of his or her family—measured by the kind of comprehensive SES indicator that often dominates statistical explanations of student achievement. In addition, family SES has a chance to influence achievement through the student body of the school.

If the school itself matters for achievement, then, it must make its

TABLE 4-7. Structure and Measurement of Basic Model of Student Achievement Gains

Concept	Measures	Major components of measures[a]
Dependent variable		
Total gain in student achievement	Index of IRT log gain scores	IRT log gain scores in reading, writing, vocabulary, math, science
Independent variable		
Student's academic ability	Index of sophomore IRT scores	Sophomore IRT scores in reading, writing, vocabulary, math, science
Family background of student	Index of family socioeconomic status	Family income; mother's education; father's education; father's occupation; home learning tools
Background of student body	Average family socioeconomic status index for students in school	Same as above
	Percentage of black students	
School financial situation	Index of school resources	No components
		Per pupil school and district expenditures; student-teacher ratio
School organization	Comprehensive index of four organizational dimensions: goals, leadership, personnel, and practice	Graduation requirements; priority of academic excellence; principal's motivation; principal's teaching esteem (principal's dedication to teaching, estimated excellence of teachers); teacher professionalism (teacher influence, teacher efficacy, teacher absenteeism); staff harmony (teacher collegiality, teacher cooperation, principal's vision); percentage of students in academic track; homework assignments; classroom administrative routines; disciplinary fairness and effectiveness
Selection bias correction	Estimated probability of leaving school early	See appendix C

a. The survey items, index formulas, and measurement metrics are detailed in appendix B.

effects felt while students and families make their influences felt too. And if what is important about a school is its organization, its importance must hold even when differences in school financial resources are controlled. As we have tried to stress, this model is a balanced attempt to sort out the major influences on student achievement and to obtain a conservative estimate of the influence of school organization. It is also only the next step, and not the final one, in trying to understand school performance.

The Results

To determine the separate effects of the various influences on student achievement, we estimated a series of linear regression models. The coefficients of a regression model provide estimates of the effects of each explanatory variable on the dependent variable, when the other explanatory variables are held constant. These are the kinds of estimates that we need if we are to conclude that school organization affects student achievement independent of other factors, such as student ability and family background, that affect achievement also. It will be somewhat difficult to reduce these estimates to a single set of values, however. Regression estimates are sensitive to the specification of models and to the measurement of variables. Thus we will not try to describe the effects of the various influences on student achievement with estimates from one model. Rather, we will report a range of estimates, using alternative specifications and measures, to gauge their robustness or sensitivity.

The estimates from the first and most general set of models are reported in table 4-8. The estimates under the column labeled model 1 are for the final version of our most general model. To arrive at those estimates we eliminated from the original model variables that proved to have influences on student achievement that could not be statistically distinguished from zero. Thus in model 3 we find that school economic resources do not have a significant, independent effect on achievement gains. The unstandardized regression coefficient for school resources (.003) is less than its standard error (.005). To conclude with a high level of confidence—only a 5 percent chance of being wrong—that school resources do not have zero influence, the regression coefficient would need to be at least 1.64 times the size of the standard error. By this statistical test, which we will apply to

TABLE 4-8. Estimates of Models of Student Achievement Gains
Using Comprehensive Measure of School Organization[a]

Variable	Model[b]		
	1	2	3
Selection bias correction	−.086*	−.083*	−.087*
	(.030)	(.030)	(.030)
	−.046	−.045	−.046
Initial student achievement	.027*	.027*	.027*
	(.005)	(.005)	(.005)
	.095	.095	.095
School organization, comprehensive	.017*	.017*	.017*
	(.004)	(.004)	(.004)
	.065	.066	.065
Parent socioeconomic status	.023*	.024*	.023*
	(.005)	(.005)	(.005)
	.069	.070	.069
School socioeconomic status	.021*	.019*	.020*
	(.009)	(.010)	(.010)
	.036	.032	.034
School percent black	. . .	−.00009	. . .
		(.00015)	
		−.008	
School economic resources	. . .	. . .	.003
			(.005)
			.007
Constant	.204*	.204*	.204*
	(.007)	(.007)	(.007)
Adjusted R^2	.051	.051	.051
Sample size	7,357	7,357	7,274

* Statistically significant, $\alpha \leq .05$, $t \geq 1.64$, one-tail test.
a. Achievement gains are measured with log gain scores. Sample weighted to achieve a nationally representative sample of public and private high school seniors.
b. Coefficients are unstandardized linear regression coefficients; standard errors are in parentheses. Standardized regression coefficients (betas) are in italics.

coefficients throughout our entire analysis, school economic resources do not influence student achievement independently or directly. Although negative, this is an important finding. It shows that the simple correlation of school spending and school performance can be misleading. When other relevant factors are taken into account, economic resources are unrelated to student achievement.[29]

Another important though negative finding is reported under the column labeled model 2. There we see that the racial composition of a school's student body is not related (in a statistically significant way) to the achievement gains of its students. Once other influences on achievement are included in the model, individual gains are virtually unaffected by the percentage of the student body that is black. As we will see, individual and contextual measures of family SES are strongly associated with achievement. But these influences seem to be so strongly related to achievement that they account for much or all of the influence on achievement often attributed to race. If our models and measures are valid, the social influence of race, an important justification for school integration and busing, may not be as great as is often suggested. By our estimates the racial composition of a school has no direct influence on student achievement beyond that explained by the socioeconomic makeup of the student body or the organization of the school.[30]

We should add that race has no independent individual-level effect on achievement gains either. In a model that we do not report in this book, we found that black students learn neither more nor less than would be predicted of them based on their initial ability, family background, and the social and organizational qualities of their schools. In short, race—at least the black, non-black distinction—has no independent consequence at either the individual or the school level for student achievement.

This, of course, is a mildly controversial finding.[31] We will not elaborate on it, however, nor on several other interesting findings that emerge from our analysis—among them that achievement is not affected by the sex of the student either. To do so would require considerable amounts of additional research and would distract attention from our primary purpose, which is to build models that enable us to make fair assessments of the workings of school organizations and their environments. In pursuing that purpose we must consider alternative model specifications fully. But we do not have the luxury of reporting or exploring the results of models that ultimately make no difference for our findings.

What then seems to account for variations in student achievement? In model 1, which now excludes the racial composition of the school and school resources, we provide the most general answer. Setting aside the correction for selection bias (which has a significant negative influence on achievement), student academic gains are explained by four general factors: student ability, family SES, school SES, and school organization. The regression coefficients for all of these factors are several times larger than their respective standard errors. They are all statistically significant and thus have impacts on achievement gains that can be confidently distinguished from zero.

They all, however, have impacts that might seem rather small. The coefficients that are the most straightforward to interpret, the standardized coefficients (in italics), are indeed small.[32] Changes of one standard deviation in any of the independent variables are predicted to produce changes in achievement gains of less than one-tenth of a standard deviation.[33] By this metric, student ability is the most influential independent variable, followed by family SES and school organization, each roughly two-thirds as influential as student ability, and school SES, about one-third as influential as student ability. But all of the influences appear to be small.

Appearances, however, can be deceiving. The importance or meaning of a regression coefficient, once it is found to be significant, cannot be determined by any single statistical standard.[34] If we interpret the unstandardized regression coefficients—the first coefficients listed for each variable in table 4-8—the influences on student achievement take on new meaning and greater importance.

In the last chapter we introduced a standard for interpreting achievement gain scores that we will employ again here. This standard, a year or grade equivalent of achievement, is one-half of the average sophomore-to-senior gain for all students (or schools). It can be used to gauge the amount of change in student achievement that is associated with changes in the independent variables in the regression models. In our analysis, we use it to measure the change in achievement predicted (by the unstandardized regression coefficients) to result from a change in each of the independent variables from the median of its lowest quartile to the median of its highest quartile. We look at these quartile changes because they facilitate comparisons of the independent variables, which are measured in different and somewhat arbitrary units. The calculations of these changes are detailed in appendix C and table C-4. The results of the calculations for model 1 (and several subsequent models) are reported in table 4-9.

Looking only at the results for model 1, the strongest influence on achievement gains is student ability, as measured by initial student achievement. If a student could have his academic ability raised from the bottom to the top ability quartile, and have all else remain exactly

TABLE 4-9. Predicted Years of Achievement Gains, Sophomore Year to Senior Year, Attributable to School Organization and Other Selected Sources, by Model

Source of achievement growth[a]	Model			
	1	4[b]	9	12[b]
Initial student achievement	.65	.45	.65	.45
School organization	.45	.29	.65	.47
Parent socioeconomic status	.46	.42	.46	.40
School socioeconomic status	.24	.27	.15	.19
Academic tracking policy	. . .	.13	. . .	.14

a. Predictions compare estimated differences in achievement for students at the means of the lowest and the highest quartiles on each of the sources of achievement growth.

b. Predictions are based on models 4A and 12A described in Appendix C. These models include a dummy variable measure of each student's academic program (academic, nonacademic) instead of a measure of the school's percent academic track, which permits the estimation of the achievement effects of academic tracking policy.

the same, that student's gain in achievement over the final two years of high school would increase by .65 year. That is plainly a substantial amount.

Student ability is not the only sizable influence on achievement, however. Not far behind it in importance are two factors roughly equal in magnitude, the organization of the school and the family background of the student. If a student could be shifted from the lowest to the highest quartile on either of these factors, that student would gain roughly an additional half year of achievement. This is not surprising, perhaps, for a change in family background, but it is, in at least one respect, for a change in school organization. The results suggest not only that a well-organized school can make a meaningful difference for student achievement, regardless of the ability and background of its students, but that the influence of the school, through its organization, is comparable in size to the influence of each student's own family. What is more, the influence of school organization is twice as strong as the influence of the student body, as measured by school SES. All things being equal, then, it appears that students can really gain a great deal from attending an effectively organized school.

School Organization versus School Policy

If school organization matters so much for achievement, it is well worth asking why. There is much debate among observers of effective schools about the major sources of school success. Some argue that the key ingredients are programmatic. Students need to be made to take more rigorous courses and to apply themselves with greater diligence to academic matters.[35] Others stress that schools succeed more because of their total learning climate—because of the support and encouragement that a community of teachers, students, and parents can provide each student.[36]

There is more than theoretical importance to this debate. From a practical standpoint it matters a great deal whether one type of organizational influence is more powerful than another. It will be a great deal easier for policymakers to improve schools if improvement can be obtained by raising graduation requirements, increasing course-taking, and requiring more homework than if improvement requires the creation of more coherent, professional, and collegial teaching teams. Consequently, we attempt to determine the degree to which the influence of school organization operates through a school's academic practices and policies.

To do this we specified another set of models, the estimates of which are reported in table 4-10. There we describe the consequences of disaggregating our comprehensive measure of school organization to assess the independent influence of the discrete school policies or practices that compose it. Specifically, we created five different comprehensive measures of organization, each omitting one measure of a school policy or practice included in the original measure. Thus, for example, we created a measure of school organization including all of the original indicators except disciplinary policy. We then respecified our general model of achievement (model 1), substituting a reduced measure of organization for the full measure, and adding to the model, as an independent variable, the individual policy or practice excluded from the new index of organization. We then estimated five of these respecified models, one for each of the policy or practice measures in the comprehensive index of organization.

Generally, the results indicate that the effects of school organization on student achievement are not the product of particular school policies or practices. From the estimates of models 5–8, we learn that student achievement is not influenced to a statistically significant degree by the amount of homework assigned, by graduation requirements, by the prevalence of administrative routines in the classroom, or by the fairness and effectiveness of discipline. All of these variables have influences on student achievement that are statistically indistinguishable from zero. Moreover, the effect of school organization when each of these policies or practices is removed from the index is virtually the same as when each is a part of the index. With the various policy measures removed, the unstandardized coefficients for school organization range from .015 to .018; the coefficient for the full comprehensive measure is .017. In short, the effects of school organization do not generally work through specific—and easy to manipulate—policies or practices.

There is, however, one important exception to this generalization. We saw in the last chapter, in the comparison of high and low performance schools, that students in the top schools tend to take more academic courses than students in the schools at the bottom, and to be enrolled in an academic program of study. Students in low performance schools tend to take fewer academic courses, regardless of their track, than students in high performance schools, and their program of study is more likely to be general or vocational than academic. Among the policies and practices that we examined in chapter 3, academic course work displayed the largest differences between high and low performance schools. It is no surprise to find, then, that academic program participation has a strong, independent effect on achievement gains. The percentage of students in the academic track in a school (see model 4) has a standardized coefficient (.048) of roughly the same magnitude as school organization (minus the tracking indicator). All things being equal, academic programs promote academic achievement.

But what exactly does this mean? As tracking is measured in model 4, its effect on achievement is a reflection of two different influences. On the one hand, the percentage of students in a school enrolled in an academic track is an indicator of the programmatic orientation of the school. In this capacity, the indicator gauges the emphasis that the school places on academic work. It captures how aggressively schools track students into academic programs and how extensively academic work contributes to the school's general climate. But the percentage of students in an academic program is also an estimate of the probability that any given student in a school is tracked academically. It is a proxy for the student's own program of study. In this

TABLE 4-10. Estimates of Models of Student Achievement Gains Separating School Policies from Comprehensive Measure of School Organization[a]

Variable	Model[b]				
	4	5	6	7	8
Selection bias correction	-.088*	-.086*	-.087*	-.090*	-.086*
	(.030)	(.030)	(.030)	(.030)	(.030)
	-.047	-.046	-.046	-.048	-.046
Initial student achievement	.027*	.027*	.027*	.028*	.027*
	(.005)	(.005)	(.005)	(.005)	(.005)
	.095	.095	.095	.097	.095
School organization, comprehensive, without:					
Percent of students in academic track	.011*	...	...	...	...
	(.004)				
	.040				
Amount of homework assigned	...	.016*	...	...	...
		(.004)			
		.061			
Graduation requirements	...	...	.017*	...	...
			(.004)		
			.065		
Administrative routines in classrooms	...	...	...	.018*	...
				(.004)	
				.070	
Disciplinary policy	...	...	...	...	.015*
					(.004)
					.058

	(1)	(2)	(3)	(4)	(5)
Parent socioeconomic status	.023* (.005) *.069*	.023* (.005) *.069*	.023* (.005) *.069*	.023* (.005) *.068*	.023* (.005) *.069*
School socioeconomic status	.016* (.010) *.027*	.021* (.009) *.036*	.021* (.010) *.034*	.022* (.009) *.037*	.021* (.009) *.036*
Percent of students in academic track	.013* (.004) *.048*	...	...	...	...
Amount of homework assigned	...	.002 (.003) *.009*	...	...	...
Graduation requirements	...	...	.002 (.003) *.007*	...	...
Administrative routines in classrooms	...	...	...	.003 (.003) *.010*	...
Disciplinary policy	...	...	...	...	.003 (.004) *.011*
Constant	.204* (.007)	.203* (.007)	.204* (.007)	.205* (.007)	.204* (.007)
Adjusted R^2	.052	.051	.051	.051	.051
Sample size	6,987	7,351	7,126	7,351	7,357

* Statistically significant, $\alpha \leq .05$, $t \geq 1.64$, one-tail test.

a. Achievement gains are measured with log gain scores. Sample weighted to achieve a nationally representative sample of public and private high school seniors.

b. Coefficients are unstandardized linear regression coefficients; standard errors are in parentheses. Standardized regression coefficients (betas) are in italics.

capacity, the tracking measure in model 4 gauges the influence of a student's own course work on his or her achievement. Rather than capturing the effects of school tracking practices, it captures the effects of individual course-taking. This latter influence is of some interest, for it indicates that academic course work promotes achievement among students who do it. But it is much less interesting and important than what we are primarily concerned with: the role that school organization plays in getting all students to focus on academically rigorous work in high school.

We would like to distinguish these two influences of academic tracking from one another. To do so, we begin by removing the percentage of students in an academic track from our comprehensive measure of school organization. We included it initially because there is every reason to believe that an effective high school is one that is especially successful in placing students in academic programs and in keeping them there.[37] The estimates in model 4 support this reasoning. But if the percentage of students in an academic program were to remain in our comprehensive measure of organization, it might create problems. Most important, it would exaggerate the influence of organization. Because the percentage of students in an academic track, much more than any other indicator in our organizational index, is likely to be a function of the ability and background of students, including it in the index would allow organization to receive credit for influences that may not be organizational. We think it is prudent, therefore, to drop academic tracking from our index of organization and examine its consequences separately.

We proceed in two steps. First, we estimate a new model of achievement, identical to model 4 except that academic tracking is no longer measured at the school level. It is measured at the individual level, by means of a dichotomous variable that simply indicates whether the student is or is not in an academic program. The results are reported in appendix C and table C-2, and they are much the same as those in model 4. The only difference is that the effect of tracking has a different interpretation: it is the estimated impact that a student's enrollment in an academic program has on his or her own academic achievement. This is the individual-level effect of student course-taking.

The second step is to determine whether school tracking policy, an aspect of school organization, has an important influence on student course-taking—and thus, through the latter's causal effects, an important influence as well on student achievement. To do this, we begin by estimating a model of the probability that any given student will participate in an academic program. One of the explanatory variables, of course, is school organization. Our expectation is that schools with more effective organizations should be more likely to track students into academic courses. The other explanatory variables introduce controls for student and family-related influences that might also account for course-taking: initial student achievement, family SES, and parental expectations. The procedure and results are summarized in appendix C and table C-3.

As the findings suggest, students have very different odds of being in an academic program if they attend an effectively organized school rather than an ineffectively organized one. An average student—one with average initial ability, average family SES, and average parental expectations—has a probability of .52 of being in an academic program if he or she is enrolled in one of the schools in the upper quartile of our new comprehensive measure of organizational effectiveness. That same student in a school in the bottom quartile of organizational effectiveness has only half that chance of getting into an academic program, a probability of .27. Effectively organized schools are much more likely, in other words, to place the typical student in an academic program.

What effect does school tracking policy have, then, on student achievement? This can be figured by combining the estimates from both steps: students receive a boost in achievement owing to their academic course-taking (step 1), but only part of this boost can be credited to school organization—the amount depending on how effectively organized the school is (step 2). These calculations are summarized in table 4-9 under the column labeled model 4. There we see that the differences in school tracking policies across effective and ineffective schools are worth .13 year of achievement over the final two years of high school.[38] Placed in proper perspective, this is not a trivial influence. It indicates that tracking practices may account for as much as 30 percent of the total influence of school organization on achievement. It also indicates that the influence of tracking on achievement may be as much as half that of the student body.

A Closer Look at School Organization

If the foregoing analysis is completely correct, school organization owes a sizable share of its influence over achievement to tracking. But our analysis of the effect of school organization is not quite complete. Our estimates so far have been based on an organizational index that, while comprehensive, is also rather heterogeneous. To be sure, the index's components are all positively correlated with one another. Yet some are more strongly intercorrelated than others, and some are more closely connected, logically at least, to student achievement. As a consequence, some of the components of the organizational index may be depressing the relationship between school organization and student gains.

To explore this possibility we reestimated models 1 and 4 using a sequence of condensed measures of school organization. Each of the condensed measures excluded one and only one indicator of school organization.[39] Most of these exclusions had no impact on the estimated effect of school organization on achievement gains, but several did. Several exclusions caused the regression coefficient on school organization to increase significantly. In view of these results we constructed a new condensed index of school organization that represents all of the four major dimensions of the original index—goals, leadership, personnel, and practice—but does so more parsimoniously. Goals are indicated by the priority of academic excellence. Leadership is indicated by the principal's motivation and the principal's esteem for teaching. The attitudes and behavior of school personnel are measured by teacher professionalism and teacher cooperation. And educational practices are gauged by disciplinary policy and (for the temporary sake of comparison with model 1) the percentage of students in an academic track. The condensed measure excludes two types of indicators. It excludes three school practices—homework assignments, classroom administrative routines, and high school graduation requirements—that we already learned are of no independent significance. And it excludes two of the original three measures of staff harmony: teacher collegiality and the principal's vision, plainly the most subjective indicators of organization in the original measure.

Despite these exclusions, the condensed measure of school organization is conceptually very close to the comprehensive measure. Both measures conceive of an effective school as one characterized by an academic focus, a strong educational leader, a sharing of decisionmaking, a high level of professionalism and cooperation among teachers, and respect for discipline among students. Both conceive of an effective school as a tightly knit community or team. Both measures also lead to similar conclusions about the causes of student achievement. We see this in table 4-11, where the analyses conducted with models 1–4 are repeated using the condensed measure instead of the comprehensive one. In model 10 we find, as before, that a school's racial composition (its percentage of black students) does not exert a significant independent influence on achievement gains. In model 11 we see that school economic resources remain a nonsignificant influence on achievement. From models 9 and 12, respectively, we learn that school organization is a significant influence on achievement whether it includes or excludes tracking, which is itself significant.

The conclusions to be drawn about the production of student achievement are not insensitive, however, to the way in which school organization is measured. As we show in table 4-9, when school organization is measured in a more condensed fashion, the influence of the SES of the student body drops below generally accepted levels of statistical significance, and school organization emerges as the most important determinant of achievement gains. School organization alone is worth roughly one-half a year of achievement—about the same as student ability and family SES. When the effects of school tracking policy—an aspect of school organization—are counted, school organization is more important than either student ability or family SES.

Conclusion

It is impossible to make a precise estimate of the influence of school organization on student achievement. Overall its influence appears to be in the range of one-half to two-thirds of a year of additional achievement, if we compare ineffectively organized schools to effectively organized ones. However, some portion of that influence—25 percent to 30 percent—is exerted through a specific policy—academic tracking. This influence is still a school effect, and, as we have gauged it, a product of effective school organization. But since it is a discrete policy, it is fair to ask what residual influence the rest of school organization has. The answer to that is one-third to one-half a year of achievement.

TABLE 4-11. Estimates of Models of Student Achievement Gains Using Condensed Measure of School Organization[a]

Variable	Model[b] 9	10	11	12
Selection bias correction	−.089* (.030) −.048	−.087* (.030) −.046	−.089* (.030) −.048	−.089* (.030) −.048
Initial student achievement	.027* (.005) .095	.027* (.005) .095	.027* (.005) .095	.027* (.005) .095
School organization, condensed	.022* (.004) .084	.022* (.004) .084	.022* (.004) .084	. . .
School organization, condensed, without percent academic track	. . .	. . .	. . .	.016* (.004) .060
Parent socioeconomic status	.023* (.005) .069	.023* (.005) .070	.023* (.005) .069	.023* (.005) .069
School socioeconomic status	.013 (.010) .022	.012 (.010) .020	.012 (.010) .021	.010 (.010) .017
School percent black	. . .	−.00007 (.00015) −.006	. . .	. . .
School economic resources	. . .	. . .	.003 (.005) .006	. . .
School percent academic track	. . .	. . .	. . .	.012* (.004) .045
Constant	.205* (.007)	.205* (.007)	.205* (.007)	.205* (.007)
Adjusted R^2	.052	.052	.052	.053
Sample size	7,357	7,357	7,274	6,987

* Statistically significant, $\alpha \leq .05$, $t \geq 1.64$, one-tail test.

a. Achievement gains are measured with log gain scores. Sample weighted to achieve a nationally representative sample of public and private high school seniors. Condensed measure of organization excludes graduation requirements, homework assignments, administrative routines in classrooms, principal's vision, and teacher collegiality.

b. Coefficients are unstandardized linear regression coefficients; standard errors are in parentheses. Standardized regression coefficients (betas) are in italics.

How do these estimates add up? That depends on how one resolves two issues. The first issue is how to measure school organization. Our view is that the attributes of organizational effectiveness are inherently difficult to enumerate, include every major part of the school from the principal's office to the classroom, are highly interdependent, and work together as an organizational syndrome to influence student performance. This view is not ours alone, but we would not have embraced it had our preliminary analysis of the organizational indicators in our data sets not convinced us that there is no neat hierarchy of organizational determinants of school performance.

Accordingly, we created our comprehensive index of school organization. In it we tried to represent each of the interrelated dimensions—goals, leadership, personnel, and practice—that we thought essential, and to represent each dimension with a minimal number of reliable and valid indicators. We still believe this measure represents the most appropriate conceptualization of school organization. In any case, our construction of the measure followed the only theoretically and methodologically defensible course that it could have: we are interested in analyzing the consequences and causes of school organization independent of how it is measured.

Our analysis of student achievement revealed, however, that certain elements of our comprehensive measure of school organization are less vital than others, at least in a direct way, for the production of student achievement. Including the less vital elements in our measure of school organization consequently depressed our estimate of the effect of school organization on student achievement. Excluding the less vital elements and creating a condensed measure of organization inflated our estimate.

Which is the correct estimate? Both are—but of somewhat different things. One is the estimated impact of the full complement of organizational attributes that are related theoretically and empirically to each other and to school performance. The other is the estimated impact of those still quite numerous and closely related organizational characteristics that influence student achievement most directly. Both, however, represent the influence of organizational syndromes, very similar in concept. In our view, the two estimates should be interpreted as the endpoints of a continuum of possible influences exerted by school organization. The maximum influence of school organization is about two-thirds of a year over the final two years of high school, the minimum influence about half a year.

Some of this influence, though, is not exerted entirely through a complex of organizational factors but through a single organizational practice—tracking. How the influence of tracking should be interpreted is the second issue that complicates our assessment of organizational influence. We have shown that aggressive tracking of students into academic programs is a practice that distinguishes effectively organized schools from ineffectively organized ones. In our view, effectively organized schools are able to track aggressively because their organizations thoroughly support and encourage academic performance. If an ineffectively organized school were to try to track students aggressively into academic programs, it would probably fail. The students and teachers would lack the support and encouragement that is necessary for a vigorous academic program to work for average or below-average students. If this is true, it makes little sense, except for accounting purposes, to distinguish the influence of tracking practices from the influence of effective school organization more generally. Rigorous programs of study cannot be forced on students; such programs must be provided as part of a well-rounded, schoolwide effort to stimulate and reinforce academic learning.[40]

Where does this leave us? It leaves us with three major causes of student achievement—student ability, school organization, and family background—in roughly that order of importance. And it provides us with an important piece of the puzzle of school performance—school organization. All things being equal, a student in an effectively organized school should achieve at least a half year more than a student in an ineffectively organized school over the last two years of high school. If that difference can be extrapolated to the normal four-year high school experience, an effectively organized school may increase the achievement of its students by more than one full year. That is a substantial school effect, indeed.

Chapter Five

Institutional Context and School Organization

WHILE IT IS important to understand how an effective school is organized, it is even more important to understand why some schools are organized so much more effectively than others. Schools cannot be anything they may want to be. They do not choose their goals, leadership, personnel, and practices with complete freedom. Parents, students, and external authorities constrain their choices and even impose organizational decisions on them. If we want to get to the root of the problem of school performance, then, we cannot stop with school organization. We must work our way out of the school and into the school environment where many of the forces that shape school organization are to be found.

In considering this environment, we will take special note of its institutional structure. If we are correct, different institutions give rise to different relationships between schools and their environments, and in turn to different school organizations. In particular, institutions of direct democratic control promote ineffective school organizations. Driven by politics, these institutions encourage the bureaucratization and centralization of school control and discourage the emergence of coherent, strongly led, academically ambitious, professionally grounded, teamlike organizations. Institutions of market control encourage pretty much the opposite.

Of course, there is no denying that American education has become more bureaucratized and centralized in its organization and control. The federal government administers scores of elementary and secondary education programs, state governments now provide more money to schools than local governments do, school districts have become larger and far less numerous (fewer than 16,000 today compared with more than 100,000 in 1945), and administrative costs and employment have been rising many times faster than student enrollments.[1] We are hardly the first to criticize these developments. While some education authorities still cling to the view that schools and school systems can best be run as rational bureaucracies—from the top down—there is an emerging consensus among scholars and reformers that centralization and bureaucratization are substantially at odds with the effective organization of schools and the successful provision of education.[2]

We count ourselves as part of this consensus. But we believe something more controversial also to be true. We believe that excessive bureaucratization and centralization are no historical accident. We believe they are inevitable consequences of America's institutions of democratic control. We also believe that efforts to reverse these developments—to promote school autonomy and professionalism—are doomed to fail unless accompanied by fundamental reform of the institutions through which education is controlled.

In this chapter we want to explore the evidence for our perspective on school organization. First we want to consider whether the bureaucratization of school control is in fact an important source of ineffective school organization. For all of the criticism that has been heaped on school bureaucracy by scholars and reformers, and for all of the effort now being made to decentralize educational administration and replace bureaucratic control with school-site management, there is as yet little systematic evidence that bureaucracy has been bad for education. Indeed, the fact is that schools have become bureaucratized over time mostly as a result of efforts to make them better.

The first half of this chapter examines the consequences of bureaucratic control for school organization. It asks whether schools that are subjected to greater amounts of bureaucratic control are organized less effectively than schools that are subjected to less bureaucratic control, all else being equal. In the second half of the chapter we look at the grounds for our more controversial belief, asking whether the bureaucratization of school control is primarily a consequence of the system of institutions by which schools are governed.

Control and Organization in America's Schools

Our search for an explanation of effective school organization will follow much the same course as our search for an explanation of student achievement. We will look separately at a number of possible explanations and then use statistical models to evaluate their comparative strengths.

As we did in chapters 3 and 4, we begin by using the explanatory variables to profile schools at opposite ends of the distribution of the variable we are trying to explain. In chapters 3 and 4 we looked at schools at opposite ends of the distribution of achievement gain scores. In this chapter we will consider schools at opposite ends of the distribution of school organization. For convenience, schools in the top quartile of the distribution will be referred to as effective schools (or effectively organized schools), those in the bottom quartile of the distribution as ineffective schools.

Schools will be classified using one of the two comprehensive indexes of school organization analyzed in the last chapter—the one that excludes academic track enrollments. We use the comprehensive index rather than the condensed index because the comprehensive version best represents our original conception of an effective school organization.[3] We exclude academic track enrollments because, as we try to account for school organization, we want to avoid any confusion about precisely what we are trying to explain. While aggressive academic tracking appears to be an integral part of an effective school organization, our primary interest is in the syndrome of organizational characteristics that together promote achievement and that may well make aggressive academic tracking workable.

Economic Resources

It seems obvious that economic resources should have something to do with whether a school is able to organize effectively. Large, understaffed schools paying poor wages might find it difficult to develop the kind of camaraderie and commitment, the spirited teamwork, that seems to characterize effective schools. To see if this might be so, we calculated the average levels of various economic resources found in effective and ineffective schools. The results are reported in table 5-1.

Consider school size first. As we mentioned in chapter 4, there is considerable controversy about the appropriate size of high schools.[4] For decades it was believed that larger high schools offered clear advantages, primarily in the form of specialization, diversity, and economies of scale. But today there is increasing emphasis on the

TABLE 5-1. Economic Characteristics of Effective and Ineffective
School Organizations[a]
Salaries and expenditures in dollars

Characteristic	Ineffective school organization	Effective school organization
Mean tenth grade enrollment	179.0	167.7
Economic resources, above average (percent)	38.3	49.2
Mean student-teacher ratio	15.0	14.0
Mean per pupil expenditure[b]	1,507	1,804
Mean minimum teacher salary[c]	14,577	17,157
Mean maximum teacher salary[c]	28,681	27,932
Mean salary range midpoint[c]	21,629	22,544

a. Sample weighted to achieve a nationally representative sample of public and private high schools.
b. Data are from 1980.
c. Data are from 1984.

apparent disadvantages—fragmentation, alienation, the lack of community.

None of these tendencies has proven to be consistently strong,
however. And that is what we find too. We find a weak tendency for
effectively organized schools to be smaller than ineffectively organized
ones, but by only eleven students per grade. That's a difference of
only 6 percent. If school size makes a meaningful difference for school
organization, it does not make the kind of difference that stands out
amidst other influences on school organization.

Much the same must be said about other school resources. Reformers
often think that an effective school is something that money can buy.
Money can be used to shrink class sizes and thereby encourage closer
relationships between teachers and students. It can be used to give
teachers more time away from their classrooms to work with and
support one another. Money can also be used to increase teacher
compensation and, through it, teacher satisfaction. To be sure, research
has never found a systematic relationship between school spending
and student achievement.[5] But the relationship between spending and
school organization is more direct and presumably stronger than the
relationship between spending and achievement.

In the ATS schools resources and organization are indeed related,
but not unambiguously. Schools with effective organizations spend
about 20 percent more per pupil on average than schools with ineffective
organizations. As we explained in the last chapter, that is a potentially
meaningful difference. The difference does not produce obvious ma-

terial advantages, however. Schools with effective organizations have an edge of only one student per teacher in staffing ratios—14-to-1 in effective schools as opposed to 15-to-1 in ineffective schools. And schools with effective organizations pay their teachers only slightly more than schools with ineffective organizations pay theirs. Effective schools offer noticeably higher starting salaries than ineffective schools, but the midpoints of their respective salary ranges differ by less than one thousand dollars.

Overall, then, schools with effective organizations have only somewhat more resources than schools with ineffective organizations. This is evident when schools are classified using the general index of economic resources introduced in chapter 4. Economic resources are above average in only 11 percent more of the effective schools than of the ineffective ones. And even more to the point: schools with effective organizations are not generally rich. A shade more than half of the effective schools have *below*-average levels of economic resources. Although our more complex analysis may yet show otherwise, effective schools do not seem to be things that money can easily buy.

Student Bodies

Effective schools may be difficult to obtain by other means, too. School improvement has long been stymied by the influence that factors largely beyond school control exert over educational outcomes. Prime among these factors is the composition of the student body. It is well known that students influence one another, good ones encouraging and bad ones discouraging achievement by fellow students. It is likely that students influence teachers, principals, and school organization also. It ought to be relatively easy to organize an academically focused school that vigorously pursues excellence and that cultivates feelings of efficacy among its teachers if the school is serving well-behaved, academically accomplished students from well-educated, economically successful families. If this is true, it may be difficult to create effective schools for educationally disadvantaged students.

In fact, this difficulty may be real. The student bodies of effective and ineffective schools tend to be rather different. As we report in table 5-2, the vast majority of schools with effective organizations serve students whose families are above average in socioeconomic status (SES)—in education, income, occupational status, and home

TABLE 5-2. Student Body Characteristics of Effective
and Ineffective School Organizations[a]
Percent

Characteristic	Ineffective school organization	Effective school organization
Socioeconomic status, above average	32.9	83.0
Tenth grade academic achievement, above average	41.8	75.3
Levels of disciplinary problems, below average	18.6	67.3
Below-average levels of students		
Not attending school	29.3	65.3
Cutting classes	32.9	61.7
Talking back to teachers	30.1	70.6
Disobeying instructions	19.9	66.2
Fighting	21.4	67.3
Schools reporting no problem or only minor problem with		
Physical conflicts among students	85.4	99.3
Conflicts between students and teachers	94.7	99.6
Robbery or theft	74.9	84.0
Vandalism of school property	66.0	80.2
Student use of drugs or alcohol	51.5	65.2
Rape or attempted rape	100.0	100.0
Student possession of weapons	99.2	99.9
Verbal abuse of teachers	84.7	95.6

a. Sample weighted to achieve a nationally representative sample of public and private high schools.

learning tools. The majority of schools with ineffective organizations serve students whose families are below average in SES. Three-fourths of the schools with effective organizations have sophomores who are above average in their mean achievement level. Less than half of the schools with ineffective organizations enjoy this advantage.

In addition, roughly two-thirds of the schools with effective organizations have less trouble than average with various forms of misbehavior: students not attending school, cutting classes, talking back to teachers, disobeying instructions, and fighting. In schools with ineffective organizations the numbers are almost exactly reversed. Similarly, effective schools are less likely than ineffective schools to have more than minor problems with violent or illegal student behavior. For most such behavior—physical conflicts among students, robbery or theft, vandalism, alcohol or drug usage, and verbal abuse of teachers—the incidence of moderate or serious problems is roughly 10 percent higher in ineffective schools than in effective ones.[6] When all forms of misbehavior are combined into one index, moreover, organizational differences become even more pronounced. The number of schools with a below-average level of disciplinary problems is 50 percentage points higher—67.3 percent versus 18.6 percent—for effective schools than for ineffective ones.

All of this suggests, of course, that school organizations may benefit enormously—or suffer badly—from the kinds of students they enroll. Yet even if further analysis shows this to be so, table 5-2 reveals that schools can also fail or succeed regardless of their student bodies.[7] More than 40 percent of the schools with ineffective organizations have the benefit of students whose tenth grade achievement is above average. A third of the schools with ineffective organizations have the luxury of teaching students from families above average in SES. In contrast, a quarter of the schools with effective organizations teach students whose sophomore scores are below average. A third of the schools with effective organizations teach students with above-average levels of various behavior problems. In sum, "good" students do not always produce good schools, and good schools do not only serve "good" students.

Parent Involvement

Schools with effective organizations nevertheless appear to have certain advantages. One is better students, another may be more supportive parents. Parents who unite behind a school, trust it to do what is best, and support its objectives and programs in the home can be a real asset to a school that wants to build an effective school organization. Parents who regularly challenge school priorities, frequently object to tracking policies or course assignments, and disagree with personnel decisions can cause real problems for the development of a coherent, ambitious, professional organization. Parents also have many sources of influence. They can meet directly with principals and teachers. They can reach the school indirectly through school boards, superintendents, and other external authorities. They can also affect the school through their influence—or lack thereof—on children in the

TABLE 5-3. Characteristics of the Parental Environments
of Effective and Ineffective School Organizations[a]
Percent

Characteristic	Ineffective school organization	Effective school organization
Schools with above-average frequency of parent contacts	49.8	76.9
Students whose parents "often" or "once in a while"		
Attend a PTA meeting	20.6	33.3
Attend a parent-teacher conference	46.2	52.8
Visit classes	21.0	24.0
Phone the school about problems	48.2	44.8
Schools that contact parents		
By newsletter once a semester	73.4	87.9
If a student is absent 2–3 days	74.0	92.1
If student grades become low	94.1	96.9
Schools whose parental relationships are above average	56.0	62.2
Schools whose relationships with parents are		
Predictable[b]	66.5	74.4
Cooperative[b]	78.9	85.5
Unconstrained by rules[b]	62.9	76.2

a. Sample weighted to achieve a nationally representative sample of public and private high schools.
b. Percent of principals giving response of 5 or 6 on a 6-point scale.

home. We therefore expect to see differences in the parents of effective
and ineffective schools. In effective schools, we expect to find parents
who are more supportive and who place a higher value on education.
We also expect to see differences in school efforts to reach out to
parents, to educate them about school progress and problems, and to
encourage them to be helpful and understanding. Schools that want
to succeed will no doubt recognize the need to get parents on their
side. An effective school will not wait for parents to choose sides.

As we see in table 5-3, effective schools are indeed more likely to
have supportive parents, though the differences are not always as
large as might be expected. The smallest differences are in direct
parent involvement. In effective and ineffective schools, parents are

about equally likely to attend parent-teacher conferences, visit classes, and phone the school about problems. Parents do attend more PTA meetings at effective schools than at ineffective ones, but at both types of schools only a small minority of parents attend.

The differences between schools are greater when we look at parent involvement from the other direction. As we said, schools have incentives to reach out to parents, not necessarily to involve parents directly in the school—which can become burdensome—but to promote parental support and understanding. Effective schools are, in fact, more likely to reach out to parents than are ineffective ones. Effective schools are substantially more likely to send parents a newsletter each semester and to notify parents if their child is absent two to three days. Effective schools are slightly more likely to notify parents if a student's grades become low, even though this is a nearly universal practice.

Schools that make these extra efforts are also likely to have higher levels of parent involvement of the kinds mentioned initially. Because of this, we created a general index out of all of the indicators of parent-school contacts. By this comprehensive measure, three-quarters of the effective schools have above-average levels of parent-school contacts; half of the ineffective schools do.

The contacts that effective schools have with parents are also of higher quality. This is important to note because schools with high levels of parent contact need not have high levels of parental support. Schools with high levels of parent involvement may have problems with parental interference. Conversely, schools with relatively low levels of parent involvement—boarding schools, for example—may enjoy strong parental support. Principals in the ATS schools were consequently asked to rate the cooperativeness, predictability, and informality of their relations with parents. On all three dimensions, as table 5-3 reports, principals in effective schools rated their relationships with parents higher than principals in ineffective schools rated theirs. These ratings are also highly correlated. When combined into an index of parental relationships, they indicate that effective organizations are somewhat more likely than ineffective organizations to enjoy parental relationships that are above average in quality. Overall, effective schools are more likely than ineffective schools to have the informed support of parents.

Bureaucratic Influence

How a school is organized ultimately depends a great deal on how a school is controlled. All schools, public and private, are subject to external authorities with various capacities to mandate or influence how schools are run. These authorities determine how many days schools must be open each year, what courses students must complete in order to receive high school diplomas, what standards teachers must meet in order to work in the schools, and so forth. They may also allocate school budgets, hire and fire school personnel, design the curriculum, furnish the classrooms, and prescribe school organization down to the finest detail. In the public sector these authorities include various units of government and public officials at the local, state, and federal levels. In the private sector government has a far less central role to play, but external authorities are nevertheless present. Private schools are subject to the authority of governing boards, and in many cases—such as Catholic diocesan and other church organizations— they are also subject to an administrative hierarchy.

In our view, the more extensive this control by external authorities, the less likely schools are to be organized effectively. In chapter 2 we explained at some length why we expect this to be so. Here we can begin to investigate issues of control—and therefore, issues of school autonomy—by comparing how schools with effective and ineffective organizations are controlled.

Principals were asked to evaluate the importance of two direct sources of bureaucratic influence—superintendents and central office administrators. They were also asked to evaluate one indirect source, teachers' unions, because of the unions' role in imposing bureaucratic constraints through union contracts. The points of reference in these evaluations were six organizational issues: establishing the curriculum, determining instructional methods used in classrooms, allocating school funds, hiring new full-time teachers, dismissing or transferring teachers, and setting disciplinary policy. Principals were asked to assess their own influence over these matters as well as the influence of superintendents, administrators, unions, and other possible influentials.[8] In addition, they were asked a number of questions specifically about their control over personnel—which, as we stressed in chapter 2, may be the crucial determinant of whether a school is able to develop a professional, teamlike organization.

Before we looked at how these various questions were answered in effective and ineffective schools, we analyzed the responses for patterns that might reveal general tendencies in how schools are run. We found two. First, we found that the influence of principals relative to central office administrators and superintendents is highly correlated across five of the six organizational issues. (Influence over school budgets fit no pattern whatsoever.) We therefore created five individual measures of administrative constraint—for curriculum, instruction, hiring, firing, and discipline—each measuring the difference between the influence of outside administrators (actually the maximum of the influences of the superintendent and the central office) and the influence of the principal.[9] The larger the value of this measure, the stronger the administrative constraint on the principal in addressing each issue. We then created a general index of administrative constraint out of the five separate measures.

The second pattern that we found involved questions having to do with personnel decisions and with the influence of unions over hiring and firing (though not over curriculum, instruction, and discipline). A principal's response to all such questions tended to be quite consistent from one question to the next. We therefore created an index of what we call personnel constraint out of the questions that produced internally consistent responses. Bureaucratic influence, then, has two dimensions in our analysis: a general one labeled administrative constraint, and a more specific one labeled personnel constraint.

In table 5-4 we take a look at administrative constraint in schools with effective and ineffective organizations. Generally, the differences between the schools are quite striking. Effective schools are subject to much less external administrative control than ineffective schools are. On every issue, effective schools experience less influence from superintendents and central office administrators than ineffective schools experience. On most issues the differences are large. On four out of five issues the percentages of schools subject to above average administrative constraint differ by at least 20 percentage points.

Since this influence is measured relative to the influence of the principal, the results in table 5-4 can also be interpreted as measures of administrative autonomy. Overall, more than 60 percent of the effectively organized schools have above average levels of administrative autonomy; less than a third of the ineffectively organized schools have such freedom. These general differences are consistent with our

TABLE 5-4. Administrative Constraints on Effective and Ineffective
School Organizations[a]
Percent

Characteristic	Ineffective school organization	Effective school organization
Schools with above-average level of administrative constraint	68.1	39.4
Schools with above-average influence by superintendent or central office staff over		
Curriculum	56.6	32.7
Instructional methods	76.6	55.0
Hiring new teachers	79.0	44.1
Dismissing or transferring teachers	92.1	43.6
Setting disciplinary policy	43.2	39.4

a. Sample weighted to achieve a nationally representative sample of public and private high schools.

view of school control. High levels of autonomy from external authority
tend to be associated with high levels of organizational effectiveness,
and vice versa.

Some of the specific differences—the differences from issue to
issue—are consistent with our perspective on school control too.
Among the reasons why direct external control may interfere with
the development of an effective school, perhaps the most important
is the potentially debilitating influence of external control over personnel. If principals have little or no control over who teaches in their
schools, they are likely to be saddled with a number of teachers,
perhaps even many teachers, whom they regard as bad fits. In an
organization that works best through shared decisionmaking and
delegated authority, a staff that is in conflict with the leader and with
itself is a serious problem. Indeed, if teamwork is the essence of an
effective school, such conflict may be a school's greatest organizational
problem. Personnel policies that promote such conflict may be a
school's greatest external burden.

The administrative constraints on the ATS schools—not to mention
the more specific personnel constraints that we shall examine next—
support this line of reasoning. The largest differences in administrative
control that effective and ineffective schools experience are in the
hiring and firing of teachers. Among schools that are ineffectively
organized, nearly all—92 percent of them—are subject to above-

average levels of administrative control over firing, and the vast majority are also subject to above-average control over hiring. Among schools that are well organized, though, only a little over 40 percent have their personnel decisions so heavily influenced by superintendents and central office administrators. Effective schools are simply much freer to build their own teams.

Effective schools are also much freer to design their own curricula and to choose their own methods of instruction. This is no surprise either, given the logic of school control and organization. As we and many others argue, education is an inherently difficult enterprise to regulate. Indeed, this is the most common basis for objections to the bureaucratization of public education. If curricula and instructional methods are prescribed too rigidly or extensively, teachers and students, who are diverse in their strengths and weaknesses, may have trouble performing successfully. The experiences of the ATS schools support such criticism. Administrative constraints on curriculum and instruction differ sharply in effective and ineffective schools. Schools that are effectively organized have much greater autonomy from bureaucratic influence on these vital matters of educational practice than schools that are ineffectively organized.

Ultimately, however, autonomy from bureaucratic influence seems most consequential for matters pertaining to personnel. This is evident in table 5-5, where we look at various indicators of personnel constraint. The first set of indicators is analogous to the indicators of administrative constraint reported in table 5-4. The indicators gauge the magnitude of union influence over personnel relative to the influence of the principal. The results are also analogous. Union influence is much stronger in schools that are ineffectively organized. Indeed, it is only the rare effective school in which union influence over hiring and firing is above average. Less than a quarter of the well-organized schools are highly constrained by unions on these personnel decisions. In contrast, about half of the poorly organized schools experience above-average union control over hiring and firing.

The second set of indicators in table 5-5 was obtained from questions asking principals about "barriers" they faced in "obtaining teachers with excellent qualifications" and in "firing or refusing to renew the contracts of poor teachers."[10] The table reports the percentages of principals saying that the barriers are "very large." Again, there are substantial disparities in external constraint. Only small fractions of

TABLE 5-5. Personnel Constraints on Effective and Ineffective
School Organizations[a]
Percent

Characteristic	Ineffective school organization	Effective school organization
Schools with above-average level of personnel constraint	45.0	8.2
Schools with above-average influence by teachers' union or association over		
Hiring new teachers	44.3	16.1
Dismissing or transferring teachers	55.8	22.7
Schools facing large personnel "barriers" of the following kinds[b]		
Union hiring constraints	52.3	13.0
Union firing constraints	61.0	21.4
Central office hiring control	52.2	26.3
Schools hiring more competent teachers over more senior[c]	60.6	92.7

a. Sample weighted to achieve a nationally representative sample of public and private high schools.
b. Percent of principals rating the size of the barrier a 5 or a 6 on a 6-point scale.
c. Percent of principals "agreeing" that they do so (a 4, 5, or 6 on a 6-point scale).

the schools with effective organizations regard the constraints imposed by unions as large obstacles to employing top-notch teachers or dismissing incompetent ones. A majority of the schools with ineffective organizations indicate that unions are large obstacles in making these key management decisions. The same pattern holds for a different barrier that we found often goes hand-in-hand with strong union influence. More than half of the principals of ineffective schools said that central office hiring controls impeded substantially their efforts to obtain excellent teachers. Only a quarter of the principals of effective schools said the same thing.

The differences are made more concrete by the final individual indicator in table 5-5. One of the most cherished personnel principles protected by unions is seniority: teachers should be compensated, promoted, and assigned to schools based primarily on their years of service. By following this principle, schools are said to be protected from destructive competition among teachers and to be guaranteed a more stable and experienced staff. Teachers are said to be protected from arbitrary evaluations by incompetent or biased administrators and politicians. Yet whatever the merits of these arguments, it must also be said that strict seniority systems can protect mediocrity among teachers and prevent principals from organizing schools according to their best professional judgment.

Principals were asked to agree or disagree with the proposition that "when two teachers with the same credentials apply for permanent transfer to this school, we decide which one to accept on the basis of their competence, not on the basis of their seniority." A majority of the principals of all schools agreed with this proposition, indicating that most seniority rules are not ironclad. But effective and ineffective schools did not support the proposition in equal numbers. Virtually all schools with effective organizations agreed that they hired the more competent applicant; only 60 percent of the ineffective schools agreed that they did the same. Seniority rules—an important aspect of educational bureaucracy—are far more prevalent and constraining in ineffective schools.

To sum up personnel constraint, we have a comprehensive index that includes all of the indicators described in table 5-5. As measured by this index, personnel constraint is above average in fewer than 10 percent of the schools with effective organizations. It is above average in nearly half of the schools with ineffective organizations. Schools with organizational problems are simply much more likely than schools without such problems to be limited by external authorities in staffing their organizations. Schools with organizational problems are also more likely to be more constrained by external administrators in all regards. Bureaucratic influence is much stronger—and autonomy is much weaker—in ineffective schools than in effective ones.

School Board Influence

A second kind of control that schools experience locally is exercised by school boards. In the public and private sectors alike, school boards are the ultimate source of legitimate local authority. In both sectors there are also higher authorities—the federal and state governments, diocesan organizations, associations of private schools—that are growing in importance. But of all relevant authorities, local boards are generally regarded as the ones most responsible for school governance. Boards also wield real power, including the authority to hire and fire superintendents and to negotiate with teachers' unions. School boards are consequently an essential place to observe how the direct democratic control of schools really works.[11]

TABLE 5-6. School Board Influence on Effective and Ineffective
School Organizations[a]
Percent

Characteristic	Ineffective school organization	Effective school organization
Schools with above-average level of school board influence	52.5	37.3
Schools with above-average influence by school board over		
Curriculum	59.4	43.1
Instructional methods	48.6	45.4
Hiring new teachers	57.9	39.7
Dismissing or transferring teachers	46.6	33.0
Setting disciplinary policy	60.8	54.2

a. Sample weighted to achieve a nationally representative sample of public and private high schools.

Our observations are based on the same kinds of questions that
principals were asked about superintendents, central administrators,
and unions—questions that gauge the influence of local boards and
principals over six areas of school organization and management. Our
expectations about the answers to these questions are also much the
same. From a school's perspective it should matter little whether
external authority is being exercised by administrators, unions, or
school boards. Whatever its source, direct external control can undermine school organization if it is increased beyond a certain limit.

In table 5-6 we look at the influence of the boards of effective and
ineffective schools. As before, we consider the five areas of school
management that displayed a consistent pattern, and we gauge board
influence in these areas relative to the influence of the principal.
Similar to bureaucratic influence, the direct influence of boards is
stronger over schools that are ineffectively organized than it is over
schools that are effectively organized. Again, the differences are larger
for hiring, firing, and curriculum—the areas that are likely to matter
most for school organization—than they are for instruction and discipline. But the differences in school board influence are unlike the
differences in bureaucratic influence in one important respect: they
are generally smaller. Overall, a little more than half of the ineffectively
organized schools experience above-average amounts of school board
influence; a little more than a third of the effectively organized schools
do. While noteworthy, this total difference is less than half the disparity

in bureaucratic influence—in administrative and personnel constraint—between effective and ineffective schools.

There are at least two reasons why the influence of school boards might not distinguish school organization as sharply as other forms of external control. One is a small school system effect. In small school systems, which are well represented in our sample, boards are more likely to represent the interests of parents than they are in medium and large systems. Parent interests are more likely to be homogeneous and more likely to be consistent with the interests of the broader community the school serves. Being more in tune with parent interests, the board in the small system will be more willing to grant the school the autonomy to make decisions that respond to student and parent needs as the school sees them. A second and probably more common reason why board influence may not sharply distinguish effective and ineffective schools is that in many school systems the influence of the board is exercised largely through the superintendent and central administrators. The board's direct influence over the school, even if the board is powerful and aggressive, is often thoroughly mediated by the board's administrative agents. Board influence could distinguish effective and ineffective schools, then, without principals being able to perceive it.

Modeling School Organization

We have now seen that school organization is associated, often strongly, with a number of variables that ought to influence it. School organization seems to be affected substantially by the students in the school and by the control exerted over it by external authorities. To a somewhat lesser degree, the school appears to be shaped by its relationships with parents, its resources, and its size. Appearances, though, can be deceiving. Factors that are closely associated with school organization may not be causes of it. The next step in the analysis is to weigh the importance of alternative causes.

This is no small step, however. Many factors that seem to influence school organization are probably influenced *by* school organization. Schools with effective organizations tend to have well-behaved, academically able students from relatively high-status families. In part this is because schools with academically oriented clienteles should find it easier to develop academically effective organizations than schools with troubled clienteles. But it is also because schools with effective organizations and reputations for success tend to attract families with relatively strong interests in education. Concerned (and financially able) parents often buy homes near effective public schools or pay tuition to effective private schools.

As we explained in chapter 4, the reciprocal causal relationships between and among school organization and the many variables associated with it make it difficult to disentangle cause and effect. In fact, there is no statistical solution to this difficulty—or, at least, none that will work with the data that we have. There is no way for us to ensure that every estimate we obtain is unbiased. Nevertheless, we can take certain precautions: we can try to ensure that the influences that interest us most are not exaggerated. In chapter 4 we took various precautions to obtain a conservative range of estimates of the effect of organization on achievement gains. Here we want to obtain a conservative estimate of the influence of external control on school organization.

To obtain such an estimate we begin by assuming that school organization is influenced by the school clientele, but not the other way around. In other words, we assume that the aptitude and behavior of the student body, and the socioeconomic status, school contacts, and school relationships of parents affect the quality of school organization, but that school organization does not affect these factors. This assumption gives several potentially major causes of school organization more than a fair opportunity to register as important influences on school organization in the statistical analysis. In so doing, the assumption stands to limit the opportunity of other variables to register their influence. In particular, it stands to limit the estimated influence of external control. In our view, this is appropriate. It is better that we perhaps overestimate the influence of the school clientele, than exaggerate the influence of school control.

Nevertheless, there is at least one remaining way in which we might overestimate the influence of school control. We do not believe that school organization and school control are reciprocally related to each other, at least to a significant degree. We believe causality runs primarily one way, from control to organization. But school organization may influence control indirectly, if student achievement, which organization helps determine, is an important determinant of school control. In that event, school organization would ultimately feed back, via a causal loop, to influence school control. Our single-equation estimate of the effect of control on organization might thereby exaggerate the effect by assuming that the relationship between the two has nothing to do with the indirect effect of organization on control.

We cannot allow for this indirect effect in our analysis of school organization. It is another problem of simultaneous causation that standard statistical methods cannot fully remedy.[12] But we can get an indication of how important this effect may be. In the last half of this chapter we will explore the causes of school control, including the influence exerted on school control by student achievement. In the last chapter we defended the equation-by-equation approach of our analysis by arguing, in part, that school control should not be heavily influenced by student achievement but should instead be determined primarily by institutional forces, which are exogenous. If school control is so determined, there is less reason to be concerned about overestimating the influence of school control on school organization in this part of the analysis.

Let us turn, then, to the second model in our analysis, a single linear regression equation of school organization. The dependent variable is our modified comprehensive index of school organization. The independent variables, at least initially, are indexes representing each of the potential influences on school organization examined in tables 5-1 to 5-6: school economic resources, school size, student tenth grade achievement, student behavior problems, parent SES, parent-school contacts, parent-school relationships, bureaucratic influence (administrative constraint and personnel constraint), and school board influence.[13] Because the analysis takes place at the school level, all of the indexes measuring characteristics of individual students or their parents are averages of the index scores for all of the students in a school.

Results

In table 5-7 we report the parameter estimates for several versions of our model of school organization. The first model that we report on, the full model, includes all of the variables that our descriptive analysis suggested were important. The model reveals that when these variables are analyzed together, some are not significantly

TABLE 5-7. Estimates of Models of School Organization[a]

Variable	Model[b]		
	Full	Reduced	Final
School economic resources	−.053	. . .	. . .
	(.059)		
	−.037		
School size	.0009*	.001*	.001*
	(.0003)	(.0003)	(.0003)
	.153	.171	.170
Student tenth grade achievement	.586*	.553*	.552*
	(.103)	(.099)	(.098)
	.247	.233	.233
Student behavior problems	−.352*	−.353*	−.353*
	(.056)	(.055)	(.055)
	−.330	−.331	−.331
Parent socioeconomic status[c]	.216*	.210*	.210*
	(.039)	(.039)	(.039)
	.209	.203	.203
Parent-school contacts	.084*	.075*	.075*
	(.040)	(.039)	(.039)
	.086	.077	.077
Parental relationships	.056	. . .	. . .
	(.064)		
	.033		
Bureaucratic influence			
Administrative constraint	−.220*	−.229*	−.227*
	(.053)	(.053)	(.047)
	−.208	−.216	−.214
Personnel constraint	−.191*	−.196*	−.195*
	(.059)	(.058)	(.058)
	−.151	−.155	−.154
School board influence	.001	.005	. . .
	(.052)	(.051)	
	.001	.004	
Constant	−.679*	−.439*	−.438*
	(.308)	(.070)	(.069)
Adjusted R^2	.518	.519	.520
Sample size	371	371	371

* Statistically significant, $\alpha \leq .05$, $t \geq 1.64$, one-tail test.

a. Dependent variable is comprehensive measure of organization without percent of students in academic track. Sample weighted to achieve a nationally representative sample of public and private high schools.

b. Coefficients are unstandardized linear regression coefficients; standard errors are in parentheses. Standardized regression coefficients (betas) are in italics.

c. Residualized variable, controlling for parent-school contacts, parental relationships, and student tenth grade achievement.

related to school organization. The coefficients estimating their influence on school organization cannot be distinguished from zero with 95 percent (or even 90 percent) confidence. The variables that have these negligible conditional effects are school economic resources, parent-school relationships, and school board influence.

In subsequent models we explored the possibility that these weak influences might not all be negligible. The importance of a marginal variable can be underestimated when variables that are correlated with it are also in the model. We therefore estimated reduced versions of the full model, in which each new model omitted one or two of the marginal independent variables. The results were essentially the same as those for the full model. School resources, parent-school relationships, and school board influence remained nonsignificant.

In table 5-7 we report the estimates of the reduced model that are most relevant to our central argument. The estimates for that model show that school board influence, even in an equation that drops the other marginal variables, is only barely related to school organization.[14] The coefficient on school board influence is only a tenth the size of its standard error, making it indistinguishable from zero. We therefore drop school board influence as well as school economic resources and parent-school relationships from our statistical model of school organization.

Our final model of school organization, which excludes these very weak variables, is described in the last column of table 5-7. All of the estimated coefficients are statistically significant; their values can be confidently distinguished from zero. The model has the added virtue of explaining more than half of the variance in organization (adjusted $R^2 = 0.52$) in this national sample of schools. Given the considerable potential for measurement error in survey research, the model provides an unusually complete accounting of school organization. The effectiveness of school organization is influenced independently by all but one of the major types of influence that are theoretically related to it. Students, parents, and external control each contribute as expected to a school's organizational effectiveness. School size, for which we had no clear expectation, turns out to enhance organizational effectiveness as it increases. Among major types of influence, only economic resources can be ruled out of an explanation of school organization. All things being equal, schools that spend more per pupil and have lower student-teacher ratios do not have more effective organizations.

TABLE 5-8. Predicted Effects of Bureaucratic Influence and Other Factors on School Organization[a]

Determinant of school organization	Predicted percentile of organizational effectiveness if determinant is at mean of		Predicted percentile change
	Lowest quartile	Highest quartile	
School size	45.2	73.4	28.2
Student tenth grade achievement	37.3	76.2	38.9
Student behavior problems	81.1	28.8	−52.3
Parent socioeconomic status	41.0	75.3	34.3
Parent contacts	49.4	63.2	13.8
Bureaucratic influence			
Administrative constraint	76.9	42.0	−34.9
Personnel constraint	67.8	42.2	−25.6
Total (administrative plus personnel constraint)	81.6	26.1	−55.5

a. Predictions use "final" model in table 5-7 and place all variables, besides the one in question, at their school-level means.

But how much impact do the variables in our final model of organization have? That is somewhat difficult to answer using the coefficients in table 5-7. The unstandardized regression coefficients are hard to evaluate and to compare because the variables are measured in different and somewhat arbitrary units. The standardized coefficients (in italics) are easy to compare, but they cannot be readily interpreted in terms of the original variables.

To overcome these problems, we created new measures of the estimated impact of each independent variable on school organization. We calculated the change in organizational effectiveness that is predicted to occur if and when each independent variable is raised in value from the midpoint of its lowest quartile to the midpoint of its highest quartile, while all other independent variables remain at their respective means. We then compared the predicted levels of organizational effectiveness to the actual distribution of organization scores and converted the predictions into percentile scores for organizational effectiveness. This method of interpretation, similar to our method for interpreting influences on student achievement, enables us to predict how far up the distribution of organizational effectiveness a school would be moved by comparable improvements in the factors that influence it. The results of these calculations are reported in table 5-8.

The results support two important conclusions. One is that, all things being equal, schools are more likely to be organized effectively if their students are relatively well behaved and well prepared for the academic work of high school, and if their students come from relatively high SES families. A change in student behavior alone can change the predicted effectiveness of a school organization by a full two quartiles. If it were possible to find two schools identical and average in all respects except that one enjoyed a very low level of behavior problems and the other suffered a very high level, the two schools would be expected to be located 52.3 percentiles apart on the distribution of organizational effectiveness. Despite differing from each other in only one way, the school with few behavior problems would likely be found around the eighty-first percentile of organizational effectiveness, the school with many behavior problems down around the twenty-ninth percentile. A substantial but less dramatic difference—a quartile and a half—would be expected between two average schools that differed sharply in student tenth grade achievement.

Clearly, schools find it easier to become academically focused institutions with real esprit de corps when their students are committed to learning. But schools benefit from one other student quality as well. If students in two otherwise average schools come from families that in one school are in the top quartile of SES, and in the second school are in the bottom quartile of SES, the organizations of these schools are likely to differ by more than one quartile in effectiveness.

The statistical importance of SES may say more about the influence of parents than of students, however. The model already includes those attributes of students that ought to influence school organization directly, student ability and behavior. And those attributes turn out to have strong effects on organization. The fact that SES, which is a good predictor of student ability and behavior, also has a substantial independent effect on organization suggests that it is not gauging a residual influence of students but rather an indirect influence of parents.

This interpretation is reinforced by the rather weak effects of the variables that try to gauge parent influence directly. One of these variables, the overall parent-school relationship, did not have a significant effect on school organization and was dropped from the final model. The other variable, parent-school contacts, has a statistically significant but substantively weak effect. A shift from the lowest to the highest levels of parent-school interaction raises the predicted effectiveness of school organization by only 14 percentiles.[15]

Overall, these results suggest that the contribution of parents to school effectiveness does not occur through direct involvement in the school. Parents evidently help or hinder schools, not through their participation but through their support of the school in other ways— ways that family SES predicts.

We can only speculate on what these ways might be, but the leading possibility is the support parents can provide a school in the home. Parents who are well educated and employed in high-paying, high-status occupations are more likely than other parents to value education and to reinforce it in the home. We saw in chapter 4, for example, that parents with children in successful schools—parents who tend to be above average in SES—tend to monitor their childrens' school work more closely and to expect more of their children academically than parents with children in unsuccessful schools. We do not want to make too much of this evidence because, as we discussed before, it is not overwhelming, and, in the case of parent expectations, has been gathered in a suspect manner. But it is reasonable to suppose that parents who are higher in SES will be at least somewhat more likely than other parents to support teachers and principals if and when they decide to impose serious academic demands on students.

Whatever its precise size, the important thing to recognize about the influence of parent SES on school organization is that it probably does not work through direct parent involvement in the school. There is currently a great deal of enthusiasm among school reformers for increasing parent involvement. Reformers are even mandating that some schools establish school councils on which parents will be represented in order to increase parent involvement. If our results are correct, however, such reform may misunderstand the proper role for parents. Schools do not seem to benefit in a large or systematic way from direct parent participation. It is more likely that they benefit from the various forms of support and encouragement parents can provide for school objectives in the home.

There is one other very good reason for believing that the key role for parents is support, not involvement: schools tend to prosper when outsiders trust them and leave them alone. Indeed, the other important conclusion that the estimates in table 5-8 support is that autonomy from bureaucratic influence is the strongest individual determinant of school effectiveness. Administrative constraint and personnel constraint are each capable of improving school organization by more than a full quartile in an average school, if they are reduced from their highest to their lowest levels.

Even more impressive are the improvements in predicted effectiveness if administrative and personnel constraints are reduced from their highest levels together. A school that is average in all respects except that it is subject to weak administrative and personnel constraints can be expected to rank in the eighty-second percentile of organizational effectiveness. The same school subject to strong bureaucratic influence can be expected to rank in only the twenty-sixth percentile.

The importance of this disparity goes well beyond its impressive magnitude. In the last chapter we gauged the influence that school organization has on student achievement by calculating the predicted difference in achievement gains for students attending schools in the top and bottom quartiles of organizational effectiveness. We calculated that over a four-year high school career, identical students attending effective and ineffective schools would differ by more than a full year in achievement gains. The influence that bureaucracy exerts over school organization is sufficiently strong that it alone is capable of producing most of this achievement difference. The shift in organizational effectiveness that we used to predict achievement gains in the last chapter compared schools in percentile 12.5 of organizational effectiveness to schools in percentile 87.5 of organizational effectiveness. A change in bureaucratic influence—from a high level to a low one—is capable of shifting organizational effectiveness from percentile 26.1 to percentile 81.6 on its own. In other words, bureaucratic influence is an important enough cause of school organization that it can make or break school performance all by itself.

To be sure, there are other factors that individually and together can also produce large differences in school organization and, in turn, student achievement: student behavior and ability, and parent SES and supportiveness. But what is important about bureaucratic influence is not only that it plays a very large role in shaping school organization. It is that bureaucratic influence is the only major factor shaping school organization that reformers can do anything about. The aptitude, behavior, and background of students who attend America's schools cannot be readily improved by reformers. Students can be sorted into different schools so that they match better what schools are trying to do. But the qualities of students and families that seem to influence school organization the most cannot be improved until the quality of schools improves first. This places reformers in a "catch-22" situation, unless they have other factors to work with.

Bureaucratic influence is quintessentially such a factor. Bureaucratic control is, after all, what reformers and others trying to make schools more effective use to implement their innovations. Bureaucratic control is therefore not only the strongest influence on school organization, it is the one influence that reformers have firmly within their grasp.

Bureaucratic control is also probably more influential than our analysis has indicated. As our analysis stands, we estimate that bureaucratic influence is powerful enough to make the difference between effective and ineffective school organization. But the full strength of this influence is almost certainly being masked by estimates of student and parent influences that are too high. Because the quality of students and parents in a school is influenced by the quality of school organization, our model, which gives the school no credit for this influence, will tend to overestimate the effects that students and parents have on schools. For the same reason, our model may underestimate the effects of external control. Unless bureaucratic control is caused indirectly by school organization, it may be an even more important influence on school effectiveness than our estimates have indicated. Let us take up that final issue, then, the causes of bureaucratic control.

Institutions and Control in America's Schools

Thus far we have found that one of the most important influences on student achievement is school organization. We have also found that the strongest influence on school organization is bureaucratic control. What we have yet to find are the major influences on bureaucratic control. In other words, what causes superintendents, administrators, and unions to impose tough constraints on some schools but only weak constraints on others? This is the final issue that our analysis will address.

It is also the most important issue. The central argument of this book is that the organization and performance of schools are profoundly shaped by their surrounding institutions. Institutions establish the ground rules that largely determine how schools and school authorities respond to demands from students, parents, and other groups with an interest in how schools are run. Institutions create the basic structures that more or less determine how everything else works. Institutions are therefore the one set of variables in the whole, complicated process of school control, school organization, and school performance that can reasonably be viewed as exogenous. They are the starting point for understanding school performance.

If we are correct, the institutions that govern America's public schools bear substantial responsibility for the bureaucratization of schools and the debilitation of their organization. Direct democratic control stimulates a political struggle over the right to impose higher-order values on the schools through public authority, and this in turn promotes bureaucracy—which is both a crucial means of ensuring that these higher-order values are actually implemented at the school level (by personnel who may not agree with them) and a crucial means of insulating them from subversion by opposing groups and officials who may gain hold of public authority in the future.

Markets offer an institutional alternative to direct democratic control. They are not built around the exercise of public authority, but rather around school competition and parent-student choice—which, for all the reasons explored in chapter 2, tend through their natural operation to discourage bureaucratic forms of organization and to promote the development of autonomy, professionalism, and other traits associated with effective schooling.

Because democratic control and markets are the institutions that distinguish the public and private sectors in American education, we ought to find in our empirical analysis that school organization is strongly influenced by sector. This is the simplest—and most funda-mental—"institutional effect" to be observed.

We do not expect every public school to be plagued by excessive bureaucracy or every private school to be free of it. The demands that are made on institutions by parents, students, and other educational interests will be important too. Schools with well-behaved, academi-cally able students will generate relatively few complaints about school performance from parents, teachers, prospective employers, and everyone else. Such schools will thereby give external authorities little reason to compel them to change what they are doing. Schools with difficult students will have just the opposite effect. Similarly, schools with concerned, supportive parents will have valuable allies to discourage outside authorities from tampering with "their" schools.

Schools with apathetic, uneducated, or incompetent parents will have less effective support against external threats.

We also expect schools in different locations to experience different amounts of control. In particular, we expect urban schools to be subject to unusually high levels of bureaucratic influence. Cities have disproportionate numbers of difficult students and uninterested parents. They also have large heterogeneous populations, which generate conflict over educational values and problems in imposing values on schools. Bureaucracy is the response to such problems.

These sorts of problems are not unique to the public sector. Problems can occur in the private sector as well. Private sector interests, especially religious interests, are often organized on a citywide basis. Catholic dioceses, for example, encompass the entire populations of most large cities. If these private organizations are interested in providing education citywide, they may have some interest in ensuring that all of their schools adhere to values that they, the governing organizations, promote. In large, heterogeneous cities, however, even private organizations will find that the imposition of higher-order values requires some measure of bureaucracy—or some willingness to compromise with schools on such values. Certainly, many urban Catholic school systems have found this out. America's four largest Catholic school systems each enroll more than 100,000 students, a number exceeded by only sixteen systems in the public sector.[16]

All urban schools, then, have three especially strong forces working to encourage bureaucratic control over them. They have difficult students, they have unsupportive parents, and they are embedded in school systems serving large, heterogeneous populations. The first two of these have already been measured in previous models and will be examined again. The third has not yet been measured but needs to be. The size, and by implication, the heterogeneity of a school system is to a great extent a basic institutional characteristic. Years ago, when school systems were rapidly being consolidated, this was not so. The proper size of a school district was a regular subject of debate. Today the issue is hardly debated at all. School districts, like school boards and superintendents, are taken for granted. Districts are permanent fixtures on the institutional landscape of American education.

If urban education is subject to excessive bureaucratic influence, then, part of this influence may occur because of the difficult clientele that city schools serve. But part of any excessive influence must also be attributed to the scope of the institutions that have been created to control city schools.[17] Much the same goes for suburban and (many) rural schools—except in reverse. If nonurban schools, serving able students from supportive families in homogeneous communities, turn out to enjoy relatively high levels of bureaucratic autonomy, part of this freedom must be attributed to the typically limited scope of nonurban educational institutions.

In sum, we expect to observe two institutional influences on the bureaucratization of school control. The first and most important is the influence that derives from the basic organizing principles of governing institutions. This is the influence that derives from direct democratic control of schools and from indirect control of schools through markets. This influence should be manifest in differences in bureaucratic influence between public and private schools. The second and less basic institutional influence is that which derives from the scope—and hence the heterogeneity—of the institutional system. It should be manifest in differences between urban schools and schools located elsewhere, when differences in students and parents are taken into account.

To observe these potential differences, let us turn to the data. As has been our custom, we will look at the data through a two-step process. First, we will describe how schools that are high and low in bureaucratic influence differ. Do they have different students, parents, and locations? Are they located in different sectors? We will do so by profiling schools that are in the top and the bottom quartiles of administrative and personnel constraint. With these pictures in mind we will then build and estimate statistical models of bureaucratic influence and use those models to sort out institutional and noninstitutional causes.

Profiles of Bureaucratic Influence

In table 5-9 we profile schools that are in the upper and the lower quartiles of the distribution of our general index of administrative constraint. These profiles reveal that schools subject to different levels of administrative constraint contain students who clearly differ as predicted. In schools with low levels of outside administrative influence, solid majorities of the student bodies are above average in tenth grade achievement and achievement gains and below average in behavior

TABLE 5-9. Characteristics of Schools with High and Low Levels of Administrative Constraint[a]

Percent

Characteristic	Schools with high administrative constraint	Schools with low administrative constraint
Students with above-average		
Tenth grade achievement	39.6	54.7
Achievement gains	35.2	70.1
Behavior problems	63.7	31.8
Parental environments above average in		
Socioeconomic status	40.7	64.2
Contacts with school	44.0	73.4
Relationships with school	54.3	67.5
Location of school		
Urban	28.3	14.3
Suburban	18.2	43.0
Rural	53.5	42.7
Type of control: private	8.7	55.2

a. Sample weighted to achieve a nationally representative sample of public and private high schools.

problems. In schools with high levels of outside administrative influence, only about a third of the student bodies exhibit these favorable qualities. Evidently, external control depends on school performance. Schools in which students are doing well seem to be granted the freedom to continue doing what they are doing. Schools in which students are performing poorly seem to be forced by external administrators to change.

Much the same is suggested by the relationships between external control and various qualities of parents. Clear majorities of the schools that are subject to low amounts of administrative influence have parents who are above average in SES, in the frequency of their school contacts, and in the quality of their school relationships. Far fewer of the schools that are subject to high amounts of administrative influence have parents with these positive attributes. It appears that administrators also tend to leave schools alone when parents are relatively high in status and are cooperatively involved in their children's schools. Administrators seem to be more willing to intervene in schools with parents who are less well educated and who demonstrate less interest in or support for their schools. Overall, it would appear that external control is substantially a response to how a school is doing with its clientele—or how well that clientele is doing itself. As we have seen many times in this analysis, however, appearances can be deceiving.

Schools that differ in external control also differ in their institutional settings. First, they differ in location.[18] Schools subject to high levels of constraint are twice as likely as schools subject to low levels of constraint to be located in urban areas, and less than half as likely to be located in suburban areas. About half of the schools of each type are rural.[19] In part, these locational differences simply reinforce what we found in looking at students and families. Urban areas tend to have more difficult students and less supportive parents. But the tendency for heavily constrained schools to be urban may indicate, as we suggested, that large, heterogeneous school systems encourage excessive amounts of bureaucratic influence. If so, the nature of school control may indeed be a product of the institutional environment.

This possibility is strongly reinforced by the data on school sector. Only 8.7 percent of the schools subject to strong administrative control are private; 55.2 percent of the schools subject to weak control are private. It remains to be seen whether this striking relationship between sector and administrative control will stand up when the effects of students and parents are taken into account. But these initial results suggest that institutions may matter a great deal.

Institutions may also be crucial to the development of a specific and especially important form of bureaucratic influence: constraints on school personnel. In table 5-10 we profile schools that are in the lowest and the highest quartiles of our index of personnel constraint. The profiles show that schools that are subject to different levels of personnel constraint are similar in all relevant respects to schools that are subject to different levels of administrative constraint more generally. This is what we would expect given our observations in chapter 2 about the compatibility of traditional democratic institutions and the major sources of personnel constraint: civil-service protections (notably, tenure) and public sector unions. These sources of constraint are simply far less compatible with institutions of market control.

There is an alternative to this institutional explanation, however. And it too is supported by the profiles of constrained and unconstrained schools. It is possible that unions, the primary source of constraint in our index, work hardest to constrain school personnel decisions when schools cause teachers the most serious problems. Thus we find that

TABLE 5-10. Characteristics of Schools with High and Low Levels
of Personnel Constraint[a]

Percent

Characteristic	Schools with high personnel constraint	Schools with low personnel constraint
Students with above-average		
Tenth grade achievement	43.2	60.9
Achievement gains	37.0	61.1
Behavior problems	84.7	23.8
Parental environments above average in		
Socioeconomic status	34.8	68.4
Contacts with school	48.0	77.4
Relationships with school	52.7	59.5
Location of school		
Urban	22.7	16.3
Suburban	32.5	38.1
Rural	44.8	45.6
Type of control: private	0.4	56.2

a. Sample weighted to achieve a nationally representative sample of public and private high schools.

constraint is much greater in schools where students are having
difficulties than in schools where students are enjoying success. More
than 60 percent of the schools that are low in personnel constraint
have students above average in tenth grade achievement and achievement gains. Only 40 percent of the schools with high personnel
constraint have students who are doing so well. The difference is even
greater for student behavior. Discipline is an above-average problem
in 84.7 percent of the schools that are strongly constrained. It is an
above-average problem in only 23.8 percent of the schools that are
weakly constrained.

Personnel decisions are also highly constrained where schools have
less support from parents. Parents are above average in SES in barely
a third of the schools with high levels of constraint. Parents are above
average in SES in two-thirds of the schools that are low in constraint.
A similar disparity characterizes parent-school contacts, though there
is little difference in parent-school relationships. Overall, these differences may indicate that teachers want unions to play a stronger role
in supporting their work when parents do not support it. The
differences may also indicate that, in communities and schools where
parents are less attentive, unions face weaker political resistance and

rise more readily to power. Whatever the reasons, teachers' unions and the constraints they seek rapidly gain in influence as parents decline in education, affluence, and occupational status.

These findings are reinforced by the locations of schools subject to different amounts of personnel constraint. Schools with tough constraints are more likely to be found in urban areas and less likely to be found in suburban areas than schools with weak constraints are. Urban areas tend to have the problem kids and uncooperative parents that prompt unions to seek protections for their teachers.

As we have said, however, urban schools are distinguished by more than their clients. They also tend to have distinctive institutions—in particular, institutions that are unusually large in scope. This distinctive characteristic is likely to be associated with personnel constraint. Union activity tends to be greater in the public and private sectors alike where the bargaining units are largest and where the rewards from successful bargaining are greatest. For this reason, large school systems are likely to experience more personnel constraint than small systems, regardless of the kinds of parents and students being served. Large systems must also deal with the political uncertainty and conflicts that heterogeneous populations bring. This too will lead to increased demands by teachers for protection and insulation, giving added force to their traditional concern for constraining the managerial discretion of their superiors.

Finally, there is strong evidence that the basic institutions of social control also determine constraints on personnel. As we explained in chapter 2, the public sector's institutions of democratic control tend to encourage the formation and entrenchment of unions, at least in comparison to the institutions of the marketplace. Many of the objectives of unions—tenure, seniority rules—are objectives that are embraced in public employment more generally. Politicians—school board members, for example—who are willing to champion those objectives can reap great electoral rewards from union support. Unions are free to pursue these same objectives in the private sector, but they do not have the assistance of politicians and administrators with political incentives to support them, and, as in the economy more generally, the competitive environment makes unionization very difficult to sell. It comes as no surprise, then, that none of the schools subject to strong unions and high levels of personnel constraint is private, but over half of the schools subject to weak unions and constraints are private. Public schools may also escape the influence of powerful unions—nearly half of the low influence schools are public—but for them it is apparently much more difficult.

Modeling School Control

To assess the relative importance of institutions and other sources of administrative and personnel constraint, we constructed linear regression models of each type of constraint. The variables to be explained, the dependent variables, are the comprehensive indexes of administrative and personnel constraint. The explanatory or independent variables are the same in each model. They include three student body measures (tenth grade achievement, total achievement gains, and behavior problems) and three schoolwide parent measures (parent SES, parent-school contacts, and parent-school relationships). The independent variables also include our primary measure of institutional structure—school sector—and a measure that does double duty as an indicator of the quality of the school clientele and of institutional structure: school location.

We want to emphasize that the student and parent variables serve two important purposes in the model. First, all of these variables work as controls on the direct relationship between institutions and bureaucratic influence, helping to ensure that we do not overestimate the strength of the relationship between institutions and influence. We have found all along that the structure of schools is important even when student and parent characteristics are taken into account. School organization is crucial for achievement above and beyond the influence of students and parents. Autonomy from bureaucracy is crucial for school organization above and beyond the kinds of students and parents being served by the organization. Now it is time to determine whether institutions are critical for bureaucratic autonomy apart from the effects that students and parents have on autonomy.

If we are correct, autonomy will also not be greatly affected by one student variable in particular—student achievement gains. In choosing to analyze school performance with a sequence of single-equation models, we argued that the causal process was anchored in institutions and that, while school performance might feed back to influence school control, such an influence was likely to be relatively small. By including student achievement gain scores as an exogenous variable—even though they are influenced indirectly by school control—our models of administrative and personnel constraint put our argument to a useful test. The test is not definitive, for it is impossible to tell through individual equations what a system of simultaneous equations might reveal. But if student achievement gains make little difference for school control in single-equation models, where the entire relationship between achievement and control is assumed to run only in one direction, it is likely that control is not substantially affected by achievement. It also suggests that it is sound to analyze school performance, as we have done, with a sequence of separate models.

Results

The estimates of the final versions of our two regression models are reported in table 5-11. The models do a reasonably good job of accounting for both administrative and personnel constraint. They explain respectable portions of the variance in the dependent variables: 43 percent of the variance in administrative constraint, and 32 percent of the variance in personnel constraint. All of the independent variables in the models work in their expected directions. The models also do a good job of clarifying the role of institutions in structuring school control and organization. They do so not only through the coefficients on the variables reported in table 5-11, but through a number of nonsignificant coefficients that, to simplify the presentation, we do not report in the table.

Consider the student variables first. To begin with, bureaucratic influence is not determined by school performance as we have measured it. In models that we do not report here, we found that student total achievement gain scores do not significantly influence administrative or personnel constraint. The only link that we could find between achievement gains and school control involved a different measure of achievement gains—a dichotomous measure that indicates whether students in a school are gaining above or below average amounts. As we show in table 5-11, this measure is significantly related to administrative constraint. Schools that are performing above average experience less constraint, those that are performing below average experience more constraint. Evidently, student achievement is not something that external authorities respond to in a very sensitive way. To the extent that they respond at all, it is not to the variations

TABLE 5-11. Estimates of Final Models of Administrative
and Personnel Constraint[a]

Variable[b]	Administrative constraint[c]	Personnel constraint[c]
Student tenth grade achievement	n.s.	−.186*
		(.092)
		−.099
Student achievement gains[d]	−.186*	n.s.
	(.078)	
	−.095	
Student behavior problems	n.s.	.139*
		(.045)
		.164
Parent contacts	−.094*	n.s.
	(.038)	
	−.103	
Urban location	.580*	.501*
	(.108)	(.105)
	.213	.219
Private control	−1.526*	−.838*
	(.106)	(.119)
	−.610	−.399
Constant	.233*	−.098
	(.056)	(.040)
Adjusted R^2	.431	.320
Sample size	388	389

n.s. Variable was statistically nonsignificant in preliminary models and was therefore excluded from final model.
    * Statistically significant, $\alpha \leq .05$, $t \geq 1.64$, one-tail test.
    a. Sample weighted to achieve a nationally representative sample of public and private high schools.
    b. The full models also included a dummy variable for rural location and two other parent variables: parent socioeconomic status and parental relationships. The coefficients on the variables consistently proved to be nonsignificant, so they were dropped from the final models reported here.
    c. Coefficients are unstandardized regression coefficients; standard errors are in parentheses. Standardized regression coefficients (betas) are in italics.
    d. Dummy variable with gains dichotomized at school mean.

in achievement that our analysis has explained, but to crude indications that performance is good or bad. Moreover, administrative constraint does not respond to other indications of student performance at all. When everything else is held constant, constraint does not increase as tenth grade achievement decreases or as behavior problems increase.

Personnel constraint is somewhat more responsive to students. Constraint becomes stronger as student tenth grade achievement declines and as student behavior problems grow. Evidently teachers do demand and acquire greater job protection when their clientele is more difficult to manage. But constraint does not depend on how well students do academically over their high school years. Schools in which student achievement gains are high are no less likely to be constrained in their personnel decisions than schools in which gains are low. School control does respond somewhat, then, to indicators of school performance. But the response is quite uneven and quite insensitive to gains in student achievement.

The influence that parents have on bureaucratic influence is also less than impressive. Personnel constraint is not independently affected by any parental attribute—parent SES, parent-school contacts, or parent-school relationships—and administrative constraint is affected by only one, parent-school contacts. This is an especially important finding with regard to parent SES. It indicates that schools may be given the freedom to make their own decisions about personnel, curriculum, instruction, and discipline even when their clienteles are not well educated. It might seem that only schools working with economically and educationally advantaged parents would be capable of developing programs and practices that are suitable for students and schools alike. Schools working with disadvantaged parents might seem to require external intervention, either to keep such schools from selling their disadvantaged students short, or to protect teachers and principals from the unreasoned demands of poorly educated parents. This perspective, however, seems to be wrong. Schools can be subject to high or low levels of external control regardless of the SES of the parents.

These rather mixed findings about the importance of parents and students suggest that other factors may have more to do with whether schools are subjected to high or low levels of bureaucratic influence. That is what we find. School sector is associated as predicted with administrative constraint and with personnel constraint. All things being equal—same students, same parents, same location—private schools are subject to significantly less bureaucratic influence than public schools are. School location is also a consistently significant predictor.[20] Urban schools experience significantly more administrative and personnel constraint than schools located elsewhere, even when the kinds of students and parents in these schools are taken into

TABLE 5-12. Predicted Effects of Institutions and Other Conditions on Administrative and Personnel Constraint[a]

Contrasting school conditions	Administrative constraint		Personnel constraint	
	Percentiles	Difference	Percentiles	Difference
Below-average achievement gains/ above-average gains	33.9/17.2	− 16.7	n.s.	. . .
Lowest quartile tenth grade scores/ highest quartile scores	n.s.	. . .	51.6/21.6	− 30.0
Lowest quartile behavior problems/ highest quartile problems	n.s.	. . .	20.4/63.7	43.3
Lowest quartile parent contacts/ highest quartile contacts	42.8/17.2	− 25.6	n.s.	. . .
Urban location/nonurban location	89.3/17.2	− 72.1	90.3/24.0	− 66.3
Public control/private control	68.3/12.1	− 56.2	64.1/12.2	− 51.9

n.s. Variable was statistically nonsignificant in preliminary models and was therefore excluded from final model used to make predictions in this table.

a. Predictions use models in table 5-11 and place all variables, besides the one in question, at their school-level means. Quartile conditions are given by their means.

account separately, and even when the basic form of control—public or private—is held constant too.

But just how important are school sector and school location as compared with the school clientele? To answer that question we turn to a now familiar interpretive device. We calculated the size of the change in the dependent variable that would be predicted from a change in the independent variable, if all of the other independent variables are at their respective means. The changes in the independent variable that we examine are from the median of the bottom quartile to the median of the top quartile for each continuous independent variable. For the dichotomous independent variables—achievement gains, sector, and location—we examine changes from one category to the other. The predicted changes in the dependent variables are then interpreted, in percentiles, by comparing the changes with the distributions of the dependent variables. We use this technique once again because the units of measurement for the independent variables are not comparable.

The predictions, reported in table 5-12, make one thing abundantly clear. Bureaucratic influence—or school autonomy—is determined primarily by sector and location, not by students and parents. This is especially true of administrative constraint, which no parent or student variable is capable of shifting more than one quartile with a shift in its own value from the bottom of its distribution to the top. A change in student achievement gains from below average to above average reduces administrative constraint only 17 percentiles. An analogous change in parent-school contacts reduces administrative constraint one quartile. In sharp contrast, a move from an urban to a nonurban location reduces administrative constraint by nearly three quartiles and a shift from the public to the private sector reduces it by more than two quartiles. Differences are not quite so dramatic for personnel constraint. Vast improvements in student achievement levels or in student behavior are capable of reducing constraints on personnel decisions by a quartile to a quartile and a half. Changes in school sector or school location can reduce constraint by as much as twice these amounts.

We should note, however, that the figures in table 5-12 are somewhat misleading in what they seem to say about the relative effects of sector and location. As the basic regression results reported in table 5-11 clearly suggest, sector actually has a far greater effect on bureaucratic control than school location does. Because the dependent variables in these models are standardized, the unstandardized coefficients on school sector tell us that a shift from public to private control reduces administrative constraint by 1.526 standard deviations and personnel constraint by .838 standard deviation. A shift from urban to nonurban yields changes in bureaucratic constraint of .580 and .501 standard deviation, respectively. The impact of school sector on administrative constraint is thus almost three times that of school location, while its impact on personnel constraint is some 60 percent greater. These are big differences.

Normally, of course, these sorts of differences are picked up in our method of comparing variables according to how many percentiles they are able to shift a school's ranking on the dependent variable. In this case, however, a plot of the actual distribution of schools would show that they are oddly strung out at the low-constraint end of the continuum, and that, for this particular sample of schools, big reductions in constraint can sometimes change a school's ranking by only a few percentiles. Thus, while reference to percentile rankings usually helps us illustrate our statistical results, in this instance it happens to mask the relative impacts of our variables rather than making them easier to appreciate.

In other respects, though, the predictions in table 5-12 still help clarify the role of institutions. As we went into this analysis we said that schools in urban locations may be subject to more bureaucratic influence than schools in other locations for several reasons: urban schools have more difficult students, they have less supportive parents, and they are often embedded in large, heterogeneous school systems. In the analysis, we controlled directly and extensively for the kinds of students and parents in each school. Indeed, we included three controls for students and three controls for parents in each model of bureaucratic influence. In light of the analysis, it appears that the key thing about schools in urban areas may not be that they have especially troublesome students and parents, but that they tend to be embedded in large, heterogeneous school systems. We do not want to exaggerate this conclusion, since schools in urban locations do tend to have rather troublesome clienteles. And by our own estimates, student and parent problems clearly do make a difference for bureaucratic control. But the fact that an urban location influences bureaucratic control when student and parent characteristics are held constant certainly indicates that the key characteristic of urban schools may be their large institutional settings.

There is no ambiguity, moreover, about the more basic influence of institutions. When all else is equal—when schools are serving the same kinds of students and dealing with the same kinds of families, when schools are situated in the same locations, including urban locations where large educational institutions are conducive to bureaucratization—schools in the private sector are likely to experience far less administrative and personnel constraint than schools in the public sector. When all of the conditions that promote bureaucracy are average, private schools rank well into the bottom quartile of bureaucratic influence—or well into the top quartile of bureaucratic autonomy, if we want to view it the other way around. Under average conditions, public schools experience above-average levels of bureaucratic influence—below-average levels of bureaucratic autonomy. Indeed, the only way a public school enjoys the kind of autonomy routinely enjoyed by private schools is if the public school is lucky enough to be located outside an urban area and serving able students and parents.

Through the several steps of our analysis, then, this is what we have found. School organization alone is capable of shifting student achievement gains by more than one full year during four years of high school. By itself, autonomy from bureaucracy is capable of making the difference between effective and ineffective organizations—organizations that would differ by a year in their contributions to student achievement. The institutions of school control, without the assistance of any other influences, are capable of raising bureaucratic autonomy to the level necessary for effective school organization. Market control tends to promote autonomy through its natural operation, while democratic control tends to allow for it only under the most favorable circumstances—outside of urban areas with able and interested students and parents. Under any comparable set of circumstances, autonomy will be far greater under markets.

If, by limiting the bureaucratization of school control, market forces tend to promote more autonomous schools, then our data ought to show that school organization is in fact more effective in private schools than in public schools, when all else is held constant.[21] Because we have already modeled school organization, this is straightforward to determine. In table 5-13 we consider whether private schools are better organized than public schools by reestimating the final model of school organization estimated earlier in this chapter in table 5-7. The only difference in the new version is that it includes a measure of school sector and excludes the measures of bureaucratic influence—administrative and personnel constraint—that according to our theory are the means by which school sector achieves its effects on school organization.[22]

The estimates are striking indeed. With the exception of parent-school contacts, all of the influences on school organization that were statistically significant in the original model remain significant, though slightly weaker in their respective impacts. School sector, though, is clearly the most important influence on school organization. Its standardized influence is at least three times the magnitude of the standardized influence of any of the other variables. Moreover, it alone is capable of shifting school organization from the middle of the distribution of effectiveness to the top.[23] When all else is average—average student achievement and behavior problems, average parent SES and school contacts, average school size—schools subject to market control tend to have highly effective organizations while schools subject to direct democratic control have organizations that are merely average.[24]

The structure of school control is critical, then, not only for the

TABLE 5-13. Estimates of Model of Effective School Organization, Controlling for Sector[a]

Variable	Estimates[b]
School size	.0009*
	(.002)
	.151
Student tenth grade achievement	.416*
	(.086)
	.175
Student behavior problems	− .201*
	(.050)
	− .188
Parent socioeconomic status[c]	.086*
	(.036)
	.084
Parent contacts	.046
	(.034)
	.048
Private sector	1.536*
	(.113)
	.579
Constant	− .567*
	(.062)
Adjusted R^2	.672
Sample size	371

* Statistically significant, $\alpha \le .05$, $t \ge 1.64$, one-tail test.

a. Dependent variable is comprehensive measure of organization without percent of students in academic track. Sample weighted to achieve a nationally representative sample of public and private high schools.

b. Coefficients are unstandardized linear regression coefficients; standard errors are in parentheses. Standardized regression coefficients (betas) are in italics.

c. Residualized variable, controlling for parent-school contacts and relationships, and student achievement.

autonomy of schools but for the development within schools of the requisites for school success. Clear academic goals, strong educational leadership, professionalized teaching, ambitious academic programs, teamlike organizations—these effective school characteristics are promoted much more successfully by market control than by direct democratic control. The kinds of qualities that contemporary school reformers would like public schools to develop, private schools have developed without external reform at all. Bureaucratic autonomy and effective school organization are natural products of the basic institutional forces at work on schools in a marketplace. They are products of school competition and parental choice. Success is built into the institutional structure of private education. As public education is now structured, institutions make success almost unnatural.

Conclusion

We began this chapter with a good, yet incomplete, understanding of effective school organization. We saw in chapter 3 that academically successful schools have distinctive organizational characteristics. And we determined in chapter 4 that academic success is a product of effective school organization. Yet we still had to examine how effective schools come about.

We had strong expectations that effective school organization cannot flourish without substantial school autonomy from direct external control. Like many observers of contemporary American education, we believe that the bureaucratization of educational governance and administration has simply gone too far. Many public school systems seem to have become so bureaucratized that their schools cannot possibly develop clear objectives and high academic expectations or attract and keep the kinds of principals and teachers that are required for effective performance.

We have a different theory than other observers, however, about why all of this has happened. Our reasoning is that much of it is an inevitable and logical consequence of the direct democratic control of schools. Except under special conditions, we believe, the existing institutions of democratic control are simply inconsistent with the autonomous operation and effective organization of schools.

The data that we examined in this chapter are consistent with our expectations. Autonomy has the strongest influence on the overall quality of school organization of any factor that we examined. Bureaucracy is unambiguously bad for school organization. But bureaucracy is not the most fundamental impediment to more effective schools. That distinction belongs to direct democratic control.

Autonomy turns out to be heavily dependent on the institutional structure of school control. In the private sector, where schools are controlled by markets—indirectly and from the bottom up—autonomy is generally high. In the public sector, where schools are controlled by politics—directly and from the top down—autonomy is generally low. Under special circumstances—in nonurban systems with good students and able parents—autonomy can be high in the public sector too. But the fact remains, institutions of democratic control work systematically and powerfully to discourage school autonomy and, in turn, school effectiveness. If public schools are ever to become substantially more effective, the institutions that control them must first be changed.

Chapter Six

Better Schools through New Institutions: Giving Americans Choice

THIS IS A book about the causal foundations of effective schools. In chapter 2, we set out a theoretical perspective linking the organization and performance of schools to their institutional environments. In chapters 3 through 5, we brought evidence to bear from a massive survey of American high schools in assessing key questions of causal importance. Throughout, we tried to fashion a coherent picture of what effective schools look like, what conditions promote or inhibit their development, and how these conditions reflect the institutions in which schools operate.

This is also a book about public policy and educational reform. While we have yet to talk much about these things, the fact is that the causal issues concerning us in past chapters are precisely the same issues that reformers must address and answer if they are to engineer better schools through public policy. Educational reform, if it is done right, is essentially an exercise in harnessing the causes of effective performance. It is an application of theory. Similarly, a theory of effective performance is the analytical basis for designing public policy, as well as for judging which kinds of reforms are likely to succeed and which are likely to fail.

Here in this final chapter, we want to put our theory to use in thinking about reform. A lot of rather complicated ground has been covered in getting us to this point, so we will begin by pulling together the basic components of our analysis and summarizing our perspective on schools. Once we have done so, we will move on to two new tasks.

First, we will take a look at the ambitious and, many say, revolutionary reforms of the 1980s and evaluate their prospects for success. While some of these reforms are more promising than others, we think the recent reform movement as a whole is destined to fail in its mission to bring significant improvement to America's public schools, and we will explain in some detail why we think so.

Second, we want to outline a proposal for reform that, in our view, is likely to succeed—in the event that it is ever adopted. In today's vernacular, it is a "choice" proposal. More descriptively, it is a proposal for a new system of public education, one that is built on school autonomy and parent-student choice rather than direct democratic control and bureaucracy.

Schools and Institutions

Three basic questions lie at the heart of our analysis. What is the relationship between school organization and student achievement? What are the conditions that promote or inhibit desirable forms of organization? And how are these conditions affected by their institutional settings? With regard to the first and second, virtually everything we have to say is compatible with the mainstream ideas of education scholars and policymakers. It is only in paying serious theoretical attention to institutions and in what we conclude about their causal importance for schools that our own ideas depart from the norm. We regard this departure, of course, as fundamental to an understanding of schools. But even so, it is not a departure that contradicts mainstream theory and research. The social science of education simply has little to say about the role of institutions. We depart from the mainstream because we try to address issues that have largely gone unaddressed.

Our perspective on organization and student achievement is in agreement with the most basic claims and findings of the effective schools literature, which, throughout the 1980s, served as the analytical base of the education reform movement. We believe, as most others do, that how much students learn is not simply determined by their aptitude or family background—although, as we show, these are certainly influential—but that school organization has a significant impact all its own. By our own estimates, the typical high school student tends to learn considerably more, comparable to an extra year's worth of study, when he or she attends a high school that is effectively organized rather than one that is not.

Generally speaking, effective schools have the kinds of organizational characteristics that the mainstream literature would lead one to expect: strong leadership, clear and ambitious goals, strong academic programs, teacher professionalism, shared influence, and staff harmony, among other things. These are best understood as integral parts of a coherent syndrome of organization. They go together. When this syndrome is viewed as a functioning whole, moreover, what is most striking about it is that it seems to capture the essential features of what people normally mean by a team—principals and teachers working together, cooperatively and informally, in pursuit of a common mission.

How do these kinds of schools develop and take root? What causes them? Here again, our own perspective dovetails with a central theme of educational analysis and criticism: the dysfunctions of bureaucracy, the value of autonomy, and the inherent tension between the two in American public education. Bureaucracy vitiates the most basic requirements of effective organization. It imposes goals, structures, and requirements that tell principals and teachers what to do and how to do it—denying them the discretion they need to exercise their expertise and professional judgment, and denying them the flexibility they need to develop and operate as teams. The key to effective education rests with unleashing the productive potential that is already present in the schools and their personnel. It rests with granting them the autonomy to do what they do best. As our study of American high schools documents, the freer schools are from external control—the more autonomous, the less subject to bureaucratic constraint—the more likely they are to have effective organizations.

It is only at this late stage of the game that we begin to part company with the mainstream. While most observers can agree that the public schools have become too bureaucratic and would benefit from substantial grants of autonomy, it is also the standard view that this transformation can be achieved within the prevailing framework of democratic control. The implicit assumption is that, although these institutions have acted in the past to bureaucratize, they can now be counted on to reverse course, grant the schools autonomy, and support and nurture this new population of autonomous schools. Such an assumption, however, is not based on a systematic understanding of how these institutions operate and what their consequences are for schools. It begs the important causal issues instead of addressing them.

Our institutional perspective is an attempt to address these issues. What it suggests, among other things, is that America's traditional institutions of democratic control cannot be relied on to solve the schools' bureaucracy problem—for it is not the schools but the institutions that are the real problem. They inherently breed bureaucracy and undermine autonomy. This is not something that is temporary or the product of mistakes. It is deeply anchored in the most fundamental properties of the system.

Democratic governance of the schools is built around the imposition of higher-order values through public authority. As long as that authority exists and is available for use, public officials will come under intense pressure from social groups of all political stripes to use it. And when they do use it, they cannot blithely assume that their favored policies will be faithfully implemented by the heterogeneous population of principals and teachers below—whose own values and professional views may be quite different from those being imposed. They have little choice but to rely on formal rules and regulations that tell these people what to do and hold them accountable for doing it.

These pressures for bureaucracy are so substantial in themselves that real school autonomy can have little chance to take root throughout the system. But they are not the only pressures for bureaucracy. They are compounded by the political uncertainty that is inherent in all democratic politics: those who exercise public authority know that other actors with different interests may gain authority in the future and subvert the policies they worked so hard to put in place. This gives them additional incentives to embed their policies in protective bureaucratic arrangements—arrangements that reduce the discretion of schools and formally insulate them from the dangers of politics.

These pressures, arising from the most fundamental properties of democratic control, are compounded yet again by another special feature of the public sector. Its institutions provide a regulated, politically sensitive setting that is conducive to the power of unions, and unions protect the interests of their members through formal constraints on the governance and operation of schools—constraints that strike directly at the schools' capacity to build well-functioning teams based on informal cooperation.

All the major participants in democratic governance—including the unions—complain that the schools are too bureaucratic. And they mean what they say. But they are the ones who bureaucratized the schools in the past, and they will continue to bureaucratize the schools in the future, even as they tout the great advantages of autonomy and professionalism. The incentives to bureaucratize are built into the system. The institutions of democratic control ensure that, in the politics and governance of public education, bureaucracy is almost everyone's dominant strategy when the key decisions actually get made. People may genuinely believe in autonomy and professionalism. But what they do—quite rationally, given their institutional setting— is bureaucratize.

This kind of behavior is not something that Americans simply have to accept, like death and taxes. People who make decisions about education would behave differently if their institutions were different. The most relevant and telling comparison is to markets, since it is through democratic control and markets that American society makes most of its choices on matters of public importance, including education. Public schools are subject to direct control through politics, private schools are subject to indirect control through markets. What difference does it make?

Our analysis suggests that the difference is considerable, and that it arises from the most fundamental properties that distinguish the two systems. A market system is not built to enable the imposition of higher-order values on the schools, nor is it driven by a democratic struggle to exercise public authority. Instead, the authority to make educational choices is radically decentralized to those most immediately involved. Schools compete for the support of parents and students, and parents and students are free to choose among schools. The system is built around decentralization, competition, and choice.

Although schools are free to organize any way they want, bureaucratization tends to be an unattractive way to go. Part of the reason is that virtually everything about good education—from the knowledge and talents necessary to produce it to what it looks like when it is produced—defies formal measurement through the standardized categories of bureaucracy. The more fundamental point, however, is that bureaucratic control and its clumsy efforts to measure the unmeasurable are simply *unnecessary* for schools whose primary concern is to please their clients. To do this, they need to perform as effectively as possible—which induces them, given the bottom-heavy technology of education, to favor decentralized forms of organization that take full advantage of professionalism, discretionary judgment, informal cooperation, and teams. They also need to ensure that they are providing the kinds of services parents and students want, and that they have the capacity to cater and adjust to their clients' specialized needs and interests—which this same syndrome of organization allows them to do exceedingly well.

While schools controlled only by the market are free to organize any way they want, then, an environment of competition and choice gives them strong incentives to move toward the kinds of "effective-school" organizations that academics and reformers would like to impose on the public schools. Of course, not all schools in the market will respond equally well to these incentives. But those that falter will find it more difficult to attract support, and they will tend to be weeded out in favor of schools that are better organized. This process of natural selection, based on ease of entry and performance-based attrition, complements the incentives of the marketplace in propelling and supporting a population of autonomous, effectively organized schools.

No institutional system can be expected to work perfectly under real-world conditions. Just as democratic institutions cannot offer perfect representation or perfect implementation of public policy, so markets cannot offer perfect competition or perfect choice. But these imperfections, which are invariably the favorite targets of each system's critics, tend to distract attention from what is most crucial to an understanding of schools: as institutional systems, democratic control and market control are strikingly different in their most fundamental properties. As a result, they structure individual and social choices about education very differently, and they have very different consequences for the organization and performance of schools. Each system puts its own, indelible stamp on the schools that emerge and operate within it.

What this institutional perspective suggests, in the most practical terms, is that American society offers two basic paths to the emergence of effective schools. The first is through markets, which scarcely operate in the public sector, but which act on private schools to discourage bureaucracy and promote desirable forms of organization through the natural dynamics of competition and choice. The second is through "special circumstances"—homogeneous, problem-free environments—which, in minimizing the three types of pressures just discussed, prompt democratic governing institutions to impose less bureaucracy than they otherwise would. Private schools therefore tend to be effectively organized because of the way their system naturally works. When public schools happen to be effectively organized, it is in spite of their system—they are the lucky ones with peculiarly nice environments.

As we showed in chapter 5, the power of these institutional forces is graphically reflected in our sample of American high schools. Having cast our net widely to allow for a full range of noninstitutional factors that might reasonably be suspected of playing causal roles, we found that virtually all of them fall by the wayside. The extent to which schools are granted the autonomy they need to develop more effective organizations is overwhelmingly determined by their sector and the niceness of their institutional environments.

Viewed as a whole, then, our effort to take institutions into account builds systematically on mainstream ideas and findings—but, in the end, puts a very different slant on things. We agree that effective organization is a major determinant of student achievement. We also agree that schools perform better the more autonomous they are and the less encumbered they are by bureaucracy. But we do not agree that this knowledge about the proximate causes of effective performance can be used to engineer better schools through democratic control. Reformers are right about where they want to go, but their institutions cannot get them there.

The way to get schools with effective organizations is not to insist that democratic institutions should do what they are incapable of doing. Nor is it to assume that the better public schools, the lucky ones with nice environments, can serve as organizational models for the rest. Their luck is not transferable. The way to get effective schools, rather, is to recognize that the problem of ineffective performance is really a deep-seated institutional problem that arises from the most fundamental properties of democratic control.

The most sensible approach to genuine educational reform is therefore to move toward a true institutional solution—a different set of institutional arrangements that is compatible with, and indeed actively promotes and nurtures, the kinds of schools people want. The market alternative then becomes particularly attractive, for it provides a setting in which these organizations can flourish and take root.

Educational Reform during the 1980s

As they try to gain perspective on the turbulent developments of the 1980s, educators find themselves distinguishing between two "waves" of educational reform. The first wave began several years before the spate of commission reports in 1983, picked up considerable momentum at that point, and continued for several years thereafter. During this time, the states carried out hundreds of studies, shifted through and debated countless proposals for reform, and enacted a good many of them. These reforms launched direct attacks on what appeared to be the most obvious and tractable problems—money, academic standards, teacher pay and quality—and they did so in the most traditional way: by imposing new regulations on schools and local districts and providing them additional financial resources.[1]

The fact that so much study and legislation was accomplished in so short a time was itself an astonishing political development. Remarkably, however, the pressures for change did not die down. Popular support for educational reform remained high, and, with most of the traditional ground already covered, reformist energies were increasingly directed to far more difficult problems that much of the academic mainstream saw as more fundamental: the need to reduce bureaucracy, the need to grant schools more autonomy.

Whatever its benefits, the first wave of reforms not only skirted these problems, it made them a bit worse by opting for regulatory solutions that added to bureaucracy and centralized control. The second wave has generally left these earlier reforms intact and sought to add new, more innovative reforms that would reduce unnecessary bureaucracy and decentralize important decisionmaking powers to the local level.[2] Because these reforms are just beginning to catch on around the country—and because they tend to be both expensive and potentially threatening to some of the established interests—it is still unclear how far they will go or exactly what forms they will take when and if they are fully developed. At this point, the restructuring movement has largely been a movement of ideas and proposals. Of these, the most popular have to do with school-based management, teacher professionalism, and "choice."[3]

In our view, the second wave is clearly more promising than the first, but the sum total of these efforts cannot bring about the kind of transformation in America's public schools that reformers want. In this section, we will take a closer look at some of the basic reforms that both waves have introduced and suggest why we think this is so.

Traditional Reforms: More Money

One thing mainstream educational reformers can always agree on is that more money—lots more money—needs to be spent. In part, this is just an unavoidable part of politics. Teachers, administrators, school boards, and everyone else in the educational establishment are better off when educational budgets go up, and they take reformist swings in public opinion as golden opportunities to lobby hard for more money. But the intellectual grounds for more money also appeal to common sense. Many of the policy changes reformers have sought—better pay for teachers, longer school days and years—cost additional money to provide. And even if no policy changes were introduced, more money would still mean more teachers, more equipment, smaller class sizes, and all sorts of other good things for schools.

During the 1980s, governments responded to these pressures with handsome increases in funding.[4] The problem is that, common sense notwithstanding, there is no evidence that increases of even this magnitude stand to have important effects on school performance. In fact, the relationship between resources and performance has been studied to death by social scientists, and their consistent conclusion has been that resources do not matter much, except perhaps in cases of extreme deprivation or gross abundance.[5]

Our own analysis of American high schools affirms this well-established finding. While it is true that high performance schools have more resources to employ than low performance schools do, some 20 percent more on the average, the apparent causal connection turns out to be spurious when controls are introduced for factors like social class and student aptitude. Money is not what makes some schools more effective than others. To this we should add that private schools—which outperform public schools, on the average—also tend to spend less than the public schools do in educating their students. They get better schools for less money.[6]

If money does not make much difference, then it must mean that many of the things money can buy do not have the kinds of beneficial consequences that educators and reformers think they do. Better schools probably do not require lots of expensive equipment or huge new buildings or vast libraries. Nor do they require paying teachers substantially more or hiring an army of them to teach a diverse array of courses. In our view, the performance problems of the public schools have little or nothing to do with inadequate funding, and they cannot be corrected by digging deeper into the public purse.

Traditional Reforms: More Controls

Money aside, the first wave was an effort to "make" schools better through new controls. The schools had not performed well in the past, and it was now up to policymakers to impose the kinds of changes that seemed to be needed for academic excellence. The rules and regulations eventually adopted varied from state to state, and they targeted virtually every aspect of the schools—curriculum, discipline, personnel, textbooks, instructional methods, and more.

Several basic reforms stand out, however, as uniformly popular and representative of what was going on: the states sought to ensure a more rigorous academic curriculum through stricter graduation requirements, they sought to ensure that this curriculum was more effectively taught by raising teacher quality, and they sought to hold schools accountable for effective teaching by requiring new formal tests of student performance. Better courses, better teachers, better accountability.

Because their objectives are admirable, these sorts of reforms seem to make good sense. Just like spending more money does. But there is little reason to think they will have any significant impact on how much students learn—and they may make things worse rather than better.

The imposition of stricter graduation requirements is, in our view, the least troubling.[7] Academic excellence does call for a rigorous curriculum in which students actively participate. But laws of this sort can only do so much. They can mandate that courses with certain titles and subject matters be taught and that students spend time physically sitting in the classroom. But they cannot mandate a high-quality learning experience. Teachers and students can go through the motions, each following state-imposed rules to the letter, without students gaining much of anything in the process. This, of course, is where the other bureaucratic controls come in: by controlling teacher quality and by demanding evidence of student learning, reformers try to guarantee that course requirements are not meaningless. Thus stricter academic requirements would essentially figure as benign impositions—not very promising, but unlikely to be very harmful— were they not just the tip of the iceberg.[8]

To engineer more effective teaching, reformers have tried a number of things. One is to pay teachers bigger salaries as a means of attracting better people into the field over the long haul. This is the least bureaucratic approach, and it will doubtless do at least some good. But it is also fiscally painful for state and local governments, extremely costly to taxpayers—and, as we pointed out, there is no evidence that it will do enough good to justify the costs. We are not talking here about how much teachers "should" get paid—a normative question that has no objective answer—but only about the connection between teacher pay and effective schools. Within the salary ranges that are feasible, how much teachers get paid simply does not appear to be a key part of the problem.[9]

Because taxes are unpopular, offering attractive salaries is not the normal governmental approach to teacher quality (or anything else). The normal approach is to regulate. Traditionally, this has been done through teacher certification: educational and testing requirements that candidates must satisfy before they are deemed sufficiently well qualified to teach in the public schools. When the quality of teaching became a matter of public debate and concern in the early 1980s, the reflexive response was to strengthen these requirements—by calling for more units of postgraduate training, for specific kinds of course work, for demonstrations of knowledge in fields of emphasis, for more serious and broadly administered tests of competency.[10]

In general, this is a bureaucratic approach that has little to recommend it. People who surmount the nearly countless hurdles that certification places in their paths will probably emerge better equipped to teach than they were when they started. But there is no guarantee that even a reasonable percentage of these survivors will make good teachers—for the true essentials of the job cannot be formally measured through course-taking and test-passing. Whether duly certified teachers turn out to be good or bad is ultimately revealed in the classroom through the informal, experience-based judgments of principals, other teachers, students, and parents. By this time, however, in a bureaucratic world that grants the schools almost no discretion in hiring and firing, it is usually too late.

Certification raises problems not just because it fails to screen out the mediocre and the bad. It also raises problems because it sets up formidable barriers to entry that keep many excellent prospects out of the job pool. People who are well educated, bright, enthusiastic, creative, and good with children cannot simply pursue a latent interest in teaching by giving it a try. Nor can talented people already working in other lines of endeavor shift into teaching, or perhaps move in and out of it, as they might other jobs. Instead, potential teachers are asked by the state to foreclose other options, make a substantial investment of time and resources, and jump through formal hoops. American society is full of people who could make excellent teachers, but burdensome certification requirements are the best way to ensure that most of them never teach.

In some states, teacher "shortages"—which these barriers to entry, of course, help cause—have prompted public officials to relax certification rules a bit, allowing for the hiring of uncertified people on temporary or emergency bases, for programs that enable on-the-job training, and for out-of-field placement.[11] These are promising developments, but they are little more than a chink in the bureaucratic armor. The conventional democratic response to the effectiveness problem has been to "strengthen" certification requirements—adding to the bureaucratization of teaching and exacerbating a host of already serious problems that threaten in the aggregate to stifle teacher quality instead of raising it.

While certification and its focus on job qualifications have been the most popular approach to the regulation of teacher effectiveness, some states have also sought more innovative changes designed to give teachers stronger on-the-job incentives for effective performance. One is merit pay, which is supposed to provide special rewards to high-performing teachers. Another involves the creation of "career ladders" within schools, which essentially introduce new hierarchies of responsibility and pay among teachers—allowing, for instance, for "mentor" or "master" teachers who, having achieved their positions based on experience and performance, would lead and supervise other teachers and receive additional compensation.[12]

Attempts to base rewards on performance are steps in the right direction. And, as public officials are well aware, they certainly strike a responsive chord among taxpayers. But the problem is that these sorts of reforms cannot work well in a system of direct democratic control. The only way to measure performance adequately is to rely on the discretion of those who work in the school—which is precisely what the unions and democratic authorities are strongly inclined not to do, and what the whole system is built to prevent. The result is that merit systems tend to get bureaucratized. Pay and promotion are supposed to be performance based, but, in design and practice, every effort is made to reduce the discretionary component of these evaluations as far as possible and base them on objective measures. With discretion squeezed out, teachers are left with more hierarchy, more rules, and precious few incentives to do a better job than they were doing in the past.[13]

Finally, there is the matter of accountability. Schools can guarantee that students take what appears to be a more rigorous curriculum. They can hire teachers who have met strengthened certification requirements. They can adopt innovative new programs for enhancing teacher incentives. But all of these may look much more impressive on paper than they do in practice. The bottom line is, how much are students learning?

Schools have always been held accountable, by means of rules and reporting requirements, for their implementation of policies, their expenditure of money, their handling of personnel, and most everything else their democratic superiors cared about (and were themselves accountable to their constituents for). Now, in a reformist atmosphere centered on academic excellence, public officials increasingly demanded concrete evidence of results.

These demands translated into requirements for new, expanded, or more rigorous formal tests of student competency and achievement. Through competency tests, officials sought to ensure that schools could not pass along students who had failed to meet certain minimum standards—which many schools were clearly guilty of in the past. Schools would now be held accountable for really teaching these students something. Achievement tests served the more general purpose of indicating how well or poorly the schools were doing.[14]

We believe, as almost all educators do, that testing is a necessary and important part of the educational process. The social science of testing is quite advanced, and, for most students most of the time, test results can provide reliable information about learning. Competency tests, moreover, while measuring only the most basic types of knowledge and skills, can be extremely useful in allowing schools to identify students with serious learning deficiencies and to provide them with remedial help and special training.

Nonetheless, statewide testing of students can also be a misleading and counterproductive means of evaluating the performance of schools.[15] There are three basic problems at work here. The first is that statewide tests are uniform, one-shot measures of learning. As such, they cannot help but leave some types of knowledge and reasoning untapped, and what they do tap they will measure imperfectly. Their results will nonetheless become the official yardstick by which school performance is assessed. The second is that schools and teachers, wanting positive evaluations, will adapt their practices to conform to these imperfect yardsticks. They will "teach to the tests," regardless of what they think good education consists of and requires. The third is that student test scores are due in part to schools, but also to student aptitude, social class, and other causes. Figuring out what test scores properly have to say about school performance is a complicated methodological undertaking: one that may excite researchers in departments of education, but that seldom finds its way into the politics of educational decisionmaking. The reality is that people look at a school's average test scores and jump to conclusions—unwarranted conclusions—about school performance, with far-reaching consequences for their assessments of problems and solutions.

In the end, testing requirements are a lot like certification requirements and many other traditional reforms. They seem to make good sense, and they do indeed offer certain benefits. But they are clearly deficient as solutions to the problems they are addressing, and they stand little chance of improving schools in any significant way. Worse, they create still more bureaucracy, and they unleash new bureaucratic pathologies that divert people and resources from the pursuit of quality education. The danger is not just that these reforms will fail to accomplish their lofty goals, but that they will actually hurt the schools more than help them over the long run.

Innovative Reforms: School-Based Management

As the 1980s wore on, reformers increasingly called for bolder, more innovative actions that could strike at the heart of the schools' problems. The early period of reform, they believed, was an exciting new beginning for the public schools—but it was only a beginning. The schools had to be granted more autonomy. Teachers had to be professionalized and empowered. Bureaucracy had to be reduced. These ends could not be accomplished by continuing along the traditional path of stricter regulatory controls. Nor, in fact, would reform succeed if it left the basic structure of the public system intact—for the fundamental problems were structural in origin, having to do with who controls whom and who makes what decisions. To liberate schools and teachers from their bureaucratic straightjackets, reformers had to "restructure" the system.

While the notion of restructuring has gained widespread popularity since the mid-1980s, there has been little agreement about what it really means or how it should be carried out. Educational theory and research clearly suggest that bureaucracy is bad and that autonomy and professionalism are good, but they do not have much to say about how these things are caused by institutional structure, nor, therefore, about what structural changes are needed to bring about the desired ends. With no clear analytical foundation to guide them—and unwilling to fall back on traditional controls—reformers have been open to a variety of innovative ideas.[16]

One of the most influential is school-based management. First proposed during the 1970s in reaction to rapid growth in state funding and control, it offers a comprehensive plan for decentralizing important educational choices to the school level. While only one state—Hawaii—has adopted a full-blown system of school-based management, a number of school districts have done so (often in conjunction with other decentralizing reforms). Perhaps the most prominent applications have come in Chicago, Dade County (Florida), and Rochester (New York), where the public schools were in genuine crisis, plagued by problems so severe and deep-seated that the traditional system could offer no real hope for improvement.[17] Something dramatically innovative, like school-based management, did; and reformers embraced it with the enthusiasm of a drowning man for a life preserver.

In its structural details, this approach to reform means different things to different people and has been outlined and applied in various ways. Broadly speaking, though, a plan for school-based management might look as follows. States and districts would continue to make general policies, with schools delegated substantial authority and budgetary flexibility in making the operational decisions about how these general policies are to be carried out—decisions that may range from how much money to spend on athletic equipment to "policy" decisions about school discipline or academic programs. The principal, as the school's chief executive, would make these decisions with the advice and active participation of formally constituted councils of "stakeholders": teachers and parents, at a minimum, and possibly students and relevant members of the community. (Sometimes these councils are not just advisory, but have decisionmaking authority.) Through oversight, mechanisms for approval and veto, rules for budgeting and accounting, and annual performance reports—in which the school provides a compendium of data on its activities, staff, student test scores, parent and staff satisfaction, and future plans— authorities at the district and state level hold school decisionmakers accountable for the school's choices and performance.[18]

In our view, decentralization is preferable to central control, and systems that move toward school-based management are likely to create conditions better suited to effective education than those that existed originally. But the institutional change it introduces is not nearly as dramatic or fundamental as its enthusiasts tend to claim, and the consequences for student achievement are likely to prove far less impressive than they hope.

School-based management leaves the traditional institutions of democratic control intact. The schools remain subordinates in a democratic hierarchy. Their superiors have decentralized by delegating some of their own authority, but it is the superiors who are held accountable by the public at large for what happens in the schools. If the schools perform poorly, if they spend public money unproductively or unwisely, if they make politically controversial choices—and, in general, if they use their "autonomy" to do things that generate political opposition—the schools' superiors will come under intense pressure to use their higher-level authority to take charge and turn matters around. They will even be blamed for failing to prevent these problems from arising in the first place.

Acutely aware of all this from the outset, the authorities are motivated to control and monitor how the schools exercise their autonomy—they need to know what is going on, they need to be able to derail bad decisions before they happen, they need to be able to intervene and make corrections, they need to be able to ensure that schools will use their autonomy wisely in making good decisions, they need to make plans for the system as a whole. They do these things not by telling the schools what their decisions will be, but by imposing a host of new rules, regulations, and requirements. Parts of the old bureaucracy are jettisoned, only to be replaced by new ones.

School-based management, then, is another way of controlling the schools within an essentially bureaucratic system. Its very name, in fact, is wonderfully appropriate, for what it suggests is that principals, teachers, and others at the lower reaches are fundamentally engaged in the "management" of schools—a bureaucratic conception, if there ever was one, of what effective education is all about.

The decentralization it achieves within the bureaucratic system, moreover, is sometimes deceptive; and it threatens to be inherently unstable. It is sometimes deceptive because, except in rather unusual circumstances (crises, for instance), higher-level authorities are jealous of their powers, reluctant to give them up under reformist pressure, and thus inclined to make delegations that are more apparent than real. Some applications of school-based management, as a result, place most of their emphasis on shared influence *within* the schools rather than on delegations of important powers from states and districts *to* the schools.[19]

When important delegations to schools are made, on the other hand, they are vulnerable to instability. For as soon as problems arise—as soon as the schools make bad decisions or are perceived to be performing poorly or are faced with difficult situations that seem beyond their control—the authorities will find themselves under pressure to reassert their powers. Unless all goes well, then, there is a built-in tendency for decentralized systems to gravitate toward greater centralization. As long as higher-level authority exists, it will eventually get used.[20]

Innovative Reforms: Teacher Professionalism and Empowerment

The reforms of the early 1980s sought to increase the quality of teaching through higher pay, stricter controls, and new incentives, but they did not seriously attempt to change the subordinate status of teachers in the public system. Teachers remained lowly bureaucrats. As time went on and support gathered for innovative reforms generally, it was inevitable that the role of teachers would become a central issue. The common understanding that less bureaucracy, more autonomy, and more professionalism are good for schools, and that restructuring is necessary to achieve them, was but another way of saying the traditional status of teachers had to go.

A major thrust of this movement has been to empower teachers by granting them greater individual control over their own jobs, as well as greater collective say in shaping the policies and practices of their schools.[21] In the abstract, this emphasis on empowerment is entirely consistent with effective schools research and richly deserving of support. The specific forms it takes in political practice, however, are another matter. While helpful in some ways, they empower teachers by creating all sorts of new problems and failing to solve most of the old ones.

To proponents of teacher empowerment, the job at hand is to reallocate power within the current system of democratic control: from states to districts, from districts to schools, from administrators (including principals) to teachers.[22] They seek to carry this out by shifting the locus of decisionmaking downward and by introducing an onerous array of new formal mechanisms—committees, councils, career ladders, rules, processes—that, by force of law, guarantee teachers specific types of educational roles and governing responsibilities. For obvious reasons, these proposals to empower teachers are often pursued within more comprehensive plans for school-based management, although the different goals and scopes of the two movements sometimes produce conflict (regarding, for example, the discretionary powers of principals).

In important respects, reforms to empower teachers are rightly seen as progressive. They do indeed grant teachers more autonomy in the performance of their jobs, greater say in the running of their own schools, and more influence in educational policymaking and administration. All of this, especially given the stifling effects of hierarchical control, is doubtless for the good, other things being equal. Moreover, the path to teacher empowerment has not always entailed additional bureaucracy. Aggressive expansion of career ladder schemes within schools, for instance, has sometimes included important dimensions of flexibility and discretionary judgment—as in apprenticeship programs (where teachers train teachers on the job) and peer review (where teachers evaluate the quality of one another's teaching).

For the most part, however, the movement to empower teachers has been a characteristic exercise in democratic control. Proponents have tried to "make" teachers more powerful by relying on new bureaucratic arrangements that specify precisely who gets to do what and how they have to go about doing it. This whole approach to empowerment is a gross distortion of the kind of shared influence that prevails within effective schools, where teachers are powerful not because rules and regulations dictate that they must be, but because they naturally come to be influential participants in decisionmaking when schools are founded on teams, informal cooperation, collegiality, and mutual respect. The qualities of effective organization that naturally bring power to teachers cannot be imposed by bureaucratic fiat. They have to develop on their own, freely and informally. Trying to make teachers powerful through bureaucracy is the best way to guarantee that they can never achieve the kind of professionalism they really want, and that good schools require.

A second major thrust of the teacher reform movement has been to create a credentialing superstructure that would help transform teaching as a whole into what proponents consider a bona fide profession. In the early 1980s reformers saw their efforts to strengthen certification requirements as an important step in this direction. Like doctors and lawyers, teachers would have to go through a strict, uniform regimen of education and training at accredited institutions before they could be certified to practice. But these steps did not seem to go far enough, for doctors and lawyers were true professionals in a way that teachers were not: they designed and controlled their own certification procedures—they regulated themselves—while teachers were regulated by public officials and agencies. As the reform movement in general turned increasingly to ideas for restructuring the system, demands for stricter certification requirements blossomed into demands for self-regulation.

Two proposals have attracted most of the attention. The first, championed by the National Education Association, is for the creation of teacher-controlled licensing boards within each of the states that would set legally binding standards and requirements for admission to the profession. In effect, government would delegate public authority to teachers, who would then use that authority to regulate themselves and control entry.[23] The second, popularized by the Carnegie Forum on Education and the Economy, calls for a teacher-controlled national board that would certify individuals as having attained a high level of professional knowledge and mastery of teaching.[24] National certification would be voluntary and not required for entry into the profession; but, as a concrete indicator of achievement, it would presumably be used—by states, districts, schools, and unions—to qualify teachers for higher pay and more responsibility. A well-known proposal along these lines comes from Albert Shanker, head of the American Federation of Teachers, who argues for a career-ladder arrangement in which nationally certified "lead" teachers play major supervisory and policymaking roles within each school.[25]

The proposal for state licensing boards is a bad idea. In the name of professionalization, it essentially retains the top-heavy bureaucratic arrangements already in place—arrangements that cannot do a good job of measuring and promoting good teaching, and whose numerous, time-consuming formal hurdles discourage entry into the field and vitiate what ought to be a dynamic, exciting market for teachers. The only real difference is that teachers, rather than public officials and agencies, would be able to exercise this authority. But this does not solve anything. Regulation would still be just as bureaucratic and just as inappropriate and counterproductive as before. Worse, as political scientists have complained for decades, these self-regulating boards—whether for doctors and lawyers or for cosmetologists, plumbers, and dog groomers—tend to use public authority in their own self-interest to restrict entry and enhance their incomes.[26] And worse still, it would not really be "teachers" who would control the boards, but almost surely organized teachers—and far-and-away the largest, most geographically dispersed organization of teachers is the National Education Association. No wonder, then, that the NEA is the chief advocate of this regulatory proposal, and that the much smaller, less dispersed American Federation of Teachers, its main competitor, has not endorsed it.[27]

The proposal for a national standards board has more to recommend it. Its great advantage is that it is voluntary, providing information about teacher quality without putting public authority behind a new bureaucracy to control entry. But there are several very serious drawbacks here. First, no certification scheme, especially not a national one, can possibly provide much valid information on the quality of an individual's teaching; assessments will inevitably rely too heavily on standard formal measures and too little on school-level discretionary judgment. Second, voluntary national credentialing would doubtless become cloaked in public authority anyway, as states, districts, and collective bargaining agreements make board certification a requirement for increased pay and educational responsibilities. It would be voluntary only in the sense that it would not constitute a legal barrier to entry. It would, on the other hand, become a legal barrier to career advancement. Third, credentialing by a national board would, in the end, create yet another bureaucracy that teachers and schools would have to contend with in doing their jobs. Making it private or voluntary or teacher controlled does not change its essentially bureaucratic approach to the problem of teacher quality and professionalism. And fourth, this board would be strongly influenced and perhaps dominated by the National Education Association and the American Federation of Teachers, adding to their already stifling hold on educational personnel.

All of these reforms to empower and professionalize teaching are institutionally crippled from the outset; they are destined to disappoint. The kind of power that teachers have in effective schools cannot be imposed by formal rule. Nor can the kind of professionalism they exercise in effective schools be imposed by licensing and standards boards. Democratic control cannot "make" teachers into the efficacious professionals they want to be—for democratic control is the real problem. It is what caused their bureaucratic subordination in the first place, and the only kind of restructuring it can offer is a different set of bureaucratic arrangements in which teachers play new formal roles and have more formal powers. This is an artificial version of the real thing. And it leaves the most fundamental problem untouched.

Innovative Reforms: Choice

The most innovative and promising reforms to have gained momentum during the late eighties fall under the heading of "choice." In the past, educators tended to associate this concept with the privatization of public education, aid to religious schools, and racial segregation, portraying it as a subversive notion that threatened the common school ideal and virtually everything else the public system had traditionally stood for. In recent years, however, choice has come to be viewed very differently, even by many in the educational establishment.

This new movement puts choice to use as part of a larger set of strategies for reform *within* the public sector. It is not about privatizing the public schools, nor is it a surreptitious way of giving aid to religious schools. Choice is being embraced by liberals and conservatives alike as a powerful means of transforming the structure and performance of public education—while keeping the public schools public. In the process, it is being used to combat racial segregation; indeed, it has become the preferred approach to desegregation in districts throughout the country—in Rochester and Buffalo (New York), Cambridge (Massachusetts), and Prince George's County (Maryland), to name a few.[28]

Support for public sector choice is widespread. Surveys reveal that the vast majority of public school parents want to choose the schools their children attend—and that, when choice plans are implemented and people have a chance to exercise their newfound freedom, popular support for choice grows.[29] Not surprisingly, many public officials are also singing the praises of choice, with support running particularly strong among political executives. Their broad, heterogeneous constituencies, their uniquely central role in policymaking, and the public's inclination to hold them singularly responsible for effective government all make them more willing (than legislators) to take bold, unconventional actions that provoke opposition from the established interests.

At the federal level, Presidents Ronald Reagan and George Bush have been enthusiastic supporters of educational choice, although there is not a great deal the federal government can do on its own. More consequentially, given the primary role of the states in public education, the National Governors' Association has come out strongly for choice in its recent report on education, *Time for Results*[30]—and reformist governors, Democrats and Republicans alike, have typically been in the forefront in pressing for real change.

They have many allies. Maverick legislators have played leading roles in public debate and coalition building. Respected groups of academics and reformers, less satisfied than before with the intellectual mainstream, are increasingly arguing the advantages of choice.[31] So are business groups, which have been disappointed in past reforms and are increasingly calling for more innovative approaches that take greater advantage of market-based incentives.[32] And many groups speaking for minorities and the poor have become supporters as well, embracing choice as a crucial means of escaping from the intolerably bad urban schools that the traditional system of fixed boundaries and assignments forces on them.[33] Despite the opposition that unions have offered to choice proposals generally, some aspects of choice have been endorsed, at least provisionally, by a few key union leaders, including Albert Shanker, president of the American Federation of Teachers, and Adam Urbanski, president of the Rochester Teachers Association.[34]

Yet all this enthusiasm has not translated into truly successful reform, and it may never do so, at least if current efforts are projected into the future. There are three basic problems at work. The first is that choice means many different things to its supporters. They all claim to favor choice, but when it comes to the specifics of actual choice plans, their superficial consensus breaks down. To the extent the movement for choice can be called a movement at all, it is an extremely fragmented and conceptually shallow one. It lacks mission.

The second is that virtually all choice plans are entirely demand focused: they offer parents and students a measure of choice among schools. Period. Rarely do these plans take any steps to free up the supply side by decontrolling—or, at least, encouraging and promoting through official actions—the emergence of new and different types of schools, so that people really have an attractive and dynamically responsive set of alternatives from which to choose. Instead, choice is usually restricted to a fixed set of existing schools, which reformers hope to improve through the "competition" that choice will presumably stimulate. All these schools, however, have their existence and financial support guaranteed; actions are inevitably taken to ensure that no schools are "underenrolled" (a bureaucratic euphemism for what happens when schools are so bad no one wants to attend them); schools that do the worst are implicitly rewarded, because they tend to be the first in line for bigger budgets and more staff; and all the usual formal rules and democratic controls continue to apply in constraining what the schools are able (and want) to do in changing their behavior. Under these conditions, giving parents and students choice among schools cannot in itself be expected to produce vigorous, healthy competition among schools. The supply side has to be freed up if that is to happen.

Third, any choice plan that upsets the traditional structure of public education generates intense opposition from established groups. As a result, most of the choice plans that get put into effect (or, for that matter, even gain serious attention) are grafted onto the traditional system and make only marginal changes in it. Choice becomes part of a big compromise among contending political powers—no one loses jobs, no bad schools are closed down, vested interests remain securely vested, the basic structure of the system stays the same. In a nutshell, this is why reforms always focus on giving parents and students choice, but never free up the supply and governance of schools. Parent-student choice is popular, and it can be accomplished with minimal disruption to traditional structures, while real change on the supply side is fundamentally threatening to established interests and hence never gains political acceptance. The reality, therefore, is that choice plans fail to take advantage of what choice really has to offer—and they leave intact the crippling institutional causes of the schools' past problems.

What passes for choice takes diverse forms. Most often, districts offer choice through one or more alternative schools, usually with special programs targeted at special clienteles—dropouts, the gifted, students needing remedial education, parents seeking open learning environments for their children. Students can choose to attend (or may be shunted into) an alternative school instead of their regular schools of assignment. Almost always, however, there are too few alternative schools to accommodate more than a small percentage of a district's students; and, if the schools are any good, there tend to be far more applicants than the schools can accept. The vast majority of students in these "choice" systems continue to attend schools of assignment, and all the usual institutions of democratic governance remain in place, doing their usual jobs.[35]

In many districts, choice plans are built around "magnet" schools.

This is particularly true of districts that have been under pressure, whether internally or from the courts or the state, to take aggressive action in achieving racial balance. Magnet schools are alternative schools that are set up with special programs and often granted additional funds and equipment in order to attract students from throughout the district. They tend to be located in minority areas, thus offering minority kids an attractive alternative to their neighborhood school (or to taking buses to the suburbs), and offering incentives to white or suburban children for choosing a racially mixed school in the city. As part—often the core—of a desegregation plan, magnet schools are a means of achieving racial balance through voluntary choice. And evidence suggests that in many districts they have worked well in that regard.[36]

They have worked less well in promoting districtwide improvement in school effectiveness. Like alternative schools generally, magnets typically offer choices to just a small portion of the district's students, and they leave the traditional system as a whole intact. Moreover, they can have a negative impact on the rest of the schools. Their additional funding and equipment may (depending on their source) result in a smaller pie for the remaining schools to divide up. Magnets tend to attract the best, most innovative teachers away from regular schools of assignment, which then threaten to become dumping grounds for the district's mediocre teachers (especially if magnets are allowed to rid themselves of staff they do not want). Magnets also tend to attract the best, most interested students and parents, making the job of the regular schools still more difficult.[37]

These choice plans are disappointing because they are too limited in scope to achieve significant reform. We should emphasize, however, that there is strong and mounting evidence that the introduction of choice through alternative and magnet schools does indeed have positive consequences for those who are lucky enough to be direct participants. Broadly speaking, schools of choice tend to be more informal, professional, and unified around a common mission than regular schools of assignment are. Their teachers are more autonomous, more excited about their work, more influential in decision-making, and happier with their overall situations. Students are more satisfied with their chosen schools; dropout and absenteeism rates are down; achievement scores are up. Parents are better informed, more supportive, and participate more actively.[38]

These are clearly steps in the right direction. Yet the fact remains that most schools, even in so-called choice systems, are *not* schools of choice. The vast majority of teachers, students, and parents are stuck in regular schools of assignment—and the availability of choice elsewhere in the district is of little benefit to them and may actually cause them new problems.

The most promising choice systems now in operation are those that have moved aggressively toward the elimination of fixed jurisdictions and assignments. Carried to their full extent, such systems make every school a school of choice. This is the cutting edge of the current reform movement, pioneered by just a few systems.

Broadest in scope are recent reforms carried out in the state of Minnesota.[39] Elementary and secondary students are allowed to attend schools outside their own districts, with state and local money—up to a minimum or "foundation" set by the state—following them, as long as the receiving district has room and racial balance is not adversely affected. State law grants districts the right to decide whether free choice will reign within their boundaries, but districts have been encouraged to move in this direction and some are in the process of doing so. In addition, high school students are also allowed to opt out of their own schools and receive credit for taking courses at colleges of their choosing, with state and local money following them. The Minnesota reforms are so new that it remains unclear how many students and schools will be affected by choice and what the consequences will be. The preliminary results are positive. Those directly involved are happy with how the new system is working and seem to be benefiting from it. Like virtually all choice-based reforms, however, the Minnesota reforms do not go nearly far enough, failing to free up the supply of schools, continuing to control them from above, and leaving all the traditional institutions in place.

Just as Minnesota has been a pioneer among states, so a small number of districts have taken the lead in building their own systems around choice. One of the boldest has been Cambridge, Massachusetts. The Cambridge system emerged incrementally over the years, beginning in the late 1960s, as the district responded to pressures for desegregation. Its authorities initially relied on magnet schools, then began resorting to various kinds of controls (redrawing jurisdictional boundaries, imposing involuntary transfers on students); but the cumulative effects on racial balance were unsatisfactory, and whites were bailing out of the system into private schools and other districts. By 1981 these failures had prompted a shift to something new and more radical, a districtwide "controlled choice" system, which a year later had taken over as the district's programmatic attack on desegregation.[40]

The concept is simple. There are no neighborhood schools or attendance areas. Parents and students are free to choose any schools in the district. To assist them in gaining information and making wise decisions, the district provides a Parent Information Center complete with parent liaisons, whose job it is to know about the special characteristics of individual schools, to discuss with parents the special needs of their children, and to facilitate the application process. Parents and students can rank order up to four schools in submitting their applications to the district's assignment officer, who is responsible for assigning each student to a school, and who gives weight to racial balance as well as proximity and siblings in making his determinations.

While one might think that all students would try to get into the same schools, this has not happened—in part because students often prefer schools that are close to their homes, but also because the Cambridge schools offer distinctive programs that have differential appeal.[41] The end result is that the great majority of students receive their first-choice school, and almost all receive one of their picks. The remaining students are assigned; but they have the right to appeal to the district's Hardship Appeal Board, and in any event are free to apply for transfer during the next year.

The Cambridge choice plan has been a huge improvement over the district's troubled past. The perennial problem of racial imbalance has dramatically changed for the better. Student achievement scores are up, and achievement differences between the worst and best schools are significantly down. Teachers are more satisfied with their jobs, parents and students are happier with their schools. And, not surprisingly, the public schools are now winning back the students they lost in earlier years to the private sector—by 1987, 89 percent of the district's newly entering students (kindergarten aged) were choosing to enroll in public schools, compared with 78 percent in 1979. This is perhaps the most concrete of all measures of success: people are choosing public schools because they prefer them.[42]

There is little doubt that the Cambridge plan works. In our view, it is one of the most exciting developments in American public education. Yet it does not go far enough. The demand side has essentially been freed up by giving parents and students choice. But the supply side—the set of alternatives from which they choose—remains firmly under the control of all the usual democratic institutions. Schools do not emerge in response to what parents and students want. Nor are schools truly free to organize, staff themselves, and design their curricula in ways they think will most appeal to their clients. All these matters remain subject to control from above. District authorities decide, through the usual political and administrative processes, what the supply of public schools will be. The central office and its resident experts continue to spin out programs and policies. The district remains fundamentally responsible for what its schools are, what they do, and how well they perform—and it continues to take those hierarchic responsibilities very seriously. The schools have been granted somewhat more flexibility, but everyone knows who is really in charge.

The most radical—and most promising—exercise in public sector choice is to be found in Manhattan's District No. 4 in East Harlem, New York, which serves some 14,000 students from prekindergarten through the ninth grade.[43] Here, as in many other districts, the stimulus for reform was crisis: the educational system was a disaster. Out of New York City's thirty-two school districts in 1973, District No. 4 ranked last in reading and mathematics. The demographics of the district make this kind of failure seem predictable and inevitable. More than half of all families are headed by single females. Almost 80 percent of all students qualify for free-lunch programs because of low income. Almost all students are minorities—60 percent are Hispanic, 35 percent are black.[44]

But District No. 4 was also lucky. It had dynamic leaders who were willing to take risks and follow innovative paths to reform almost unthinkable to their mainstream colleagues in the larger educational community. Beginning in 1974, they oversaw the creation of an expanding number of alternative schools built around distinctive themes, philosophies, and programs. This expansion arose from a special source: the district encouraged teachers with ideas and initiative to put forward their own proposals, and, with the district's involvement and consent, form their own schools. Teachers were only too happy to take advantage of these opportunities, and schools sprouted up like mushrooms. To make this proliferation of schools possible, district officials also rejected the traditional notion that each school must have its own building. In East Harlem, schools were henceforth to be identified with programs, not with buildings. A given building, therefore, often houses a number of very different schools, each with its own "director" (a teacher with the responsibilities of principal), staff, and student body.

These schools have been granted very substantial autonomy. To begin with, district authorities do not seek centralized control over student admissions. They assist parents through orientation sessions, information on each school, lessons in decisionmaking, and meetings with school representatives. But the schools control their own admissions—they set their own criteria and make their own decisions about whom to accept and reject. More generally, the schools are largely (but not entirely) free to make their own decisions about programs, methods, structure, and virtually everything else pertaining to the kind of education they provide; and with teachers running their own shops, many of the preexisting formal rules imposed through collective bargaining and democratic control have either been waived or ignored. Teachers, parents, and students are all encouraged to think of themselves as their schools' "owners" and to take the responsibilities— and the pride and involvement—that real ownership entails.

The district has pursued innovation and diversity, and that is what it has achieved. The names of some of its junior high schools help illustrate just how spectacular the variety can be when the supply side is liberated: the Academy of Environmental Science, the Creative Learning Community, the East Harlem Career Academy, the East Harlem Maritime School, the East Harlem School for Health and Bio-Medical Studies, the Jose Feliciano Performing Arts School, Music 13, the Isaac Newton School for Math and Science, Northview Tech for Communication Arts and Computer Science, Rafael Cordero Bilingual School, the School of Science and Humanities.[45] From the list alone, one would think this is a system of private schools.

Freeing up the supply and governance of schools has not led to the kind of chaos or unfairness that critics of market arrangements invariably predict. The system appears to work smoothly, effectively, and fairly. While schools have control over their own admissions, their distinctiveness and their sheer need for students—the district puts them out of business if they fail to attract enough clients—has meant that schools and students tend to match up quite well on their own.

In recent years, 60 percent of the students have received their first choices, 30 percent their second choices, and 5 percent their third choices.

On virtually every relevant dimension, the East Harlem reforms have been a tremendous success. There are lots of schools, emphasizing everything from music to science. Teachers are enthusiastic about their work and largely in control of their own schools. They are empowered, professional, and satisfied—all achieved through the natural dynamics of the system, not through the artificiality of bureaucratic rules. School organizations are small and informal, built around team cooperation and coherence of mission. Parents are active, well informed, and take pride in "their" schools.

Meantime, student achievement is way up. While only 15.9 percent of the district's students were reading at or above grade level in 1973, 62.6 percent were doing so by 1987. Its scores now put it around the middle for New York City school districts, rather than at the bottom— quite remarkable, given how heavily the sociological odds are stacked against it. Students are also dramatically more successful in gaining admission to New York's selective high schools. Whereas in the past they were essentially shut out of these schools, now they are accepted at rates that far exceed the citywide average. Some of this progress may be attributable to an influx of students from throughout New York City who have chosen to transfer from their districts to the schools of East Harlem. But these transfers represent only a small portion of District 4's enrollments, and are yet another indicator of the attractiveness of East Harlem's schools.

If there is a single district in the country that deserves to be held up as a model for all the others, it is East Harlem. Nonetheless, its system still suffers from what may turn out to be a fatal flaw. Beginning in the 1970s and continuing throughout the eighties, the East Harlem reforms have been driven by a small group of visionaries who used district authority not only to provide parents and students with choice, but also to liberate the supply and governance of schools from district control. This freeing up of the supply side is what makes the East Harlem system so bold and unique. But its creation is entirely dependent on the visionaries themselves and their hold on power. The structures of democratic authority remain in place, and, if they become occupied by people with different beliefs or constituencies, the same public authority that liberated the schools could then be used to regain control over them.

This is not an idle fear. A recent scandal at the district level, involving allegations of mishandling of funds for personal benefit and giving rise to widespread media coverage, prompted city officials to initiate a shakeup of district personnel.[46] The new leadership appears to be intent on reasserting certain district controls and moving toward more traditional forms of governance and administration.[47] How far this will go remains to be seen. The up side is that East Harlem's radical system is well established; the schools have vocal, active, supportive clienteles, and they will fight any attempt to reduce their autonomy. But their problem, when all is said and done, is that they are subordinates in the hierarchy of democratic control, and what authority they have been privileged to exercise to this point has been delegated to them by their superiors—who have the right to take it back.

A Proposal for Reform

It is fashionable these days to say that choice is "not a panacea." Taken literally, this is obviously true. There are no panaceas in social policy. But the message this aphorism really means to get across is that choice is just one of many reforms with something to contribute. School-based management is another. So are teacher empowerment and professionalism, better training programs, stricter accountability, and bigger budgets. These and other types of reforms all bolster school effectiveness in their own distinctive ways—so the reasoning goes—and the best, most aggressive, most comprehensive approach to transforming the public school system is therefore one that wisely combines them into a multifaceted reformist package.[48]

In practice, then, choice is rarely treated as a self-contained strategy for reform. It is one element among many. Parents and students are sometimes given a modicum of choice, often through one or more alternative schools or magnets; but this is typically part of a larger stream of reforms in which efforts are also made to decentralize governance through some (though usually not all) of the elements of school-based management, to make teachers more professional (through career ladders or new decision responsibilities, say), to monitor school performance more closely (through stricter accounting requirements, formal tests of student achievement, parent surveys), and so on. Even when choice is an important part of the package, the result is not really a choice system at all. It is a more decentralized version of the traditional system of democratic control in which parents and students have more options.[49]

Politics is of course partly responsible for this. A true choice system strikes at the foundations of democratic control, and the established interests have every reason to throw their weight behind a more conventional grab-bag of marginal changes. In addition, democratic politics promotes compromise solutions anyway: if there are lots of reformist ideas with political support, the system tends to generate policies that borrow a little from each.

Politics aside, however, there are intellectual reasons for this grab-bag approach as well. People opt for combinations of reforms when they do not know what to think—when they have no coherent notion of what causes the problems they are concerned about and what might be done to address them. They cast about for answers, and their uncertainty prompts them to entertain whatever plausible-sounding ideas happen to come along. Just as investors do in the financial world, reformers respond to uncertainty by diversifying their portfolios.

As we have suggested, we do not think that all these ideas are bad. They have their pluses and minuses, and some combinations have in fact been responsible for tangible improvements in many schools and districts around the country. School-based management is better than centralized management. Having a few alternative schools is better than having none at all. Giving teachers more control over teaching is better than allowing administrators to tell them what to do. But as an "approach" this is precisely the wrong way to go about transforming American public education. The schools' most fundamental problems are rooted in the institutions of democratic control by which they are governed; and, despite all the talk about "restructuring," the current wave of grab-bag reforms leaves those institutions intact and in charge. The basic causes of America's educational problems do not get addressed.

Of all the sundry reforms that attract attention, only choice has the capacity to address these causes. The others are system preserving. They fully embrace direct democratic control and simply put its authority to use in ways somewhat different from the past. The schools remain subordinates in the structure of public authority—and they remain bureaucratic. In principle, choice offers a clear, sharp break from the institutional past. In practice, however, it has been forced into the same mold with all the others. It has been embraced half-heartedly, in bits and pieces, as a means of granting parents and students additional options or of giving schools more incentives to compete—popular moves that can be accomplished without changing the existing system in any fundamental way. Choice has simply been part of the grab-bag, one of many system-preserving reforms that presumably make democratic control work better.

Without being too literal about it, we think reformers would do well to entertain the notion that choice *is* a panacea. This is our way of saying that choice is not like the other reforms and should not be combined with them as part of a reformist strategy for improving America's public schools. Choice is a self-contained reform with its own rationale and justification. It has the capacity *all by itself* to bring about the kind of transformation that, for years, reformers have been seeking to engineer in myriad other ways. Indeed, if choice is to work to greatest advantage, it must be adopted *without* these other reforms, since the latter are predicated on democratic control and are implemented by bureaucratic means. The whole point of a thoroughgoing system of choice is to free the schools from these disabling constraints by sweeping away the old institutions and replacing them with new ones. Taken seriously, choice is not a system-preserving reform. It is a revolutionary reform that introduces a new system of public education.

What would such a system look like? Within the educational establishment, any serious consideration of choice automatically raises the much-hated specter of a "voucher" system—a system in which government would provide funding directly to students in the form of vouchers, and students would use their vouchers to pay for education in the public or private school of their own choosing. For the last thirty years or so, advocates of choice have come up with many voucher proposals, and the educational community has consistently and vehemently opposed them, portraying vouchers as the embodiment of everything that is threatening to public education.[50]

Fortunately, the growing popularity of choice and its incremental adoption in districts and states around the country have helped break the stereotypical identification of choice with vouchers—and helped dissociate it, as well, from the unwarranted stigma that the establishment has succeeded in attaching to the very concept of vouchers. The fact is that all sorts of diverse arrangements are compatible with the basic principles on which choice is founded. Vouchers are not even necessary. Whether private schools are included is simply a matter of policy—they need not be. Similarly, choice systems can be designed differently depending on how reformers want to deal with issues of racial integration, religion, funding equalization, the educationally disadvantaged, and whatever other special concerns they may have.

This does not mean, of course, that all choice plans are somehow on an equal footing. As we have seen in evaluating what passes for choice in the current reform movement, some arrangements are clearly better than others, particularly as they attack or (most often) fail to attack the institutional causes at the root of the problem. It does mean, on the other hand, that there is no fixed or uniformly best system of choice, and that reformers have lots of flexibility and options at their disposal. Choice offers an array of institutional possibilities, not a determinate formula.

Without pretending to have an optimal plan up our sleeves, we would now like to outline a brief proposal for a choice system that we think is equipped to do the job. Offering our own proposal in this way has a certain practical value, for it allows us to illustrate in some detail what a full-blown choice system might look like, as well as to note some of the policy decisions that must be made along the way in building one. But more important, it also allows us to suggest in specific terms what our institutional theory of schools actually entails for educational reform—and to emphasize, once again, how essential it is that reforms be founded on theory. The absence of a clear, well-developed theory—and the triumph, in its stead, of platitudes and surface plausibility—leads inevitably to the grab-bag. And to failure and disappointment.

Our guiding principle in the design of a choice system is this: public authority must be put to use in creating a system that is almost entirely beyond the reach of public authority. Because states have primary responsibility for American public education, we think the best way to achieve significant, enduring reform is for states to take the initiative in withdrawing authority from existing institutions and building a new system in which most authority is vested directly in the schools, parents, and students. This restructuring cannot be construed as an exercise in delegation. As long as authority remains "available" at higher levels within state government, it will eventually be used to control the schools. As far as possible, all higher-level authority must be eliminated.[51]

What we propose, more specifically, is that state leaders create a new system of public education with the following properties.

The Supply of Public Schools

—The state will have the responsibility for setting criteria that define what constitutes a "public school" under the new system. These criteria should be quite minimal, roughly corresponding to the criteria many states now employ in accrediting private schools—graduation requirements, health and safety requirements, and teacher certification requirements.

—Any group or organization that applies to the state and meets these minimal criteria must then be chartered as a public school and granted the right to accept students and receive public money.

—Existing private schools will be among those eligible to participate. Their participation should be encouraged, since they constitute a ready supply of often-effective schools. (Our own preference would be to include religious schools as well, as long as their sectarian functions can be kept clearly separate from their educational functions.) Any private schools that do participate will thereby become public schools, as such schools are defined under the new system.

—District governments can continue running their present schools, assuming the latter meet state criteria. They will have authority, however, only over their own schools and not over any of the others that may be chartered by the state.

The Funding of Public Education

—The state will set up a Choice Office in each district, which, among other things, will maintain a record of all school-age children and the level of funding—the "scholarship" amounts—associated with each child. Schools will be compensated directly by this office based on the specific children they enroll. Public money will flow from funding sources (federal, state, and district governments) to the Choice Office and then to schools. At no point will it go to parents or students.

—As it does now, the state will have the right to specify how much, or by what formula, each district must contribute for each child. Our own preference is for an equalization approach that requires wealthier districts to contribute more per child than poor districts do and that guarantees students in all districts an adequate financial foundation. The state's contribution can then be calibrated to bring total spending per child up to whatever dollar amount seems desirable; under an equalization scheme, this would mean a larger state contribution in poor districts than in wealthy ones.

—While it is important to give parents and students as much flexibility as possible, we think it is unwise to allow them to supplement their scholarship amounts with personal funds. Such "add-ons" threaten to produce too many disparities and inequalities within the public system, and many citizens would regard them as unfair and burdensome.

—Complete equalization, on the other hand, strikes us as too stifling and restrictive. A reasonable trade-off, we believe, is to allow for collective add-ons (much as the current system does). The citizens of each district can be given the freedom to decide whether they want to spend more per child than the state requires them to spend. They can then determine how important education is to them and how much they are willing to tax themselves for it. This means that children from different districts may have different-sized scholarships.

—Scholarships may also vary within any given district, and we strongly think that they should. Some students have very special educational needs—arising from economic deprivation, physical handicaps, language difficulties, emotional problems, and other disadvantages—that can only be met effectively through specialized programs that are costly to provide. State and federal programs already appropriate public money to address these problems. Our suggestion is that these funds should take the form of add-ons to student scholarships. At-risk students would then be empowered with bigger scholarships than the others, making them attractive clients to all schools (and stimulating the emergence of new specialty schools).

—The state must pay to support its own Choice Office in each district. Districts may retain as much of their current governing apparatus as they wish—superintendents, school boards, central offices, and all their staff. But they have to pay for them entirely out of the revenue they derive from the scholarships of those children who voluntarily choose to attend district-run schools.[52] Aside from the governance of these schools (which no one need attend), districts will be little more than taxing jurisdictions that allow citizens to make a collective determination as to how large their children's scholarships will be.

Choice among Schools

—Each student will be free to attend any public school in the state, regardless of district, with the relevant scholarship—consisting of federal, state, and local contributions—flowing to the school of choice. In practice, of course, most students will probably choose schools in reasonable proximity to their homes. But districts will have no claim on their own residents.

—To the extent that tax revenues allow, every effort will be made to provide transportation for students that need it. This is important in helping to open up as many alternatives as possible to all students, especially the poor and those located in rural areas.[53]

—To assist parents and students in choosing among schools, the state will provide a Parent Information Center within its local Choice Office. This Center will collect comprehensive information on each school in the district, and its parent liaisons will meet personally with parents in helping them judge which schools best meet their children's needs. The emphasis here will be on personal contact and involvement. Parents will be required to visit the center at least once, and encouraged to do so often. Meetings will be arranged at all schools so that parents can see first-hand what their choices are.

—The applications process will be handled in simple fashion by the Parent Information Center. Once parents and students decide which schools they prefer, they will fill out applications to each, with parent liaisons available to give advice and assistance (including filling out the applications themselves, if necessary). All applications will be submitted to the Center, which in turn will send them out to the schools.

—Schools will make their own admissions decisions, subject only to nondiscrimination requirements.[54] This is absolutely crucial. Schools must be able to define their own missions and build their own programs in their own ways, and they cannot do this if their student population is thrust on them by outsiders. They must be free to admit as many or as few students as they want, based on whatever criteria they think relevant—intelligence, interest, motivation, behavior, special needs—and they must be free to exercise their own, informal judgments about individual applicants.

—Schools will set their own "tuitions." They may choose to do this explicitly—say, by publicly announcing the minimum scholarship they are willing to accept. They may also do it implicitly by allowing anyone to apply for admission and simply making selections, knowing in advance what each applicant's scholarship amount is. In either case, schools are free to admit students with different-sized scholarships, and they are free to keep the entire scholarship that accompanies each student they have admitted. This gives all schools incentives to attract students with special needs, since these children will have the largest scholarships. It also gives schools incentives to attract students from districts with high base-level scholarships. But no school need restrict itself to students with special needs, nor to students from a single district.

—The applications process must take place within a framework that guarantees each student a school, as well as a fair shot at getting into the school he or she most wants. It is important, however, that such a framework impose only the most minimal restrictions on the schools. We suggest something like the following. The Parent Information Center will have the responsibility for seeing that parents and students are informed, that they have visited the schools that interest them, and that all applications are submitted by a given date. Schools will then be required to make their admissions decisions within a set time, and students who are accepted into one or more schools will be required to select one as their final choice. Students who are not accepted anywhere, as well as schools that have yet to attract as many students as they want, will participate in a second round of applications, which will work the same way. After this second round, some students may remain without schools (although, judging from the East Harlem experience, probably very few). At this point, parent liaisons will take informal action to try to match up these students with appropriate schools. If any students still remain, a special safety-net procedure will be invoked to ensure that each is assigned to a specific school.[55]

—Schools must also be free to expel students or deny them readmission when, based on their own experience and standards, they believe the situation warrants it (as long as they are not "arbitrary and capricious"). This is essential if schools are to define and control their own organizations, and it gives students a strong incentive to live up to their side of the educational "contract."[56]

Governance and Organization of the Public Schools

—Each school must be granted sole authority to determine its own governing structure. It may be run entirely by teachers or even a union. It may vest all power in a principal. It may be built around committees that guarantee representation to the principal, teachers, parents, students, and members of the community. Or it may do something completely different. The state must refrain from imposing *any* structures or rules that specify how authority is to be exercised within the school. This is meant to include the district-run schools: the state must not impose any governing apparatus on them either. These schools, however, are subordinate units within district government—they are already embedded in a larger organization—and it is the district authorities, not the schools, that have the legal right to determine how they will be governed.

—More generally, the state will do nothing to tell the schools how they must be internally organized to do their work. There will be no requirements for career ladders, advisory committees, textbook selection, in-service training, preparation time, homework, or anything else. The schools will be organized and operated as they see fit.[57]

—Statewide tenure laws will be eliminated, allowing each school to decide for itself whether or not to adopt a tenure policy and what the specifics of that policy will be. This is essential if schools are to have the flexibility they need in building a well-functioning team. Some schools may not offer tenure at all, relying on pay and working conditions to attract the kinds of teachers they want, while others may offer tenure as a supplementary means of compensating and retaining their best teachers. Teachers, meantime, may demand tenure in their negotiations (individual or collective) with schools—and, as in private colleges and universities, the best teachers are well positioned to get it (since they can take their valued services elsewhere). District governments may continue to offer districtwide tenure, along with transfer rights and seniority preference and whatever other personnel policies they have adopted in the past. But these policies apply only to district-run schools and the teachers who work in them.

—Teachers will continue to have a right to join unions and engage in collective bargaining, but the legally prescribed bargaining unit will be the individual school or—as in the case of the district government— the larger organization that runs the school. If teachers in a given school want to join a union or, having done so, want to exact financial or structural concessions, that is up to them. But they will not be allowed to commit other schools or teachers to the same things, and they must suffer the consequences if their victories put them at a competitive disadvantage in supplying quality education. Similarly, if teachers at district-run schools want to remain unionized, their unions may continue to bargain centrally for all of them. But their decisions will not apply to any other public schools in the district.

—The state will continue to certify teachers, but requirements will be minimal—corresponding to those that, in many states, have historically been applied to private schools. In our view, individuals should be certified to teach if they have a bachelor's degree and if their personal history reveals no obvious problems. The question of whether they are truly good teachers will be determined in practice, as schools determine whom to hire, observe their own teachers in action over an extended period of time, and make decisions about merit, promotion, and dismissal. The schools may, as a matter of strategy, choose to pay attention to certain formal indicators of past or future performance, among them: a master's degree, completion of a voluntary teacher certification program at an education school, or voluntary certification by a national board. Some schools may choose to require one or more of these, or perhaps to reward them in various ways. But that is up to the schools—which will be able to look anywhere for good teachers in a now much larger and more dynamic market.

—The state will hold the schools accountable for meeting procedural requirements. It will ensure that schools continue to meet the criteria presumed by their charters, that they adhere to nondiscrimination laws in admissions and other matters, and that they collect and make available to the public—via the Parent Information Center—certain types of information: on their mission, their staff and course offerings, parent and student satisfaction, staff opinions, standardized test scores (which we would make optional), and anything else that would promote informed choice among parents and students.

—The state will not, on the other hand, hold the schools accountable for student achievement or other dimensions that call for assessments of the quality of school performance. When it comes to performance, schools are held accountable from below, by parents and students who directly experience their services and are free to choose. The state plays a crucial supporting role here in monitoring the full and honest disclosure of information by the schools—but it is only a supporting role.

Overview: Choice as a Public System

This proposal calls for fundamental changes in the structure of American public education. Stereotypes aside, however, these changes have nothing to do with "privatizing" the nation's schools. The choice system we have outlined here would be a truly public system—and a democratic one.

We are proposing that the state put its democratic authority to use in creating a new institutional framework. The design and legitimation of this framework would be a democratic act of the most fundamental sort. It would be a social decision, made through the usual processes of democratic governance, by which the people and their representatives specify the structure of a new system of public education.

This framework, as we set it out, is quite flexible and admits of substantial variation on important issues, all of them matters of public policy to be decided by government. Public officials and their constituents would be free to take their own approaches to taxation, equalization, supplementary funding for the disadvantaged, treatment of religious schools, parent add-ons, and other controversial issues of public concern, thus designing choice systems to reflect the unique conditions, preferences, and political forces of their own states.

Once this structural framework is democratically determined, moreover, governments would continue to play important roles within it. State officials and agencies would remain pivotal to the success of public education and to its ongoing operation. They would provide funding, approve applications for new schools, orchestrate and oversee the choice process, elicit full information about schools, provide transportation to students, monitor schools for adherence to the law, and (if they want) design and administer tests of student performance. School districts, meantime, would continue as local taxing jurisdictions, and they would have the option of continuing to operate their own system of schools.

The crucial difference is that direct democratic control of the schools—the very *capacity* for control, not simply its exercise—would essentially be eliminated. Most of those who previously held authority over the schools would have their authority permanently withdrawn, and that authority would be vested in schools, parents, and students. Schools would be legally autonomous: free to govern themselves as they want, specify their own goals and programs and methods, design their own organizations, select their own student bodies, and make their own personnel decisions. Parents and students would be legally empowered to choose among alternative schools, aided by institutions designed to promote active involvement, well-informed decisions, and fair treatment.

Politics, Ideas, and America's Schools

We have no illusions that a true choice system of this type stands a good chance of being adopted in any single state, much less throughout the country. Almost everyone in the reform movement has something nice to say about choice nowadays as long as "choice" means little more than giving parents and students additional freedom in selecting among schools. Choice is politically attractive when it is not designed to do much. But when it is designed to get to the root of the problem— when it seeks to liberate the schools by means of a thorough transformation of public institutions—it generates fierce opposition from every nook and cranny of the educational establishment. And this is enough to dim the prospects for real reform.

Still, we are cautiously optimistic. As the Progressive movement demonstrated many years ago, attempts to transform political institutions are not doomed to fail. They may succeed when they have widespread support and when the resources of powerful social groups can be mobilized behind change. Something of the sort could happen during the next decade. The fact is that choice is highly popular among ordinary citizens and is gaining adherents among reformers and state officials, particularly governors. Bold executive leadership and broad popular support, especially if combined with the concentrated power of a unified business community—which, in effect, might reassume the historical role it played during the Progressive era as the political vanguard of reform—could succeed in overturning the established order and creating a new system of public education.

Cautious optimism is better than no optimism at all. Just a few years ago, the suggestion that choice might succeed in restructuring American education would have been regarded as pure fantasy. Times have changed. Important as this is, though, expectations about the future have to be based on reality, and the reality is that the American political deck is stacked against institutional reform. As we look ahead, the most reasonable scenario is for limited success: choice will likely gain in popularity during the 1990s, but it will be adopted in bits and pieces along with lots of other reforms that, in the aggregate, decentralize but preserve the traditional system of democratic control.

We did not write this book, however, to complain about how democracy works or to urge public officials to get their acts together and make it work differently. It works the way it works—which, in shorthand, is precisely the point we have been trying to make from the beginning. We wrote this book to develop an argument about the causal connection between schools and institutions, and to show that the normal, routine operation of educational institutions, whatever form they might take, has pervasive consequences for the organization and performance of schools. The key to understanding why America's public schools are failing is to be found in a deeper understanding of how its traditional institutions of democratic control actually work. The nation is experiencing a crisis in public education not because these democratic institutions have functioned perversely or improperly or unwisely, but because they have functioned quite normally. Democratic control normally produces ineffective schools. This is how it works.

Reformers have paid little attention to institutions. All the talk in recent years about "restructuring" would seem to express a recognition that institutions are important, yet it really does not. Most reformers agree that top-down control is bad, that it promotes bureaucracy, and that something has to be done to make schools more autonomous and teachers more professional. But in trying to bring about such a transformation, they simply take it for granted that the public schools will continue to be governed by the same institutions they have always been governed by, and that "restructuring" within this familiar framework will do the job. The public debate is not about direct democratic control as a form of governance. The debate is about finding more enlightened ways to exercise it.

The ideas about schools that have guided reformers are basically correct, in our view. They are just incomplete. They focus on the micro-world of schools and have a good deal to say about the makeup and immediate causes of effective organization; but they have almost nothing to say about institutions. The most fundamental questions, as a result, have generally gone unasked and have not been an integral part of reformist thinking. In what ways do schools reflect their institutional settings? How does this come about and why does it happen? Do some institutions tend to promote and nurture effective organizations? Do others, perhaps in spite of everyone's best intentions, promote and nurture ineffective organizations? What are the consequences of direct democratic control for the public schools? These are the sorts of issues that strike to the heart of what educational theory and research have left unexplored over the years, producing a giant gap in the knowledge base that reformers have relied on in figuring out how to improve the nation's schools.

We do not expect everyone to accept the argument we have made here. In fact, we expect most of those who speak with authority on educational matters—leaders and academics within the educational community—to reject it. But we will regard our effort as a success if it directs attention to America's institutions of democratic control and provokes serious debate about their consequences for the nation's public schools. Whether or not our own conclusions are right, the fact is that these issues are truly fundamental to an understanding of schools, and they have so far played no part in the national debate. If educational reform is to have any chance at all of succeeding, this has to change.

In the meantime, we can only believe that the current "revolution" in American public education will prove a disappointment. It might have succeeded had it actually been a revolution, but it was not and was never intended to be, despite the lofty rhetoric. Revolutions dismember old institutions and replace them with new ones. The 1980s reform movement never seriously thought about the old institutions, and certainly never considered them part of the problem. They were, as they had always been, part of the solution—and, for that matter, part of the definition of what democracy and public education are all about.

This identification has never been valid. There is nothing in the concept of democracy to require that schools be subject to direct control by school boards, superintendents, central offices, departments of education, and other arms of government. Nor is there anything in the concept of public education to require that schools be governed in this way. There are many paths to democracy and public education. The path America has been trodding for the past half-century is exacting a heavy price—one the nation and its children can ill afford to bear, and need not. It is time, we think, to get to the root of the problem.

Appendix A

Data

THE ANALYSES reported in this book are based on two data sets, the High School and Beyond 1980 Sophomore Cohort First Follow-up, which was assembled in 1982, and the High School and Beyond Administrator and Teacher Survey, which was assembled in 1984. The first contains data that were collected from schools and students in surveys conducted in 1980 and 1982. The students participating in these surveys were sophomores in 1980 and seniors in 1982. Throughout this book we refer to the data provided by students and schools in these surveys as High School and Beyond (HSB) data. The second data set contains information that was collected from teachers and principals in a subsample of the HSB schools in the spring of 1984. We refer to these data as Administrator and Teacher Survey (ATS) data. Because both data sets, now publicly available, are described in full detail in user's manuals, we will describe them only briefly here.[1] The purpose of this appendix is to explain how we prepared the data for this analysis.

The HSB study began in 1980 with a national sample of 1,015 high schools and nearly 60,000 students: 30,030 sophomores (class of 1982) and 28,240 seniors. The students were random samples, numbering up to 36 sophomores and 36 seniors in each school. In 1982, 1984, and 1986 the students in the class of 1982 were resurveyed. Our analysis focuses on a subsample of the class of 1982—the students who attended ATS schools—and the 1980 and 1982 surveys of that class. The ATS sample was drawn from the 975 HSB schools that were still in existence in the winter of 1982–83. Resources limited the ATS sample to a maximum of 540 schools, roughly half the number in the original HSB sample.

The ATS sample was constructed as follows. All of the HSB schools that participated in a separate Parent Survey (which was a component of the 1980 HSB study) were included first. This provided an unbiased HSB subsample of 312 schools, of which 293 were open at the time the ATS data were collected. Next, the remaining 83 Hispanic schools, which were heavily oversampled in the original HSB sample, were excluded. All non-Hispanic private schools—75 of them—were then included, to ensure enough private schools for statistical analysis. From the remaining 520 public, non-Hispanic schools, 166 schools were then added to the ATS sample by random selection. This brought the ATS sample to 538 schools, of which 532 were open at the time the data were collected. Properly weighted, this final sample of 532 schools can be used to estimate population characteristics for public and private high schools that were in existence in the United States from 1980 through 1984.

In each of the ATS schools, questionnaires were completed by the principal or head, and a random sample of up to 30 teachers (and a guidance counselor, a vocational education director, and a community service director). Questionnaires were returned by 402 principals, for a total completion rate of 76 percent, and by 10,370 teachers in 457 schools, for a total completion rate of 86 percent. The response rates were actually higher than these percentages suggest, however. Because final questionnaires were mailed to only 505 of the original 532 schools (27 schools were used for pretests), responses were received from principals in 80 percent of the schools and teachers in 90 percent.

The sample of schools analyzed in this book includes all of those schools for which we have at least ATS data from principals. Our maximum sample size, then, is 402 schools. Of these schools, 402 also have HSB school data, 399 have ATS teacher data, and 389 have complete HSB student data—in particular, senior as well as sophomore test data. The descriptive statistics reported in the book were based on the largest samples available to measure the characteristics in question: 402 schools for principal and (HSB) school characteristics, 399 schools for teacher characteristics, and 389 schools for student characteristics. The multivariate analyses are based on the sample of 389 schools with valid data on schools, principals, teachers, and students. Properly weighted, each of the samples examined in the book is representative of American high schools that were open from 1980 to 1984, or of the students attending American high schools during those years.

All of the analyses in this book are conducted on weighted data sets. The student-level analyses are based on data weighted to create a representative sample of high school seniors in 1982 (who were also sophomores in 1980). The weighting variable, "PNLTSTWT," was designed (by the National Center for Education Statistics, which prepared the data for public use) to create a representative sample out of those students who completed questionnaires and took achievement tests in both 1980 and 1982.[2] The school-level analyses are based on data weighted to create a representative sample of high schools open from 1980 through 1984. This weighting was accomplished using the variable that in the public ATS data file is now labeled "ATSWT." This weight was applied to all school-level measures, whether they were obtained from student, teacher, principal, or HSB school questionnaires. Teacher responses were always averaged to the school level before being analyzed, so they were never weighted to represent national samples of teachers. The only weights used in the analysis, then, are for schools and for students.[3]

Throughout our analysis we combine the information provided in the ATS and HSB data sets to provide well-rounded pictures of schools and their students. Doing so, however, raises a final issue about the appropriate use of these data. Because the ATS data were collected in 1984, and the HSB data in 1980 and 1982, there is some question whether the ATS data can be used to explain variation in the HSB data, and vice versa. For example, is it valid to explain student achievement with school characteristics that are observed nearly two years after the achievement has occurred? The answer is that it depends on the stability of the school characteristics to be used in the explanation.

Our view is that the ATS and HSB data can be analyzed as if they were gathered contemporaneously. Schools are complex organizations that are often governed by complex administrative systems. They have great longevity, and, especially in the public sector, very stable staff. Generally speaking, schools do not change rapidly. And more specifically, the organizational characteristics that most interest us— for example, leadership and professionalism—tend not to change over short periods at all. To be sure, we would prefer data that were collected on schools and students over precisely the same time interval. But that was not an option once the original HSB study was under way. If it were ever going to be possible for us or for other researchers to determine whether effective schooling had anything to do with the achievement of the HSB students, it was necessary for us to proceed as we did.

It is reasonable to suspect, of course, that the early 1980s might present special problems. It was at that time that a massive wave of school reform began to sweep the nation's public schools. Schools may therefore have changed more during the early 1980s than they would be expected to change over a short period ordinarily. The ATS data were designed to measure changes in school practices. Specifically, principals were asked whether their schools had made any of a number of changes in their operations "since the 1980–81 school year." This is not a perfect measure of whether schools changed after the HSB students graduated. The measure allows for changes that occurred in time to affect the 1981–82 school year when the HSB students were seniors.[4] Still, the odds are two out of three that the reported changes occurred after the HSB students graduated.

To see whether school changes might have caused problems for our analysis, we calculated the percentages of public schools in the top quartile and in the bottom quartile of student achievement gains (as described in appendix D) that reported changes in their operations. Changes are unlikely to present a problem for our analysis unless they are systematically related to school quality. If high and low performance schools are equally likely to have made changes, those changes are unlikely to have anything to do with the differences in school performance or organization that we observed.

Table A-1 reports the changes made by public schools in the top and bottom quartiles of achievement gains. The percentages indicate that public schools were indeed making many changes in their operations during the early 1980s. But they also indicate these changes were about equally likely in successful and unsuccessful schools. Some efforts at improvement were more likely to be made by top public schools, other kinds of efforts were more likely to be made by public schools at the bottom. It is also important to recognize that these changes represent practices that may not be closely connected to the organizational qualities that we used to characterize effective schools. Overall, it seems safe to say the 1984 measures of school organization introduce little or no bias into an analysis of 1980–82 schools and students.

TABLE A-1. Changes in School Practices, 1980–81 to 1983–84, by School Achievement Gain Quartiles, Public Schools[a]
Percent answering "yes"

School practice	Lowest quartile	Highest quartile
Increased graduation requirements	84.0	81.4
Increased homework	37.5	37.5
Longer school day	24.4	15.6
Longer school year	18.4	8.8
Established teacher career ladder	23.9	6.8
Established teacher performance evaluation	55.7	62.5
Established teacher financial incentives	2.5	4.2
Established new student conduct code	86.2	82.5
Grouped students by academic need	55.6	45.0
Adopted eleven-month teacher contract	2.6	0.1
Background of students changed	20.7	20.9
New desegregation plan	3.1	10.1
Instituted graduation tests	38.8	46.6
Major curriculum change	21.7	25.2

a. Sample weighted to achieve a nationally representative sample of public high schools.

Appendix B

Measures and Indicators

T HIS APPENDIX contains the definitions of measures and the survey indicators used in our study.

Definitions of Measures

Unless otherwise indicated, all indexes were constructed by standardizing the indicators, averaging the standardized indicators, and then standardizing the averages. For cases with missing data, indexes were based on whatever subset of indicators had valid responses. When teacher and student indicators were aggregated to the school level, the responses of teachers and students within each school were averaged without weighting.

Academic excellence is top priority: P06E
  If P06H GT P06E Then P06E = P06E-1
Academic track enrollment, percent of tenth grade: SB017BY
Academic track of student, dummy variable: 0 if (BB002 NE 2), 1 if (BB002 EQ 2)
Achievement gains in number of items:
  Math: Sum(FYMTH1RT,FYMTH2RT) – Sum(YBMTH1RT, YBMTH2RT)
  Science: FYSCINRT-YBSCINRT
  Reading: FYREADRT-YBREADRT
  Vocabulary: FYVOCBRT-YBVOCBRT
  Writing: FYWRITRT-YBWRITRT
Achievement IRT scores, tenth and twelfth grades:
  Math: MATH10,MATH12
  Science: SCI10,SCI12
  Reading: READ10,READ12
  Vocabulary: VOC10,VOC12
  Writing: WRIT10,WRIT12
Achievement log gain scores, individual:
  Math: MATHLOG
  Science: SCILOG

Reading: READLOG

Vocabulary: VOCLOG

Writing: WRITLOG

Achievement log gain score, total: Mean(MATHLOG,SCILOG, READLOG, WRITLOG,VOCLOG) Unstandardized

Administrative constraint: Mean(Superintendent or Central office influence over Curriculum, Instruction, Hiring, Firing, Discipline)

Administrative constraint in public schools: Mean(Superintendent or Central office influence over Curriculum, Instruction, Hiring, Firing)

Administrative routines in classrooms: Mean(T19U,T21B,T25A,T25B,T26C1, T26C2)

    Recode T21B $(1=0)$ $(2=1)$ $(3=2)$ $(4=3)$ $(5=4)$ $(6=6.5)$ $(7=7.5)$ $(8=9.5)$ $(9=12.5)$ $(10=17.5)$ $(11=25)$

              T25A T25B $(1=4.5)$ $(2=19.5)$ $(3=39.5)$ $(4=59.5)$ $(5=79.5)$ $(6=95)$

              T26C1 T26C2 $(1=0)$ $(2=1.5)$ $(3=5)$ $(4=10)$ $(5=15)$ $(6=20)$ $(7=25)$

                  $(8=30)$ $(9=35)$ $(10=40)$ $(11=45)$ $(12=50)$ $(13=55)$

Annual per pupil expenditure by district: SB053A

Annual per pupil expenditure by school: SB053B

Central office hiring control: P19H

    Recode P19H $(99=1)$

Changes in school practice:

  Increased graduation requirements: P40A

  Increased homework: P40B

  Longer school day: P40C

  Longer school year: P40D

  Established career ladders for teachers: P40E

  Established performance evaluation for teachers: P40F

  Established financial incentives for performance: P40G

  Established new codes of student conduct: P40H

  Grouped students by academic need: P40I

  Adopted eleven-month teacher contracts: P40J

  Changes in social background of students: P40K

  New desegregation plan implemented: P40L

  Competency test for graduation: P40M

  Major curriculum change: P40N

Classroom disruption: Mean(T06,T23)

    Recode T06 $(1=0)$ $(2=.5)$ $(3=2)$ $(4=5)$ $(5=10.5)$ $(6=20)$

           T23 $(2=4)$ $(3=7)$ $(4=10)$ $(5=13)$ $(6=16)$ $(7=19)$ $(8=25.5)$ $(9=35)$

Course work completed:

  Mathematics: FY4A

  English: FY4B

  Foreign language: Sum(FY4C,FY4D,FY4E,FY4F) unstandardized

History: FY4G

Science: FY4H

Recode FY4A FY4B FY4C FY4D FY4E FY4F FY4G FY4H
(1 = 0) (2 = 1) (3 = 2) (4 = 3) (5 = 4) (6 = 5) (7 = 6) (8 = 7)

Disciplinary constraint in public schools: Mean(Superintendent or Central office influence over Discipline)

Disciplinary practices, fairness and effectiveness: Mean(BB053F, BB053G)
Recode BB053F BB053G (5 = missing)

Dropouts, percent of student body: SB014

Economic resources: Mean(Per pupil expenditure, − Student-teacher ratio)

Economically disadvantaged students, percent of student body: SB037

Family income: BB101

Family socioeconomic status: BYSES

Father closely monitors school work: BB046B

Father's education: BB039

General track enrollment, percent of tenth grade: 100 percent − Sum(Academic track enrollment, Vocational track enrollment)

Goal clarity: T19M

Graduation requirements: Mean(P01A1,P01B1,P01C1,P01D1,P01E1)

English: P01A1

Mathematics: P01B1

Science: P01C1

History: P01D1

Foreign Language: P01E1

Home learning tools: Mean(BB104C,BB104D,BB104G,BB104I)
Recode BB104C BB104D BB104G BB104I (2 = 0)

Homework assigned, in minutes, 1980–1981: T24C
Recode T24C (1 = 0) (2 = 7.5) (3 = 23) (4 = 38) (5 = 53) (6 = 75)

Initial (tenth grade) student achievement, total: Mean(MATH10,SCI10, READ10, WRIT10,VOC10)

Mother closely monitors schoolwork: BB046A

Mother's education: BB042

Mother worked while student in high school: BB037A

Parent involvement: Mean(FY58A,FY58B,FY58C,FY58D)

Parent involvement indicators:

Attended PTA meetings: FY58A

Attended parent-teacher conferences: FY58B

Visited classes: FY58C

Phoned the school about problems: FY58D

Parental relationships: Mean(P37A1,P37B1,P37C1)

Parental relationship indicators:

Unconstrained by rules (Informal): P37A1

Predictable: P37B1

Cooperative: P37C1

Parent-school contacts: Mean(School contacts parents, Parent involvement)

Parents closely monitor schoolwork: Mean(Father closely monitors schoolwork, Mother closely monitors school work)

Parents' education: Mean(BB039,BB042)

Recode BB039 BB042 (1,11 = missing) (2 = 10) (3 = 12) (4 = 13) (5 = 14) (6 = 13) (7 = 14) (8 = 16) (9 = 18) (10 = 20)

Parents' expectations: Mean(BB050A,BB050B,BB066)

Recode BB050A BB050B (1 = 1) (Otherwise = 0)

BB066 (1 = 10) (2 = 12) (3 = 13) (4 = 14) (5 = 13) (6 = 14) (7 = 16) (8 = 18) (9 = 20) (10 = missing)

Per pupil expenditures: Mean (SB053A,SB053B)

Personnel barriers faced by school:

Central office hiring control: P19H

Union hiring constraints: P19I

Union firing constraints: P27E

Recode P19H P19I P27E (99 = 1)

Personnel constraint: Mean(Teacher union or association influence over Hiring and Firing, Central office hiring control, Union hiring constraints, Union firing constraints, School hires competent teachers over teachers with seniority)

Principal's dedication to teaching: Mean(Principal's teaching experience, Principal's administrative aspirations)

Principal's teaching experience: P49

Principal's administrative aspirations: P58

Recode P58 (1 = 2) (2 = 3)

Principal's motivation: Mean(Preference for control, Preference for career advancement)

Preference for career advancement: 4-P59G

Preference for control: Min(P59D,P59E,P59F)

Recode P59D P59E P59F P59G to maintain original ordering on a one to four scale

Principal's vision: Mean(T19K,T19R,T19HH,T19JJ,T19M,T03A)

Race of student: BB089

Racial composition of the student body, percent black: SB0094S

Racial composition of the student body, percent Hispanic: SB0093S

School board influence: Mean(School board influence over Curriculum, Instruction, Hiring, Firing, Discipline)

School board influence over:

Curriculum: P32F1 – P32A1

Discipline: P34F2 – P34A2

Hiring: P33F2 – P33A2

Firing: P34F1 – P34A1

Instruction: P32F2 – P32A2

    Recode P32A1 P32A2 P33A2 P34A1 P34A2 P32F1 P32F2 P33F2 P34F1
    P34F2 (99 = 1)

School contacts parents:

  By newsletter once a semester: P39A

  If student is absent 2-3 days: P39B

  If grades become low: P39C

    Recode P39A P39B P39C (2 = 0)

School hires competent teachers over teachers with seniority: P35S

    Recode P35S (1,2,3 = 0) (4,5,6 = 1)

School objectives:

  Basic literacy: P06A

  Citizenship: P06B

  Specific occupational skills: P06C

  Good work habits: P06D

  Academic excellence: P06E

  Personal growth and fulfillment: P06F

  Human relations skills: P06G

    Recode (If P06H GT P06? Then P06? = P06? – 1)

School organization, comprehensive measure: Mean(– Priority of excellence,
  – Principal's motivation, Teaching esteem, Teacher professionalism, Staff
  harmony, Disciplinary fairness and effectiveness, – Administrative routines in classroom, Graduation requirements, Homework assignments,
  Academic track enrollment)

School organization, condensed measure: Mean(– Priority of excellence,
  – Principal's motivation, Teaching esteem, Teacher professionalism, Teacher
  cooperation, Disciplinary fairness and effectiveness, Academic track
  enrollment)

School region: SCHREGN

School sector: SCHSAMP

    Recode SCHSAMP (0,1,2,3 = 0) (5,6,7,8,9 = 1)

Size of high school (high school enrollment): Sum(P62A1,P62A2, P62A3,
  P62A4) Unstandardized

Staff harmony: Mean(Principal's vision, Teacher collegiality, Teacher cooperation)

Student disciplinary problem indicators:

  Not attending school: YB019A

  Cutting classes: YB019B

  Talking back to teachers: YB019C

  Disobeying instructions: YB019D

Fighting: YB019E

Student disciplinary problems: Mean(−Student reports of disciplinary problems, −School reports of student violence)

Student reports of disciplinary problems: Mean(YB019A,YB019B,YB019C, YB019D,YB019E,YB019F)

School reports of student violence: Mean(SB056G,SB056H,SB056I, SB056J,SB056K,SB056L,SB056M,SB056N)

Student expected to attend college:

By father: BB050A

By mother: BB050B

Student status, senior year (In school, Dropout, Transfer, Early Graduate): FUSTTYPE

Student-teacher ratio: Sum(P62A1,P62A2,P62A3,P62A4)/P62B

Student violence indicators:

Physical conflicts among students: SB056G

Conflicts between teachers and students: SB056H

Robbery or theft: SB056I

Vandalism of school property: SB056J

Student use of drugs or alcohol: SB056K

Rape or attempted rape: SB056L

Student possession of weapons: SB056M

Verbal abuse of teachers: SB056N

Student's own disciplinary problems: Mean(BB059B, BB059D, BB059E)

Recode BB059B BB059D BB059E (2 = 0)

Superintendent or Central office influence over:

Curriculum: Max(P32B1,P32C1) − P32A1

Instruction: Max(P32B2,P32C2) − P32A2

Hiring: Max(P33B2,P33C2) − P33A2

Firing: Max(P34B1,P34C1) − P34A1

Discipline: Max(P34B2,P34C2) − P34A2

Recode P32A1 P32B1 P32C1 P32A2 P32B2 P32C2 P33A2 P33B2 P33C2 P34A1 P34B1 P34C1 P34A2 P34B2 P34C2 (99 = 1)

Suspensions or expulsions annually: Sum (P13A1,P13B1,P13C1,P13D1,P13A2, P13B2,P13C2,P13D2)/Sum(P62A1,P62A2,P62A3,P62A4)

Teacher absenteeism problem: Mean(−P63/P62B, −SB044,SB056E,SB056F)

Teacher collegiality: Mean(T19D,T19E,T19DD,T19GG,T12)

Recode T12 (1 = 0) (2 = 1.5) (3 = 4) (4 = 7.5) (5 = 15) (6 = 25)

Teacher cooperation: Mean(T19C,T19KK,T13,T03D)

Recode T03A T03D (7 = 0)

T13 (1 = .125) (2 = .375) (3 = .75) (4 = 3) (5 = 7.5) (6 = 15)

Teacher efficacy: Mean(T19F,T19II)

Teacher influence: Mean(T01A,T01B,T01C,T01D,T02D)

Teacher professionalism: Mean(Teacher influence, Teacher efficacy, Teacher
   absenteeism problem)
Teacher salary, maximum paid: P20B
Teacher salary, midpoint of salary range: Mean(P20A,P20B)
Teacher salary, minimum paid: P20A
Teacher union or association influence over:
   Firing: P34G1 – P34A1
   Hiring: P33G2 – P33A2
   Recode P33A2 P33G2 P34A1 P34G1 (99 = 1)
Teaching esteem: Mean(Principal's dedication to teaching, Teachers judged
   excellent by principal)
Teaching experience, percent of teachers with 10+ years at same school:
   SB045
Teachers judged excellent by principal: P29D
Tenth grade enrollment: P62A2
Two parents in home: 1 if (BB036B EQ 1 or BB036C EQ 1) and (BB036D EQ
   1 or BB036E EQ 1), 0 if (BB036B NE 1 and BB036C NE 1) or (BB036D
   NE 1 and BB036E NE 1)
Type of control: Same as school sector
Location of school: SCHURB
Union firing constraints: P27E
   Recode P27E (99 = 1)
Union hiring constraints: P19I
   Recode P19I (99 = 1)
Vocational track enrollment, percent of tenth grade: Sum(SB017C1Y,
   SB017C2Y, SB017C3Y,SB017C4Y,SB017C5Y,SB017C6Y,SB017C7Y)
Writing assignments per academic year: T27 × P02
   Recode T27 (1 = 0) (2 = 1.5) (3 = 3.5) (4 = 5.5) (5 = 7.5) (6 = 9.5) (7 = 12)

Survey Indicators

The variables listed include all of those employed in analyses reported
in the book and select variables employed in preliminary analyses not
reported in the book.

HSB Student Variables

BB002	High school program
BB036B	Father lives in household with student
BB036C	Other male guardian lives in household with student

BB036D	Mother lives in household with student
BB036E	Other female guardian lives in household with student
BB037A	Mother worked while student in high school
BB037B	Mother worked while student in elementary school
BB039	Father's education
BB042	Mother's education
BB046A	Mother monitors school work
BB046B	Father monitors school work
BB050A	Father's expectations
BB050B	Mother's expectations
BB053F	Effectiveness of discipline
BB053G	Fairness of discipline
BB059B	Disciplinary problems in school
BB059D	Suspended or put on probation
BB059E	Cut classes
BB066	Schooling your mother wants you to get
BB089	Race
BB090	Origin or descent
BB101	Family income by one-sevenths
BB104C	Encyclopedia in home
BB104D	Typewriter in home
BB104G	More than fifty books in home
BB104I	Pocket calculator in home
BYSES	Base year SES composite
FUSTTYPE	First follow-up student type
FY4A	Course work in Math tenth grade to twelfth grade
FY4B	Course work in English tenth grade to twelfth grade
FY4C	Course work in French tenth grade to twelfth grade
FY4D	Course work in German tenth grade to twelfth grade
FY4E	Course work in Spanish tenth grade to twelfth grade
FY4F	Course work in other language tenth grade to twelfth grade
FY4G	Course work in History tenth grade to twelfth grade
FY4H	Course work in Science tenth grade to twelfth grade
FY58A	Parents attended PTA meetings
FY58B	Parents attended parent-teacher conferences
FY58C	Parents visited classes
FY58D	Parents saw or phoned teacher
FYVOCBRT	Senior Vocabulary number right
FYREADRT	Senior Reading number right
FYMTH1RT	Senior Math level 1 number right
FYMTH2RT	Senior Math level 2 number right
FYSCINRT	Senior Science number right

FYWRITRT	Senior Writing number right
MATH10	Sophomore IRT score-Math
MATH12	Senior IRT score-Math
MATHLOG	IRT log gain score-Math
READ10	Sophomore IRT score-Reading
READ12	Senior IRT score-Reading
READLOG	IRT log gain score-Reading
SCI10	Sophomore IRT score-Science
SCI12	Senior IRT score-Science
SCILOG	IRT log gain score-Science
VOC10	Sophomore IRT score-Vocabulary
VOC12	Senior IRT score-Vocabulary
VOCLOG	IRT log gain score-Vocabulary
WRIT10	Sophomore IRT score-Writing
WRIT12	Senior IRT score-Writing
WRITLOG	IRT log gain score-Writing
YB019A	Students don't attend school
YB019B	Students cut classes
YB019C	Students talk back to teachers
YB019D	Students disobey instructions
YB019E	Students fight with each other
YB019F	Students attack or threaten teachers
YBVOCBRT	Sophomore Vocabulary number right
YBREADRT	Sophomore Reading number right
YBMTH1RT	Sophomore Math part 1 number right
YBMTH2RT	Sophomore Math part 2 number right
YBSCINRT	Sophomore Science number right
YBWRITRT	Sophomore Writing number right

HSB School Variables

SB0093S	Percent of students—Hispanic
SB0094S	Percent of students—Black
SB014	Percent of students who drop out
SB017AY	Percent of tenth grade in general program
SB017BY	Percent of tenth grade in academic program
SB017C1Y	Percent of tenth grade in agricultural program
SB017C2Y	Percent of tenth grade in business occupation program
SB017C3Y	Percent of tenth grade in distributive education program
SB017C4Y	Percent of tenth grade in health occupation program
SB017C5Y	Percent of tenth grade in home economics program
SB017C6Y	Percent of tenth grade in trade occupation program

SB017C7Y	Percent of tenth grade in technical occupation program
SB017DY	Percent of tenth grade in other program
SB037	Percent of students classified as disadvantaged
SB044	Percent of teachers absent on average day
SB045	Percent of teachers at school ten years or more
SB053A	District average per pupil expenditure
SB053B	High school per pupil expenditure
SB056E	Teacher absenteeism
SB056F	Teachers lack commitment or motivation
SB056G	Physical conflicts among students
SB056H	Conflicts between students and teachers
SB056I	Robbery or theft
SB056J	Vandalism of school property
SB056K	Student use of drugs or alcohol
SB056L	Rape or attempted rape
SB056M	Student possession of weapons
SB056N	Verbal abuse of teachers
SCHREGN	School census region
SCHSAMP	School sample type
SCHURB	School urbanization code

ATS Principal Variables

P01A1	English graduation requirements
P01B1	Math graduation requirements
P01C1	Science graduation requirements
P01D1	History graduation requirements
P01E1	Foreign language graduation requirements
P02	Number of grading periods per year
P06A	Rank of literacy as a school goal
P06B	Rank of citizenship as a school goal
P06C	Rank of occupational skills as a school goal
P06D	Rank of work habits and self-discipline as a school goal
P06E	Rank of academic excellence as a school goal
P06F	Rank of personal growth as a school goal
P06G	Rank of human relations skills as a school goal
P06H	Rank of religious values as a school goal
P13A1	Students expelled for academics
P13B1	Students suspended out of school for academics
P13C1	Students suspended in school for academics
P13D1	Students removed in other ways for academics
P13A2	Students expelled for discipline

P13B2	Students suspended out of school for discipline
P13C2	Students suspended in school for discipline
P13D2	Students removed in other ways for discipline
P19H	Too much hiring control by central office
P19I	Hiring constraints imposed by teachers' organization
P20A	Lowest teacher salary paid
P20B	Highest teacher salary paid
P27E	Firing constraints imposed by teachers' organization
P29D	Percent of teachers excellent
P32A1	Influence of principal in establishing the curriculum
P32B1	Influence of superintendent in establishing the curriculum
P32C1	Influence of central office in establishing the curriculum
P32F1	Influence of school board in establishing the curriculum
P32G1	Influence of teacher union in establishing the curriculum
P32A2	Influence of principal in determining instructional methods
P32B2	Influence of superintendent in determining instructional methods
P32C2	Influence of central office in determining instructional methods
P32F2	Influence of school board in determining instructional methods
P32G2	Influence of teacher union in determining instructional methods
P33A2	Influence of principal in hiring new full-time teachers
P33B2	Influence of superintendent in hiring new full-time teachers
P33C2	Influence of central office in hiring new full-time teachers
P33F2	Influence of school board in hiring new full-time teachers
P33G2	Influence of teacher union in hiring new full-time teachers
P34A1	Influence of principal in dismissing or transferring teachers
P34B1	Influence of superintendent in dismissing or transferring teachers
P34C1	Influence of central office in dismissing or transferring teachers
P34F1	Influence of school board in dismissing or transferring teachers
P34G1	Influence of teacher union in dismissing or transferring teachers
P34A2	Influence of principal in setting disciplinary policy
P34B2	Influence of superintendent in setting disciplinary policy
P34C2	Influence of central office in setting disciplinary policy
P34F2	Influence of school board in setting disciplinary policy
P34G2	Influence of teacher union in setting disciplinary policy
P35S	Teachers are hired on the basis of competence not seniority
P37A1	Relationship with parents unconstrained by rules

P37B1	Relationship with parents predictable
P37C1	Relationship with parents cooperative
P39A	Newsletter sent to parents
P39B	Parents notified after 2–3 days of unexcused absence
P39C	Parents informed halfway through the grading period if grades are low
P40A	Increased graduation requirements
P40B	Increased homework
P40C	Longer school day
P40D	Longer school year
P40E	Established career ladders for teachers
P40F	Established performance evaluation system for teachers
P40G	Established financial incentives for performance
P40H	Established new codes of student conduct
P40I	Grouped students by academic need
P40J	Adopted eleven-month teacher contracts
P40K	Changes in social background of students
P40L	New desegregation plan implemented
P40M	Competency test for graduation
P40N	Major curriculum change
P49	Principal's years of teaching experience
P58	Desire to move to a higher administrative position
P59D	Became principal because of desire for greater control over curriculum
P59E	Became principal because of desire for greater control over quality of personnel
P59F	Became principal because of desire for greater control over other school policies
P59G	Became principal because of desire to further career
P62A1	Grade 9 membership 1984
P62A2	Grade 10 membership 1984
P62A3	Grade 11 membership 1984
P62A4	Grade 12 membership 1984
P62B	Number of fulltime teachers 1984
P63	Person-days of substitute teaching per week

ATS Teacher Variables

T01A	Teacher influence in determining student behavior codes
T01B	Teacher influence in determining the content of inservice programs

T01C	Teacher influence in setting policy on grouping students by ability
T01D	Teacher influence in establishing the school curriculum
T02D	Teacher control over disciplining students
T03A	Teaching improvement aided by principal
T03D	Teaching improvement aided by other teachers
T06	Teaching interruptions
T12	Participated in predominantly faculty social activities
T13	Time spent meeting with other teachers on lesson planning, curriculum, and so on
T19C	Effort to coordinate course content with other teachers
T19D	Can count on other staff members to help out
T19E	Colleagues share beliefs and values about the central mission of the school
T19F	Success or failure in teaching students is beyond my control
T19K	Principal sets priorities, makes plans, and sees that they are carried out
T19M	Goals and priorities for the school are clear
T19R	Principal knows what he wants and has communicated it to the staff
T19U	Routine duties and paperwork interfere with teaching
T19DD	Great deal of cooperative effort among staff members
T19GG	School seems like a big family, everyone is so close and cordial
T19HH	Principal lets staff members know what is expected of them
T19II	Feel it is a waste of time to do my best as a teacher
T19JJ	Principal is interested in innovation and new ideas
T19KK	Familiar with the content and goals of courses taught by other teachers
T21B	Hours spent completing forms and administrative paperwork
T23	Percent of students fooling around during instruction
T24C	Homework assigned per class period, 1980–1981
T25A	Percent of completed homework recorded
T25B	Percent of homework graded or corrected and returned to students
T26C1	Class time spent reviewing an exam
T26C2	Class time spent reviewing a quiz
T27	Writing assignments per grading period

Appendix C

Special Issues in Modeling Student Achievement

IN THIS appendix we examine the following special issues: selection bias, tracking, and predicting student achievement gains.

Selection Bias

As we explained in chapter 4, estimates of the effects of schools on student achievement can be biased by problems of selection. Because students sometimes select the schools that they attend, it can be difficult to distinguish the academic benefits that schools provide students from the benefits that students bring with them when they select a school. We have tried to overcome this difficulty with several strategies. We employed an extensive array of controls for student background to try to distinguish students who would select a special school from students who would not. We measured student achievement with gain scores to avoiding crediting schools with academic achievement that occurred before students entered high school. And, in appendix D, we repeat our analysis of student achievement (and our analysis of school organization) on a sample of only public schools. By excluding private schools from that analysis, we eliminate the schools that are most likely to introduce selection bias into our results.

There is an additional way in which selection bias may affect our results, however. Students not only select themselves into schools, they select themselves out. In high schools, many students drop out before receiving a diploma. Other students, much fewer in number, graduate early or transfer to other schools. By and large, students make these moves of their own volition, but occasionally schools may encourage or force them to. Either way, early student departures can bias an analysis of student achievement. If students who leave high school early are excluded from the sample on which the analysis of student achievement is based, the analysis will not have a complete picture of the relationship between schooling and achievement. The analysis will have a picture of the relationship only for those students who stay in high school through graduation.

This limited picture of the high school experience threatens to give a distorted view of the effects of schools on achievement. If the students who are excluded from the sample being analyzed are not a random group, but are instead a group whose achievement differs systematically from the students being analyzed, the relationship between schooling and achievement for students who remain in high school will provide a biased estimate of the schooling-achievement relationship for the population of all students, as well as for the population of students who remain in school.[1] Because students who leave high school early are most likely to be dropouts, it is probable that the students who remain in school, and available for analysis, are more academically able, on average, than the students who leave school early. Analyzing only students who remain in school may therefore provide a biased estimate of the relationship between schooling and academic achievement.

The potential for such bias is evident in the ATS schools. In high performance schools (schools in the top quartile of achievement gains), the sample attrition rate between the end of the sophomore and the end of the senior years, due to dropping out, was only 10.6 percent. In low performance schools, the attrition rate due to dropping out was 16.9 percent.[2] Academic achievement and dropout rates appear to be related. If we were to estimate the relationship between schooling and achievement without taking sample attrition into account, we would therefore run some risk of misestimating the relationship.

To take attrition due to selection into account we follow a now well-established procedure.[3] It has been shown that the bias introduced into regression models by sample selection is equivalent to the bias introduced by the more general specification error of excluding relevant variables. When sample selection is a problem, the dependent variable in the regression is being determined by two processes, one due to the independent variables in the regression (the substantive process), but a second due to selection variables that limit the values of the dependent variable observed in the sample. Unless the second process (the selection process) is taken into account, the substantive process might be credited for effects on the dependent variable that are really due to the selection process. The remedy is to respecify the substantive model to include a measure of the influence of the selection process.

In particular, the substantive model must include a measure of the "hazard rate," which represents the instantaneous probability that any given observation is excluded from the sample. The hazard rate (λ_i) is obtained from the formula:

$$\lambda_i = \frac{f(z_i)}{1 - F(z_i)}$$

In this formula, z_i is the negative of the predicted value from a probit equation that models the likelihood of each observation being included in the sample. Because z_i is the negative of the predicted value, though, it will capture the likelihood of being excluded from the sample. The hazard rate is given by the ratio of the density of the predicted value, and 1.0 minus the cumulative distribution of the predicted value. The larger this ratio, the greater the likelihood of an observation being excluded from the sample.

Because the ATS-HSB students were surveyed at two points in time, it is a straightforward matter to construct hazard rates. We can use the information that we have from the sophomore survey to build a probit model of the likelihood that a sophomore will remain in school to participate in the senior survey. In table C-1 we describe the probit model that we use to calculate hazard rates. The dependent variable in the model is a dichotomy that takes the value 1.0 if the student remained in school and was retested as a senior, and the value 0 if the student left school, for any reason (dropped out, transferred, graduated early), prior to the senior tests. Among the independent variables are three that are important determinants of student achievement gains: initial student achievement, parent socioeconomic status (SES), and school SES. These variables capture the correlation between the substantive process and the selection process. The independent variables also include several measures that are not part of our models of achievement gains: the student's own disciplinary record, the student's race (black, non-black), and the monitoring of the student's schoolwork by his or her parents. These variables are included to reduce the multicollinearity between the hazard rate and the other independent variables in our models of achievement gains.

TABLE C-1. Coefficients for Probit Model of Early School Leavers[a]

Variable	Coefficient[b]
Initial student achievement	.237*
	(.028)
Parent socioeconomic status	.130*
	(.033)
School socioeconomic status	−.087
	(.057)
Student's own disciplinary problems	−.873*
	(.065)
Race of student (black, nonblack)	−.002*
	(.001)
Parents closely monitor school work	.381*
	(.055)
Constant	6.168*
	(.051)
Sample size	8,206

* Statistically significant, $\alpha \leq .05$, $t \geq 1.64$, one-tail test.
a. Dependent variable is a dummy measure, taking on the value 1.0 if student status, senior year was "in school," 0 otherwise.
b. Coefficients are linear probit estimates; standard errors are in parentheses.

As table C-1 reports, all of the variables, except school SES, are statistically significant, and most are significant by large measures. In addition, all of the statistically significant variables operate as expected. Students are more likely to stay in school—and in the study—the higher their initial achievement and family socioeconomic status (SES), and the more their parents monitor their schoolwork. Students are less likely to remain in school if they are black and if they have disciplinary problems.

When these coefficients are used to obtain predicted values, and in turn, to calculate hazard rates, the hazard rates also work as expected in our models of student achievement gains. In chapter 4, the coefficient on the selection bias correction variable (the hazard rate) was consistently negative and significant. Students at higher risk of leaving school early tend to post lower achievement gain scores. Because our models of achievement gains incorporate this tendency, the coefficients on the other variables in those models should not be biased by sample selection due to early school departures.

Tracking

Among the indicators that we used in chapter 4 to construct an index of effective school organization was the percentage of students enrolled in an academic track. We included the indicator to capture what appeared, in chapter 3, to be a clear difference in the educational practices of high and low performance schools: students in successful schools were more likely to be enrolled in an academic program of study and to take relatively heavy academic courseloads than were students in unsuccessful schools. When we analyzed student achievement, we learned that academic track enrollment is indeed related to achievement gains. The effect of school organization is stronger when the percentage of academic students in the school is part of the measure of school organization. And the percentage of academic track students has a significant independent impact on achievement when it is not part of the measure of school organization.

As we explained in chapter 4, however, the impact of academic tracking must be interpreted cautiously. Far more than any other characteristic of school organization, the level of academic track participation is likely to be a consequence of the academic caliber of the students in a school. For this reason, as much as for the independent significance of tracking, we decided to remove academic track enrollments from our measure of school organization and to analyze tracking as a separate influence on student achievement. This decision also led us to change how tracking was measured in our models of student achievement. We substituted the student's own track or program (academic, nonacademic) for the school's academic program enrollment percentage. This was the first step in trying to disentangle the school and student effects that academic track enrollments captured.

Our next step was to reestimate the two final models of student achievement gains, models 4 and 12. The coefficients for the reestimated models are reported in table C-2. Only two points need to be made about these estimates. The first is that the new measure of tracking does not substantially change the coefficients of the other independent variables. All of the coefficients remain significant and retain their relative magnitudes. The coefficients on school organization (comprehensive and condensed) in table C-2 are identical in value to the coefficients on school organization reported in tables 4-10 and 4-

TABLE C-2. Estimates of Final Models of Student Achievement Gains, with Academic Track Measured as a Dummy Variable at the Student Level, All Students[a]

Variable	Model[b]	
	4A	12A
Selection bias correction	−.075*	−.077*
	(.030)	(.030)
Initial student achievement	.019*	.019*
	(.005)	(.005)
School organization, comprehensive without percent of students in academic track	.011*	. . .
	(.004)	
School organization, condensed, without percent of students in academic track	. . .	.016*
		(.004)
Parent socioeconomic status	.021*	.020*
	(.005)	(.005)
School socioeconomic status	.024*	.017*
	(.009)	(.009)
Student in academic track	.051*	.050*
	(.006)	(.006)
Constant	.182*	.183*
	(.007)	(.007)
Adjusted R^2	.058	.059
Sample size	7,276	7,276

* Statistically significant, $\alpha \leq .05$, $t \geq 1.64$, one-tail test.
a. Achievement gains are measured with log gain scores. Sample is weighted to achieve a nationally representative sample of high school seniors.
b. Coefficients are unstandardized linear regression coefficients; standard errors are in parentheses.

11. In short, our models of student achievement gains are robust with respect to the measurement of tracking.

The other point that must be made about the results in table C-2 is that enrollment in an academic program has a significant and sizable impact on student achievement. This is evident in the model's explanatory power. The adjusted R^2 values for models 4A and 12A are 12 percent and 11 percent higher than the adjusted R^2 values for models 4 and 12 respectively, in which tracking is measured at the school level but not at the student level too.

The tracking coefficients in models 4A and 12A do not fully clarify the contribution of school tracking practices to student achievement, however. The coefficients in table C-2 only tell us that students taking an academic program achieve more than students who are not taking an academic program, all else being equal. To be sure, this indicates

TABLE C-3. Coefficients and Predicted Values for Probit Model of Academic Track Enrollment, All Students[a]

Variable	Coefficient[b]	Variable mean	Predicted value
Initial student achievement	.485* (.022)	−.003	−.0015
School organization, comprehensive, without percent of students in academic track[c]	.260* (.017)	$Q_1 = -1.132$ $Q_4 = 1.401$	−.2943 .3643
Parent socioeconomic status	.098* (.025)	.042	.0041
Parent expectations	.344* (.021)	−.054	−.0186
Constant	4.695* (.016)		4.695
Sample size 7,394	. . .	. . .	. . .
Probability of average student being in academic track in[d]			
Ineffectively organized school	. . .	. . .	.2692
Effectively organized school	. . .	. . .	.5173

* Statistically significant, $\alpha \leq .05$, $t \geq 1.64$, one-tail test.
a. Dependent variable is a dummy measure, taking on the value 1 if student is in the academic track, 0 otherwise.
b. Coefficients are linear probit estimates; standard errors are in parentheses.
c. Variable means and predicted values are provided for the lowest (Q_1) and highest (Q_4) quartiles of the distribution of school organization values.
d. "Ineffective" and "effective" schools are those in the lowest and highest quartiles, respectively, of the school organization variable. The probabilities are obtained by summing the predicted values of the variables in the probit model (minus an arbitrary constant, 5.0) and interpreting the sum with a table of values of the cumulative normal distribution.

that schools are providing academic programs and courses that are relatively effective. But the effective use of tracking means more than offering rigorous courses to some students; it means challenging all students with courses that demand that they do their best. Tracking, however, often does not do this. It often routes only the most able students into academically ambitious programs.

We are interested in this influence of tracking—the influence that schools have on which track individuals are enrolled in—as well as the influence that academic course work has on achievement. The results in table C-2 tell us only about the influence of academic course work on achievement. This effect, however, is not entirely or perhaps even mostly a result of school tracking practices. Many students in academic programs are in them only because their academic backgrounds are strong and not because their school encourages all students to participate in rigorous programs.

To determine the influence that schools have on the programs of study that students take, we estimated a probit model of a student's high school track (academic, nonacademic), in which we controlled for influences on program choice other than the influence of the school itself. To gauge the influence of the school on program choice, we employed our comprehensive measure of school organization (without academic track enrollments). If effective schools are indeed ones that are able to establish strong academic orientations, they ought to place more students into academic programs, all else being equal, than schools that are ineffective do.

In table C-3 we report the final estimates of our probit model of a student's high school track. As expected, academic track participation is significantly influenced by a student's initial achievement and family SES. A student is also more likely to be in an academic track if his or her parents have high expectations for his or her ultimate level of educational attainment. But schools themselves make a substantial difference for the programs of study in which students are enrolled. An average student in an ineffectively organized school has a probability of only .2692 of being in an academic track. An average student in an effectively organized school has a probability of nearly twice that (.5173) of taking an academic program of study. Since students in academic programs achieve more than students who are not in such programs, schools have a sizable impact on student achievement through their use of tracking. Exactly how sizable is the issue to which we now turn.

Predicting Student Achievement Gains

In chapter 4 we explained that the coefficients of our models of student achievement are difficult to interpret directly. We therefore developed an indirect method of weighing their importance. We used the unstandardized coefficients to predict differences in achievement gain scores between students at the mean of the lowest quartile and students at the mean of the highest quartile of each independent variable. We then divided these differences by the mean annual achievement gain score for all students. This provided us a measure of years of achievement gains due to each independent variable.

TABLE C-4. Predicting Student Achievement Gains in Years, All Students[a]

Predictors of achievement gains[b]	Quartile means		Model 1				Model 4A				Model 9				Model 12A			
	Lowest	Highest	B	$\hat{Q}_1$	$\hat{Q}_4$	Δ	B	$\hat{Q}_1$	$\hat{Q}_4$	Δ	B	$\hat{Q}_1$	$\hat{Q}_4$	Δ	B	$\hat{Q}_1$	$\hat{Q}_4$	Δ
Initial achievement	-1.116	1.107	.027	-.030	.030	.060	.019	-.021	.021	.042	.027	-.030	.030	.060	.019	-.021	.021	.042
Predicted two-year gain						.65				.45				.65				.45
Organization, comprehensive	-1.118	1.365	.017	-.019	.023	.042												
Predicted two-year gain						.45												
Organization, comprehensive, without percent academic	-1.132	1.401					.011	-.012	.015	.027								
Predicted two-year gain										.29								
Organization, condensed	-1.379	1.372									.022	-.030	.030	.060				
Predicted two-year gain														.65				
Organization, condensed, without percent academic	-1.320	1.414													.016	-.021	.023	.044
Predicted two-year gain																		.47
Parent socioeconomic status	-.856	.996	.023	-.020	.023	.043	.021	-.018	.021	.039	.023	-.020	.023	.043	.020	-.017	.020	.037
Predicted two-year gain						.46				.42				.46				.40
School socioeconomic status	-.502	.540	.021	-.011	.011	.022	.024	-.012	.013	.025	.013	-.007	.007	.014	.017	-.009	.009	.018
Predicted two-year gain						.24				.27				.15				.19
Academic tracking policy	.269	.517					.051	.014	.026	.012					.050	.013	.026	.013
Predicted two-year gain										.13								.14

a. The parameters reported for each model are as follows:
B = regression coefficient for predictor variable from previously estimated model.
$\hat{Q}_1$ = predicted total log gain, as a function of predictor variable, for student at the mean of the lowest quartile of the predictor variable—the product of B and the lowest quartile mean.
$\hat{Q}_4$ = predicted total log gain, as a function of predictor variable, for student at the mean of the highest quartile of the predictor variable—the product of B and the highest quartile mean.
Δ = predicted change in total log gain associated with change in predictor variable from mean of lowest quartile to mean of highest quartile.

b. To convert the predicted total log gains to years or grade equivalents, the predicted log gains (Δ) are compared to one-half the average log gain for all students over the final two years of high school, or .5 (.186) = .093. For example, the effect of initial achievement on achievement gains is given by .060/.093 = .65 year of predicted achievement over the last two years of high school.

To clarify these calculations, which are described in table C-4, it is useful to consider an example. In the first row of table C-4, under the column labeled model 1, we calculate the impact of initial student achievement on student achievement gains. The mean student achievement score for the lowest quartile of the distribution of initial student achievement is -1.116. The mean score for the highest quartile is 1.107. The unstandardized regression coefficient for initial student achievement in model 1 is 0.027. Assuming all else is equal, the difference in the predicted achievement gain scores between students in the two quartiles is the difference between the products of the regression coefficient and the respective quartile means: $(.027)(1.107) - (.027)(-1.116) = (.030) - (-.030) = .060$. Because the average achievement gain score for all students during the final two years of high school was $.186$, the average annual achievement gain score is half that, $.093$. Dividing the predicted difference in gain scores due to differences in initial achievement $(.060)$ by the average annual achievement gain for all students $(.093)$ yields a predicted difference in gain scores due to initial achievement of 0.65 year (or grade equivalent) of achievement over the final two years of high school. The same calculations provide comparable estimates of the effects of the other independent variables on achievement gains.

We use somewhat different calculations to estimate the effects of tracking, however. Because we want to know the impact that school tracking practices, as well as academic courses, have on student achievement, we cannot evaluate differences in the value of the tracking variable in models 4A and 12A. That variable—a dichotomy that cannot be divided into quartiles anyway—provides an estimate of the effect that participation in an academic program has on student achievement, once the student is in the academic program. To gauge the overall effect of tracking, we need to allow for the influence that schools have over which students are in an academic program. To do this, we calculate the expected value of academic tracking for students attending schools in the bottom and top quartiles of school organization.

The expected value of academic tracking is equal to the achievement effect of being enrolled in an academic track $(.051$ in model 4A, and $.050$ in model 12A) times the probability of being enrolled in an academic track, all else being equal. We know from the probit model (table C-3) that the probabilities of an average student being enrolled in an academic track are $.269$ and $.517$ in ineffective and effective schools respectively. Hence, the difference in the expected value of academic tracking between effective and ineffective schools is .13 year or .14 year of achievement, depending on whether model 4A or 12A is used to predict it. Because these predictions, like the other predictions in table C-4, are based on changes from the bottom quartile to the top quartile of an independent variable, they are directly comparable to the predictions for the other independent variables. As we discussed in chapter 4, these estimates indicate that while tracking makes an important contribution to student achievement, its contribution is contingent on, and much smaller than, the contribution of the organization variable. Moreover, the effect of tracking is in fact an organizational effect—the effect of school tracking policy.

Appendix D

Achievement and Organization in Public Schools

DESPITE THE sharp distinction we draw between the institutions of politics and markets, our perspective on schools is not solely intended to account for differences between public and private schools. It is based on general concepts—institutional structure, bureaucratic autonomy, and school organization—and is intended to account for differences among schools of all types. Our empirical analysis is also meant to be general. It seeks to explain the variation in achievement, organization, and autonomy among all schools. It seeks explanations in terms that are equally applicable in the public and the private sectors. Nevertheless, the fact that school sector proves to be the strongest determinant of school autonomy, and by implication, to have pervasive consequences for school organization and performance, may raise questions about the generality and validity of our analysis.

The first and most important question concerns the applicability of our findings to public schools. Because private schools are disproportionately likely to enjoy autonomy, to be organized effectively, and to post large achievement gains (38 percent of our high performance schools are private while only 2 percent of our low performance schools are private), the relationships we observe between autonomy and organization and between organization and achievement might possibly represent a "private school effect" and may not hold among schools in the public sector. We would be surprised if this proved to be the case—for neither our own perspective nor mainstream education research provides any theoretical basis for expecting effective school characteristics or autonomy to prove unimportant in public schools. Still, our empirical analysis leaves open the possibility that our results have more to do with differences between public and private schools than with differences among public schools.

Second, there is the question of selection bias. Public and private schools are difficult to compare or to analyze simultaneously because they tend to have fundamentally different relationships with their students. In private schools the relationship is generally voluntary while in public schools it usually is not. Because of this difference, which is very difficult to measure and control directly, there must always be some doubt about statistical estimates that indicate that public and private schools are different. There is always the possibility that selection—of schools by students and students by schools—is responsible for some of the differences that seem to exist between public and private schools.[1] We went to great lengths throughout our analysis to try to purge our various estimates of selection bias. We are as confident in our results as statistical precautions permit us to be. We acknowledge, however, that there is still room for doubt since school sector proves so important in our results.

The best way to address this lingering doubt is to drop private schools from our sample and repeat our analyses of student achievement and school organization using public schools.[2] To the extent that the results for public schools are the same as the results for all schools, we can have greater confidence that the findings reported in the book are general and valid.

Student Achievement

In chapter 4 we modeled student achievement for all students as a linear function of six factors: student ability, family background, peer group influence, school economic resources, school organization, and a correction for selection bias (due to sample attrition). Here we model the achievement of public school students as a function of the same factors, measured with the same indexes and indicators as in chapter 4.

The estimates for the first set of regression models are reported in table D-1. These results can be compared directly with the results for all students reported in table 4-8. By and large, the results in the two tables are the same. The unstandardized regression coefficients, which can be compared directly across samples, differ only marginally. The coefficient on school organization, for example, is .017 for all students

TABLE D-1. Estimates of Models of Student Achievement Gains Using Comprehensive Measure of School Organization, Public School Students[a]

	Model[b]		
Variable	1	2	3
Selection bias correction	−.090*	−.087*	−.090*
	(.031)	(.032)	(.032)
	−.051	−.049	−.051
Initial student achievement	.031*	.031*	.031*
	(.005)	(.005)	(.005)
	.111	.111	.111
School organization, comprehensive	.015*	.016*	.015*
	(.005)	(.005)	(.005)
	.039	.040	.039
Parent socioeconomic status	.022*	.022*	.022*
	(.005)	(.006)	(.006)
	.064	.065	.064
School socioeconomic status	.016	.013	.015
	(.010)	(.011)	(.010)
	.025	.021	.024
School percent black	...	−.00009	...
		(.00016)	
		−.009	
School economic resources	...	...	.002
			(.005)
			.004
Constant	.203*	.204*	.203*
	(.007)	(.008)	(.008)
Adjusted R^2	.044	.044	.044
Sample size	5,795	5,795	5,716

* Statistically significant, $\alpha \leq .05$, $t \geq 1.64$, one-tail test.
a. Achievement gains are measured with log gain scores. Sample weighted to achieve a nationally representative sample of public high school seniors.
b. Coefficients are unstandardized linear regression coefficients; standard errors are in parentheses. Standardized coefficients (betas) are in italics.

and either .015 or .016 for public school students. In public schools, as in all schools, the racial composition of the school (its percent black) does not have a significant effect on student achievement once other effects are taken into account.[3] The same is true of school economic resources. All things being equal, public schools do not produce higher levels of student achievement as schools increase their per pupil expenditures and reduce their student-teacher ratios. This finding is already well established in education research, but it is nonetheless useful to observe that our negative findings about school economic resources are not artifacts of analyzing public schools and private schools (which are often poorly financed) together. Indeed, the only finding that changes in a meaningful way when public schools are analyzed alone is that the influence of school socioeconomic status (SES) weakens to the point of nonsignificance. This difference is not especially important, however. In the full sample, school SES was barely significant.

In table D-2 we continue the parallel analysis of student achievement. In table 4-10 we tried to determine whether the influence of school organization on student achievement was the result of specific school practices, or whether it was the product of some more general syndrome. We therefore modeled student achievement as a function of specific school practices and various truncated measures of school organization. When we repeat this procedure for public schools, we get virtually the same results as we did for all schools. The unstandardized coefficients on the major variables—initial student achievement, parent SES, and school organization—again differ only marginally. All of the individual school practices except academic tracking are nonsignificant in both samples. And the independent effect of academic track enrollments is exactly the same for public school students as it is for all students. The effect of school organization when academic track enrollments are not part of the organizational index is .010 for public school students and .011 for all students. The only coefficients that are noticeably different in the two tables are again those for school SES. But in this set of models the coefficient on school SES is slightly stronger than it was in the first set of models, and it achieves statistical significance in models 7 and 8.

The next step in our original analysis of student achievement was to examine the robustness of the influence of school organization. To that end we estimated the influence of alternative measures of school organization, each constructed by eliminating one of that measure's original indicators. Ultimately, this led us to construct a new condensed index of school organization, containing all of the basic components of the original measure but only the strongest measures of those components.

For public schools we did not repeat the variable-by-variable tests for robustness. For the sake of comparability, we simply adopted the same condensed measure of school organization and used it to analyze public school achievement. The results, in table D-3, are essentially the same as those for all schools reported in table 4-11. As before, the condensed measure increases the estimated influence of school organization markedly—to .023 in public schools, compared with .022 in all schools. When academic track enrollments are removed from the condensed organizational measure, the influence of school organization falls—to .017 in public schools compared with .016 in all schools—and the effect of an academic program remains roughly the same (.013 in public schools versus .012 in all schools).

The only difference between the samples is, again, the weaker influence of school SES in public schools. It is not much weaker, though. When all schools were analyzed using the condensed measure of organization, school SES also became nonsignificant. Nevertheless, the influence of school SES is sufficiently weak in this set of public school models to exclude school SES from further equations. Doing so, however, has no effect on the other results. As we show in models 11 and 12, excluding school SES does not enable other variables— school percent black and school economic resources—to achieve levels even close to statistical significance.

The final step in our original analysis of achievement was to predict the differences in achievement gains between students with high values and students with low values on each of the independent variables. We did this to gauge the relative influences of the independent variables, and to obtain measures of achievement gains that could be readily converted into one clear metric: years of achievement.

This was a straightforward procedure for all of the variables except academic track enrollments. As we explained in appendix C, we had to follow an intermediate procedure to obtain a measure of the influence of tracking as a school practice. The procedure is repeated for public schools in tables D-4 and D-5. In table D-4 we reestimate two final models of achievement, models 4 and 13 (comparable to models 4 and 12 in the analysis of all schools), using a dummy variable measure of academic track. The reestimates of the public school models show much the same differences as the reestimates of the models for all schools (table C-2). The dummy measure of academic tracking weakens the influence of school organization noticeably, and weakens the influence of the other variables somewhat. The only noteworthy difference between the estimates for the two samples is that the coefficient on academic track is about 20 percent larger for all schools

TABLE D-2. Estimates of Models of Student Achievement Gains Separating School Policies from Comprehensive Measure of School Organization, Public School Students[a]

Variable	Model[b]				
	4	5	6	7	8
Selection bias correction	-.092*	-.089*	-.090*	-.094*	-.092*
	(.032)	(.032)	(.032)	(.032)	(.032)
	-.052	-.050	-.051	-.053	-.052
Initial student achievement	.031*	.031*	.031*	.032*	.031*
	(.005)	(.005)	(.005)	(.005)	(.005)
	.111	.111	.111	.113	.111
School organization, comprehensive, without:					
Percent of students in academic track	.010*	...	...	...	...
	(.005)				
	.026				
Amount of homework assigned	...	.015*	...	...	...
		(.005)			
		.038			
Graduation requirements	...	...	.016*	...	...
			(.005)		
			.041		
Administrative routines in classroom	...	...	...	.016*	...
				(.005)	
				.043	
Disciplinary policy	...	...	...	...	.015*
					(.005)
					.041

Parent socioeconomic status	.021*	.021*	.022*	.022*	.021*
	(.005)	(.005)	(.006)	(.005)	(.006)
	.064	*.062*	*.065*	*.065*	*.064*
School socioeconomic status	.017*	.017*	.015	.016	.011
	(.010)	(.010)	(.011)	(.010)	(.011)
	.027	*.027*	*.023*	*.024*	*.018*
Percent of students in academic track	⋮	⋮	⋮	⋮	.013*
					(.004)
					.044
Amount of homework assigned	⋮	⋮	⋮	.002	⋮
				(.004)	
				.007	
Graduation requirements	⋮	⋮	.0007	⋮	⋮
			(.0032)		
			.003		
Administrative routines in classroom	⋮	.004	⋮	⋮	⋮
		(.004)			
		.051			
Disciplinary policy	−.002	⋮	⋮	⋮	⋮
	(.004)				
	−.005				
Constant	.203*	.204*	.203*	.203*	.205*
	(.007)	(.007)	(.008)	(.007)	(.008)
Adjusted R^2	.044	.044	.044	.044	.045
Sample size	5,795	5,795	5,601	5,795	5,484

* Statistically significant, $\alpha \leq .05$, $t \geq 1.64$, one-tail test.
a. Achievement gains are measured with log gain scores. Sample weighted to achieve a nationally representative sample of public high school seniors.
b. Coefficients are unstandardized linear regression coefficients; standard errors are in parentheses. Standardized coefficients (betas) are in italics.

TABLE D-3. Estimates of Models of Student Achievement Gains Using Condensed Measure of School Organization, Public School Students[a]

Variable	Model[b]				
	9	10	11	12	13
Selection bias correction	−.091*	−.093*	−.088*	−.091*	−.093*
	(.031)	(.031)	(.032)	(.032)	(.032)
	−.052	−.052	−.050	−.052	−.052
Initial student achievement	.032*	.031*	.031*	.031*	.031*
	(.005)	(.005)	(.005)	(.005)	(.005)
	.113	.111	.112	.113	.112
School organization condensed	.023*	.022*	.023*	.023*	. . .
	(.004)	(.005)	(.004)	(.005)	
	.067	.064	.066	.067	
School organization, condensed, without percent academic track	. . .	. . .	. . .	. . .	.017*
					(.004)
					.051
Parent socioeconomic status	.023*	.021*	.023*	.023*	.022*
	(.005)	(.005)	(.005)	(.005)	(.005)
	.068	.064	.068	.068	.067
School socioeconomic status	. . .	.007	. . .	. . .	. . .
		(.010)			
		.011			
School percent black	. . .	. . .	−.00010	. . .	. . .
			(.00014)		
			−.010		
School economic resources	. . .	. . .	. . .	.002	. . .
				(.005)	
				.005	
School percent academic track	. . .	. . .	. . .	. . .	.013*
					(.004)
					.044
Constant	.205*	.205*	.206*	.205*	.206*
	(.007)	(.007)	(.007)	(.007)	(.008)
Adjusted R^2	.046	.046	.046	.046	.046
Sample size	5,795	5,795	5,795	5,716	5,484

* Statistically significant, $\alpha \leq .05$, $t \geq 1.64$, one-tail test.

a. Achievement gains are measured with log gain scores. Sample weighted to achieve a nationally representative sample of public high school seniors. Condensed measure excludes graduation requirements, homework assignments, administrative routines in classrooms, principal's vision, teacher collegiality.

b. Coefficients are unstandardized linear regression coefficients; standard errors are in parentheses. Standardized coefficients (betas) are in italics.

TABLE D-4. Estimates of Final Models of Student Achievement
Gains, with Academic Track Measured as a Dummy Variable
at the Student Level, Public School Students[a]

	Model[b]	
Variable	4A	13A
Selection bias correction	−.081*	−.081*
	(.032)	(.032)
Initial student achievement	.024*	.025*
	(.005)	(.005)
School organization, comprehensive, without percent of students in academic track	.009* (.005)	. . .
School organization, condensed, without percent of students in academic track	. . .	.018* (.004)
Parent socioeconomic status	.019*	.022*
	(.006)	(.005)
School socioeconomic status	.021*	. . .
	(.010)	
Student in academic track	.042*	.042*
	(.007)	(.007)
Constant	.185*	.187*
	(.008)	(.008)
Adjusted R^2	.049	.050
Sample size	5,722	5,722

* Statistically significant, $\alpha \leq .05$, $t \geq 1.64$, one-tail test.
a. Achievement gains are measured with log gain scores. Sample weighted to achieve a nationally representative sample of public high school seniors.
b. Coefficients are unstandardized linear regression coefficients; standard errors are in parentheses.

than for public schools alone. This indicates that private schools may
be providing somewhat more effective instruction in their academic
courses than public schools are in theirs.

Another difference between public and private schools emerges,
however, when we continue the analysis of tracking. In table D-5 we
report the estimates of the probit model of academic track participation
for public school students. Comparing these estimates with those for
all schools in table C-3 reveals that public schools play a much less
assertive role than private schools in assigning students to academic
programs. In both samples (all schools and public schools) a student's
chances of being in an academic track increase with his or her initial
achievement, parent SES, and parent expectations. But unlike in the
sample of all schools, where the effectiveness of the school organization
also increases the chances of academic track participation substantially,

TABLE D-5. Coefficients and Predicted Values for Probit Model of Academic Track Enrollment, Public School Students[a]

Variable	Coefficient[b]	Variable mean	Predicted value
Initial student achievement	.507* (.025)	− .079	− .0400
School organization, comprehensive, without percent of students in academic track[c]	.054* (.029)	$Q_1 = -1.208$ $Q_4 = .295$	− .0652 .0159
Parent socioeconomic status	.062* (.029)	− .034	− .0021
Parent expectations	.354* (.023)	− .243	− .0860
Constant	4.586* (.021)	. . .	4.586
Sample size 5,811	. . .	. . .	. . .
Probability of average student being in academic track in[d]			
Ineffectively organized school	. . .	. . .	.2719
Effectively organized school	. . .	. . .	.2995

* Statistically significant, $\alpha \leq .05$, $t \geq 1.64$, one-tail test.

a. Dependent variable is a dummy measure, taking on the value 1 if student is in the academic track, 0 otherwise. Sample weighted to achieve a nationally representative sample of public high school seniors.

b. Coefficients are linear probit estimates; standard errors are in parentheses.

c. Variable means and predicted values are provided for the lowest (Q_1) and highest (Q_4) quartiles of the distribution of school organization values.

d. "Ineffective" and "effective" schools are those in the lowest and highest quartiles, respectively, of the school organization variable. The probabilities are obtained by summing the predicted values of the variables in the probit model (minus an arbitrary constant, 5.0) and interpreting the sum with a table of values of the cumulative normal distribution.

in the sample of public schools, school organization increases those chances only slightly. School organization has a statistically significant effect in the public school model. But an average student's probability of being in an academic track increases from only .2719 to .2995 if a student is in an effective public school rather than an ineffective one.

Be this as it may, we can now calculate the predicted differences in achievement gains due to each of the independent variables. The calculations for public schools are reported in table D-6, exactly as they were for all schools in table C-4. The predicted differences, measured in years of achievement, are reported in table D-7. Comparing these differences with those for all schools (table 4-9) reveals mostly similarities. Initial student achievement has the strongest effect on achievement gains, ranging from .60 year to .76 year of achievement over the two-year interval of the study. This effect is

TABLE D-6. Predicting Student Achievement Gains in Years, Public School Students, Predictions Relative to Public School Distributions of Variables[a]

Predictors of achievement gains[b]	Quartile means		Model 1				Model 4A				Model 9				Model 13A			
	Lowest	Highest	B	$\hat{Q}_1$	$\hat{Q}_4$	Δ	B	$\hat{Q}_1$	$\hat{Q}_4$	Δ	B	$\hat{Q}_1$	$\hat{Q}_4$	Δ	B	$\hat{Q}_1$	$\hat{Q}_4$	Δ
Initial achievement	−1.169	1.046	.031	−.036	.032	.068	.024	−.028	.025	.053	.032	−.037	.033	.070	.025	−.029	.026	.055
Predicted two-year gain						.76				.60				.79				.62
Organization, comprehensive	−1.172	.270	.015	−.018	.004	.022												
Predicted two-year gain						.25												
Organization, comprehensive, without percent academic	−1.208	.295					.009	−.011	.003	.014								
Predicted two-year gain										.16								
Organization, condensed	−1.427	.361									.023	−.033	.008	.041				
Predicted two-year gain														.46				
Organization, condensed, without percent academic	−1.401	.436													.018	−.025	.008	.033
Predicted two-year gain																		.37
Parent socioeconomic status	−.910	.900	.022	−.020	.020	.040	.019	−.017	.017	.034	.023	−.021	.021	.042	.022	−.020	.020	.040
Predicted two-year gain						.45				.38				.47				.45
School socioeconomic status	−.553	.311	.016	−.009	.005	.014	.021	−.012	.007	.019								
Predicted two-year gain						.16				.21								
Academic tracking policy	.271	.300	.042				.042	.011	.013	.002					.042	.011	.013	.002
Predicted two-year gain										.02								.02

a. The parameters reported for each model are as follows:

B = regression coefficient for predictor variable from previously estimated model.

$\hat{Q}_1$ = predicted total log gain, as a function of predictor variable, for student at the mean of the lowest quartile of the predictor variable—the product of B and the lowest quartile mean.

$\hat{Q}_4$ = predicted total log gain, as a function of predictor variable, for student at the mean of the highest quartile of the predictor variable—the product of B and the highest quartile mean.

$\hat{\Delta}$ = predicted change in total log gain associated with change in predictor variable from mean of lowest quartile to mean of highest quartile.

b. To convert the predicted total log gains to years or grade equivalents, the predicted log gains (Δ) are compared to one-half the average log gain for all students over the final two years of high school, or .5 (.178) = .089. For example, the effect of initial achievement on achievement gains is given by .068/.089 = .76 year of predicted achievement over the last two years of high school.

TABLE D-7. Predicted Years of Achievement Gains, Sophomore to Senior Year, Attributable to School Organization and Other Selected Sources, Public School Students[a]

Source of achievement growth	Model			
	1	4[b]	9	13[b]
Initial student achievement	.76	.60	.79	.62
	(.74)	(.58)	(.76)	(.60)
School organization	.25	.16	.46	.37
	(.40)	(.25)	(.69)	(.53)
Parent socioeconomic status	.45	.38	.47	.45
	(.44)	(.38)	(.46)	(.44)
School socioecoomic status	.16	.21	. . .	. . .
	(.18)	(.24)		
Academic tracking policy	. . .	.02	. . .	.02
		(.12)		(.12)

a. Predictions compare estimated differences in achievement for students at the means of the lowest and the highest quartiles on each of the sources of achievement growth. Predictions not in parentheses use quartile means and test score means for public school students only. Predictions in parentheses employ means for all students.

b. As in table 4-9, the predictions of achievement growth for the models that include academic tracking as an independent variable are not based on the original models, but on modified models that measure tracking as a dummy variable at the student level. The predictions for models 4 and 13 reported here are based on the coefficients from models 4A and 13A.

about one-tenth of a year stronger than the effect for all schools. The effect of parent SES averages somewhat less than a half year—.44 year to be exact, virtually the same as it averages in all schools. School SES is again the weakest influence on student gains. In those public school models in which its effect is close enough to statistical significance to take seriously, its impact averages .18 year of achievement. In the models for all schools the impact of school SES averages the same.

The impact of school organization, however, is not quite the same. In all schools its impact averages just under half a year and ranges from one-third to two-thirds of a year. In public schools its impact is about a third of a year and ranges up to not quite half a year. In all schools, moreover, the lowest estimates of organizational influence are counterbalanced by strong estimates of academic tracking policy, which is itself an organizational effect. In public schools, however, this is not the case. Public schools differ from one another very little in their use of tracking. Program assignments tend to be dictated by student ability and background; average students tend not to be placed into academic programs. All in all, then, it would seem that effective school organization counts somewhat less for student achievement in public schools than the analysis of all schools would suggest. Our analysis of all schools indicates that at least a half year of achievement is due to school organization overall; the analysis of public schools indicates that no more than a half year can be attributed to organization.

Most of this discrepancy is more apparent than real, however. The estimates of the public school regression models (tables D-1 through D-4) showed that the marginal effect of school organization on student achievement is virtually identical in public schools to what it is in all schools. A change of one unit in the effectiveness of school organization is associated with essentially the same change in student achievement gains in public schools as a one-unit change in school effectiveness is in all schools. The only organizational difference between the samples is the slightly weaker influence of academic courses in public schools. In sum, school organization has almost the same conditional influence on student achievement in public schools that it has in all schools.

The reason that the predicted value of organization is less in public schools than it is in all schools is that the range of values of school organization observed in the public school sample is narrower than the range of values observed for all schools. Public schools are more alike as organizations than schools are in general. Thus the schools in the lowest and highest quartiles of school organization are not as different when the sample includes only public schools. The predicted consequences of school organization, associated with a change from the first to the fourth quartile of that variable, are therefore not as great either. School organization is no less important in its consequences, but public schools do not permit it to display its full range of influence.

This is evident in the predictions reported in parentheses in table D-7 (and calculated in table D-8). These predicted differences in achievement use the regression coefficients from public schools but the distributions of the variables from all schools. Predicted in this way, the influences of initial student achievement, parent SES, and school SES do not change. The distributions of these background variables are essentially the same for public schools as for all schools. But the predicted influence of school organization changes markedly. The influence of school organization now averages nearly half a year of achievement and ranges up to two-thirds of a year. This is virtually the same influence that we found school organization to exert in all

TABLE D-8. Predicting Student Achievement Gains in Years, Public School Students, Predictions Relative to Full Distributions of Variables[a]

Predictors of achievement gains[b]	Quartile means		Model 1				Model 4A				Model 9				Model 13A			
	Lowest	Highest	B	$\hat{Q}_1$	$\hat{Q}_4$	Δ	B	$\hat{Q}_1$	$\hat{Q}_4$	Δ	B	$\hat{Q}_1$	$\hat{Q}_4$	Δ	B	$\hat{Q}_1$	$\hat{Q}_4$	Δ
Initial achievement	-1.116	1.107	.031	-.035	.034	.069	.024	-.027	.027	.054	.032	-.036	.035	.071	.025	-.028	.028	.056
Predicted two-year gain						.74				.58				.76				.60
Organization, comprehensive	-1.118	1.365	.015	-.017	.020	.037	...	...	...	...	...	...	...	...	...	...	...	...
Predicted two-year gain						.40												
Organization, comprehensive, without percent academic	-1.132	1.401	...	...	...	...	.009	-.010	.013	.023	...	...	...	...	...	...	...	...
Predicted two-year gain										.25								
Organization, condensed	-1.379	1.372	...	...	...	...	...	...	...	...	.023	-.032	.032	.064	...	...	...	...
Predicted two-year gain														.69				
Organization, condensed, without percent academic	-1.320	1.414	...	...	...	...	...	...	...	...	...	...	...	...	.018	-.024	.025	.048
Predicted two-year gain																		.53
Parent socioeconomic status	-.856	.996	.022	-.019	.022	.041	.019	-.016	.019	.035	.023	-.020	.023	.043	.022	-.019	.022	.041
Predicted two-year gain						.44				.38				.46				.44
School socioeconomic status	-.502	.540	.016	-.008	.009	.017	.021	-.011	.011	.022	...	...	...	...	...	...	...	...
Predicted two-year gain						.18				.24								
Academic tracking policy	.269	.517	...	...	...	...	.042	.011	.022	.011	...	...	...	...	.042	.011	.022	.011
Predicted two-year gain										.12								.12

a. The parameters reported for each model are as follows:

B = regression coefficient for predictor variable from previously estimated model.

$\hat{Q}_1$ = predicted total log gain, as a function of predictor variable, for student at the mean of the lowest quartile of the predictor variable—the product of B and the lowest quartile mean.

$\hat{Q}_4$ = predicted total log gain, as a function of predictor variable, for student at the mean of the highest quartile of the predictor variable—the product of B and the highest quartile mean.

Δ = predicted change in total log gain associated with change in predictor variable from mean of lowest quartile to mean of highest quartile.

b. To convert the predicted total log gains to years or grade equivalents, the predicted log gains (Δ) are compared to one-half the average log gain for all students over the final two years of high school, or .5 (.186) = .093. For example, the effect of initial achievement on achievement gains is given by .069/.093 = .74 year of predicted achievement over the last two years of high school.

schools. If our analysis of public school achievement has revealed anything different, then, it is not that school organization exerts less of an impact than our analysis of all schools indicated. School organization has the same important impact on achievement in all schools, public and private. The only difference in public schools is that, because of their tendency toward organizational similarity, public schools do not permit organizational factors to display the full range of their influence.

School Organization

Having established the importance of effective school organization for student achievement, we turned next in our original analysis to the causes of school organization. We specified and estimated linear regression models of school organization, using our comprehensive index of school organization (excluding academic track enrollments) as our dependent variable. The independent variables included measures of bureaucratic influence (administrative constraint and personnel constraint), school board influence, school economic resources, student characteristics, and parent characteristics. The estimates of those models, reported in chapter 5, revealed that, all things being equal, bureaucratic influence has the greatest individual impact on school organization. The more autonomous the school, the more effective its organization.

In table D-9 we report for public schools the estimates of virtually the same models that we estimated for all schools. The only difference in the structure of the models that we estimate for public schools is their measuremeni of administrative constraint. In chapter 5 we observed that the issues on which administrative constraint appeared to matter most for school organization were hiring, firing, curriculum, and instruction. Administrative constraint on the issue of discipline did not distinguish effective and ineffective schools in the same dramatic way that the other issues did. This, we reasoned, could be expected. Control over hiring and firing was obviously crucial to whether a school developed a teamlike organization. Control over curriculum and instruction seemed to get at the essence of whether a school was being run as a professional organization. Control over discipline did not seem nearly so decisive for the quality of school organization.

Nevertheless, administrative constraints on disciplinary policy were

TABLE D-9. Estimates of Models of School Organization, Public Schools[a]

| | Model[b] | | |
Variable	Full	Final	Final without personnel constraint
School economic resources	−.014 (.051) −.015	. . .	. . .
School size	.0008* (.0002) .240	.0008* (.0002) .245	.0006* (.0002) .197
Midpoint of teacher salary range	−.001 (.047) −.001	. . .	. . .
Student tenth grade achievement	.241* (.091) .161	.231* (.083) .154	.273* (.085) .182
Student behavior problems	−.118* (.048) −.159	−.118* (.048) −.159	−.139* (.049) −.186
Parent socioeconomic status[c]	.119* (.034) .196	.118* (.033) .195	.127* (.034) .209
Parent-school contacts	.035 (.032) .060	.033 (.031) .057	.023 (.032) .039
Parental relationships	.014 (.052) .014	. . .	. . .
School board influence	.066 (.057) .088	.065 (.055) .086	.033 (.055) .044
Disciplinary constraint	.103* (.051) .131	.105* (.050) .131	.120* (.051) .152
Bureaucratic influence Administrative constraint	−.079 (.071) −.080	−.079 (.071) −.080	−.145* (.070) −.147
Personnel constraint	−.181* (.047) −.234	−.181* (.046) −.235	. . .
Constant	−.663* (.252)	−.604* (.056)	−.546* (.055)
Adjusted R^2	.186	.194	.155
Sample size	309	309	309

* Statistically significant, $\alpha \leq .05$, $t \geq 1.64$, one-tail test.

a. Dependent variable is comprehensive measure of organization without percent of students in academic track. Sample weighted to achieve a nationally representative sample of public high schools.

b. Coefficients are unstandardized linear regression coefficients; standard errors are in parentheses. Standardized regression coefficients (betas) are in italics.

c. Residualized variable, controlling for parent contacts, parental relationships, and tenth grade achievement.

correlated with administrative constraints on hiring, firing, curriculum, and instruction in the sample of all schools. We therefore based our original measure of administrative constraint on all five issues. In the sample of public schools, however, administrative constraints on discipline are no longer so closely related to constraints on the other organizational issues. We therefore measure administrative constraint in the public schools with an index based on control over hiring, firing, curriculum, and instruction. Administrative constraint on disciplinary policy enters the model as a separate variable.

Comparing the public school estimates with the estimates for all schools (table 5-7) again yields mostly similarities. The variables that are nonsignificant in all schools are also nonsignificant in public schools. School organizations do not become significantly more effective as public schools spend more money per pupil and reduce their student-teacher ratios, or as they raise their teacher salaries. All things being equal, the quality of parent-school relationships does not increase the quality of school organization. The frequency of parent-school contacts does not boost school effectiveness either (though in all schools it had a weak effect). Finally, the influence of school boards, though slightly stronger in public schools than in all schools, is again nonsignificant.

The variables that influence the quality of school organization most are basically the same in both samples: school size, student achievement and behavior, parent SES, and, most important for our purposes, bureaucratic influence. The strengths of these influences, however, are somewhat different in the two samples. While school size and parent SES have virtually the same unstandardized coefficients in the final models of both samples, the student variables are less than half as strong in the public school sample as in the complete sample. These differences, however, are not a great concern.

Our central concern is the influence of bureaucracy—the importance of school autonomy. In that area we find some differences. First, public schools evidently benefit from the external imposition of discipline. In public schools where the superintendent or central office plays a relatively strong role in establishing discipline, the school is likely to have a more effective organization. Why this is true, we cannot say. But we have far less reason to believe that disciplinary policy, unlike hiring, firing, curriculum, and instruction, cannot be handled effectively by authorities outside the school.

A second difference in public schools is that administrative con-

TABLE D-10. Predicted Effects of Bureaucratic Influence and Other Factors on School Organization, Public Schools[a]

| Determinant of school organization[b] | Predicted percentile of organizational effectiveness if determinant is at mean of | | Predicted percentile change |
	Lowest quartile	Highest quartile	
School size	27.6	84.7	57.1
Student tenth grade achievement	27.7	64.8	37.1
Student behavior problems	70.4	31.1	−39.3
Parent socioeconomic status	25.8	73.5	47.7
Parent-school contacts	40.3	52.8	12.5
School board influence	38.9	57.6	18.7
Disciplinary constraint	32.5	65.9	33.4
Bureaucratic influence			
Administrative constraint	56.8	39.5	−17.3
Personnel constaint	74.5	20.2	−54.3
Total (administrative plus personnel constraint)	85.6	17.2	−68.4

a. Predictions employ "final" model in table D-9 and place all variables, besides the one in question, at their school-level mean.

b. This list includes all variables from table D-9 whose regression coefficients exceeded their standard errors.

straint, while still damaging to school organization, is only statistically marginal in importance. The reason, however, is that administrative constraint and personnel constraint both measure one more general influence—the influence of bureaucracy—and are closely related to one another. This can create a problem for estimating the individual influence of each one. Unless each influence is distinctively strong—as each is in the sample of all schools—both may not achieve statistical significance when they are in a regression model together. That is what happens in the model for public schools. Personnel constraint is every bit as strong in the public school models as in the models of all schools. If personnel constraint is omitted from the model, and administrative constraint enters the model alone, administrative constraint has a significant impact, nearly the size of the impact of constraint on personnel. But when administrative constraint and personnel constraint are in the model of school organization together, only personnel constraint achieves statistical significance—administrative constraint just misses.

In light of these results it would be misleading to drop administrative constraint from our analysis and proceed as if bureaucratic influence has only one important component in public schools. Personnel constraint may well be the critical determinant of whether public school organization is affected adversely by bureaucracy. This would be consistent with our emphasis on personnel throughout the book. But the fact of the matter is, administrative and personnel constraint are closely related dimensions of bureaucratic influence. Because of this, their individual effects on school organization are difficult to disentangle. We therefore retain administrative constraint in our model, and shift our attention to the overall influence of bureaucracy, which is ultimately what really matters.

In table D-10 we compare the effects of bureaucratic influence to the effects of the other influences on school organization. As we did in table 5-8, we do so by calculating the predicted difference in organizational effectiveness for schools at the means of the first and fourth quartiles of each independent variable. As we saw in table 5-8, there are many variables that can cause major shifts in organizational effectiveness. In public schools, family background can produce a shift of nearly two quartiles in school effectiveness, and student behavior and achievement can each produce shifts of a quartile and a half. Finally, in support of the idea that comprehensive public high schools may be better than their current alternative (for example, small, inadequate rural schools), larger public schools are more effective than smaller public schools, all things being equal.[4]

The bottom line, though, is this: bureaucracy is a serious obstacle to effective organization among schools in the public sector. A change in administrative and personnel constraint from their top to their bottom quartiles is associated with an increase in organizational effectiveness of 68.4 percentiles. That is a larger change in organizational effectiveness than our analysis of all schools (see table 5-8) predicted bureaucratic influence to produce. It is also nearly the same change in organizational effectiveness that we used to estimate the impact of school organization on student achievement. In public schools, as in America's schools generally, school autonomy is important enough to school organization to produce impressive changes—changes of a year or more over four years of high school—in student achievement. What we found to be true of all schools, in other words, is also true of public schools. Autonomy from bureaucracy is crucial to effective school organization, and effective school organization is the key to superior student achievement.

Notes

Chapter One

1. For recent examples, see the National Governors' Association, *Time for Results: The Governors' 1991 Report on Education* (Washington, 1986); Business–Higher Education Forum, *American Potential: The Human Dimension* (Washington, 1988); D.C. Committee on Public Education, *Our Children, Our Future: Revitalizing the District of Columbia Public Schools* (Washington: Federal City Council, 1989); and Herbert J. Walberg and others, *We Can Rescue Our Children: The Cure for Chicago's Public School Crisis—with Lessons for the Rest of America* (Chicago: Heartland Institute, 1988).

2. Prominent early reports included the Twentieth Century Fund Task Force on Federal Elementary and Secondary Education Policy, *Making the Grade: Report* (New York: Twentieth Century Fund, 1983); Task Force on Education for Economic Growth, *Action for Excellence: A Comprehensive Plan to Improve Our Nation's Schools* (Denver: Education Commission of the States, 1983); Mortimer J. Adler, *The Paideia Proposal: An Educational Manifesto* (Macmillan, 1982); Ernest L. Boyer, *High School: A Report on Secondary Education in America* (Harper and Row, 1983); and most notably, the National Commission on Excellence in Education, *A Nation at Risk: The Imperative for Educational Reform* (Washington, 1983).

3. Denis P. Doyle and Terry W. Hartle, *Excellence in Education: The States Take Charge* (Washington: American Enterprise Institute for Public Policy Research, 1985), p. 1.

4. The most recent summary of state education reforms is William A. Firestone, Susan H. Fuhrman, and Michael W. Kirst, *The Progress of Reform: An Appraisal of State Education Initiatives*, Research Report Series, RR-014 (Rutgers University, Center for Policy Research in Education, October 1989). Earlier summaries, which offer useful analyses of these reforms, include Doyle and Hartle, *Excellence in Education;* and William Chance, *"the best of educations": Reforming America's Public Schools in the 1980s* (Washington: John D. and Catherine T. MacArthur Foundation, 1986).

5. See, for example, Lawrence A. Cremin. *American Education: The National Experience, 1783–1876* (Harper and Row, 1980); Edward A. Krug, *The Shaping of the American High School, 1880–1920* (University of Wisconsin Press, 1969); and Paul E. Peterson, *The Politics of School Reform, 1870–1940* (University of Chicago Press, 1985).

6. The important role that communities played in molding public schools,

278

and in making them effective, during their first century is brilliantly argued in James S. Coleman and Thomas Hoffer, *Public and Private High Schools: The Impact of Communities* (Basic Books, 1987), chaps. 1, 8. See also David B. Tyack, *The One Best System: A History of American Urban Education* (Harvard University Press, 1974); and Cremin, *American Education.*

7. The role of the Progressive movement (and the influence of business and education professionals) is a central feature of such major works as Ellwood P. Cubberley, *The History of Education: Educational Practice and Progress Considered as a Phase of the Development and Spread of Western Civilization* (Houghton Mifflin, 1920); Raymond E. Callahan, *Education and the Cult of Efficiency: A Study of the Forces That Have Shaped the Administration of the Public Schools* (University of Chicago Press, 1962); Lawrence A. Cremin, *The Transformation of the School: Progressivism in American Education, 1876–1957* (Knopf, 1961); and Joseph M. Cronin, *The Control of Urban Schools: Perspectives on the Power of Educational Reformers* (Free Press, 1973). All but Cubberley, however, clearly acknowledge influences other than business and professionals, and motives other than progressive reform.

8. Tyack, *One Best System,* popularized this label but does not agree that the system is best.

9. See, for example, Ellwood P. Cubberley, *Public School Administration: A Statement of the Fundamental Principles Underlying the Organization and Administration of Public Education* (Houghton Mifflin, 1916); and Samuel Train Dutton and David Snedden, *The Administration of Public Education in the United States* (Macmillan, 1912).

10. See, for example, Tyack, *One Best System*; Michael B. Katz, *Class, Bureaucracy, and Schools: The Illusion of Educational Change in America* (Praeger, 1971); Samuel Bowles and Herbert Gintis, *Schooling in Capitalist America: Educational Reform and the Contradictions of Economic Life* (Basic Books, 1976); and Peterson, *Politics of School Reform.*

11. There are some variations on the basic theme. Fourteen states have popularly elected state boards of education (though one is elected by local school boards); thirty-five states have appointed state boards (all but three of which are appointed by the governor); and only one state (Wisconsin) has no state board at all. Sixteen states have a separately and popularly elected chief state school officer; twenty-eight states have one appointed by and from the state board of education, and six have one appointed by the governor. In all but a handful of states the chief state school officer heads the department of education. Data supplied by the Education Commission of the States, Denver, Colorado, in a telephone interview, October 30, 1989.

12. On the major education reform movements of the 1960s and 1970s, see Diane Ravitch, *The Troubled Crusade: American Education, 1945–1980* (Basic Books, 1983); Diane Ravitch, *The Great School Wars: New York City, 1805–1973* (Basic Books, 1974); Gary Orfield, *Must We Bus? Segregated Schools and National Policy* (Brookings, 1978); and cf. Myron Lieberman, *Public-Sector Bargaining: A Policy Reappraisal* (Lexington Books, 1980), and Susan

Moore Johnson, *Teacher Unions and the Schools* (Harvard University, Institute for Educational Policy Studies, 1982).

13. Academic excellence was the persistent theme of the reform movement throughout the 1980s, beginning with the work of the National Commission on Excellence in Education in the early 1980s and ending with the Educational Summit in 1989. See, respectively, National Commission on Excellence in Education, *A Nation at Risk*; and "A Jeffersonian Compact, the Statement by the President and Governors," *New York Times*, October 1, 1989, p. E22.

14. James Bryant Conant, *The American High School Today: A First Report to Interested Citizens* (McGraw Hill, 1959). See also Hyman George Rickover, *Education and Freedom* (E. P. Dutton, 1959); and Rockefeller Brothers Fund, *The Pursuit of Excellence: Education and the Future of America* (Doubleday, 1958).

15. On the passage of the National Defense Education Act, see Barbara Barksdale Clowse, *Brainpower for the Cold War: The Sputnik Crisis and the National Defense Education Act of 1958* (Westport, Conn.: Greenwood Press, 1981).

16. The almost serendipitous nature of the process by which problems are placed on political agendas is discussed best in John W. Kingdon, *Agendas, Alternatives, and Public Policies* (Little, Brown, 1984).

17. The decline in SAT scores has, in fact, never been adequately explained. See Congressional Budget Office, *Educational Achievement: Explanations and Implications of Recent Trends* (August 1987). But few dispute that the decline in scores is cause for serious concern. See Diane Ravitch and Chester E. Finn, Jr., *What Do Our 17-Year-Olds Know?* (Harper and Row, 1987).

18. See, for example, Alec M. Gallup, "The 18th Annual Gallup Poll of the Public's Attitudes toward the Public Schools," *Phi Delta Kappan*, vol. 68 (September 1986), pp. 43–59.

19. The slumping economy also helped light a fire under taxpayers, whose reaction against "big government" and "bureaucratic waste" in general produced widespread resistance to new public taxing and spending—symbolized by California's Proposition 13 in 1978. This revolt, moreover, combined with high rates of inflation, caused real school spending to remain flat for several years.

20. The single best illustration of business's deep concern with education in the 1980s is a book coauthored by the chairman and chief executive officer of the Xerox Corporation, David T. Kearns. See Kearns and Denis P. Doyle, *Winning the Brain Race: A Bold Plan to Make Our Schools Competitive* (San Francisco: Institute for Contemporary Studies Press, 1988). See also National Alliance of Business, *A Blueprint for Business on Restructuring Education* (Washington, 1989); and Jeanne Allen, ed., *Can Business Save Education? Strategies for the 1990s* (Washington: Heritage Foundation, 1989).

21. See, for example, the collection of forty-four papers in Commission on Workforce Quality and Labor Market Efficiency, *Investing in People: A Strategy to Address America's Workforce Crisis, Background Papers*, vol. 1 (Department of Labor, 1989).

22. Among the most notable products of these commissions are Task Force on Education for Economic Growth, *Action for Excellence*; Twentieth Century Fund Task Force on Federal Elementary and Secondary Education Policy, *Making the Grade*; National Science Board, Commission on Precollege Education in Mathematics, Science and Technology, *Educating Americans for the 21st Century: A Plan of Action for Improving Mathematics, Science and Technology Education for all American Elementary and Secondary Students So That Their Achievement Is the Best in the World by 1995* (Washington: National Science Foundation, 1983); College Board, *Academic Preparation for College: What Students Need to Know and Be Able to Do* (New York: College Board, 1983); Ernest Boyer, *High School;* and American Council on Education, Business-Higher Education Forum, *America's Competitive Challenge: The Need for a National Response: A Report to the President of the United States from the Business-Higher Education Forum* (Washington, 1983).

23. For an overview of the major studies see J. Lynn Griesemer and Cornelius Butler, *Education under Study: An Analysis of Recent Major Reports on Education* (Chelmsford, Mass.: Northeast Regional Exchange, Inc., 1983). For a critical perspective on what the commissions had to say, see Paul E. Peterson, "Did the Education Commissions Say Anything?" *Brookings Review,* vol. 2 (Winter 1983), pp. 3–11.

24. National Commission on Excellence in Education, *A Nation at Risk,* p. 5.

25. Doyle and Hartle, *Excellence in Education,* p. 14.

26. For analyses of state reforms during the first half of the 1980s, see Doyle and Hartle, *Excellence in Education;* and Chance, *"the best of educations."*

27. For a summary of state reforms through 1989, see Firestone, Fuhrman, and Kirst, *Progress of Reform.*

28. The summit was historic because only twice before in American history, and not once since 1933, had the president met with all of the governors to work exclusively on a particular national problem. It remains to be seen whether the strong rhetoric of the summit, promising ambitious goals and structural change, will be matched by real reforms.

29. Some reformers have come close to recommending fundamental reforms. See especially John E. Coons and Stephen D. Sugarman, *Education by Choice: The Case for Family Control* (University of California Press, 1978); Joe Nathan, ed., *Public Schools by Choice: Expanding Opportunities for Parents, Students, and Teachers* (St. Paul: Institute for Learning and Teaching, 1989); Kearns and Doyle, *Winning the Brain Race;* and Myron Lieberman, *Privatization and Educational Choice* (St. Martin's Press, 1989).

30. Among political scientists it is commonly observed that political decisions are rarely concerned with fundamental issues; power and decision-making are structured in such a way that these sorts of issues do not make it onto the agenda—they are systematic victims of "nondecisions." On the concept of nondecisions, see Peter Bachrach and Morton S. Baratz, "Two

Faces of Power," *American Political Science Review*, vol. 56 (December 1962), pp. 947–52.

31. On the struggle that institutional change engenders in politics and society more generally, see Stephen Skowronek, *Building a New American State: The Expansion of National Administrative Capacities, 1877–1920* (Cambridge University Press, 1982); and John E. Chubb and Paul E. Peterson, eds., *Can the Government Govern?* (Brookings, 1989).

32. An important exception is Kearns and Doyle, *Winning the Brain Race*.

33. Again, Kearns and Doyle, *Winning the Brain Race*, is a rare exception.

34. See, for example, Robert H. Salisbury, *Citizen Participation in the Public Schools* (Lexington Books, 1980); and L. Harmon Zeigler and M. Kent Jennings, with the assistance of G. Wayne Peak, *Governing American Schools: Political Interaction in Local School Districts* (North Scituate, Mass.: Duxbury Press, 1974).

35. The important exception to this generalization is a small amount of research comparing public and private schools. This research, about which we will have much more to say, is best represented by James S. Coleman, Thomas Hoffer, and Sally Kilgore, *High School Achievement: Public, Catholic, and Private Schools Compared* (Basic Books, 1982); Coleman and Hoffer, *Public and Private High Schools*; and Arthur G. Powell, Eleanor Farrar, and David K. Cohen, *The Shopping Mall High School: Winners and Losers in the Educational Marketplace* (Houghton Mifflin, 1985).

36. James S. Coleman and others, *Equality of Educational Opportunity* (Department of Health, Education, and Welfare, 1966).

37. The most notable follow-up study was Christopher Jencks and others, *Inequality: A Reassessment of the Effect of Family and Schooling in America* (Basic Books, 1972). Much of this research is elegantly summarized in Eric A. Hanushek, "The Economics of Schooling: Production and Efficiency in Public Schools," *Journal of Economic Literature*, vol. 24 (September 1986), pp. 1141–77.

38. The best of this research includes Michael Rutter and others, *Fifteen Thousand Hours: Secondary Schools and Their Effects on Children* (Harvard University Press, 1979); Wilbur B. Brookover and others, *School Social Systems and Student Achievement: Schools Can Make a Difference* (Praeger, 1979); Theodore R. Sizer, *Horace's Compromise: The Dilemma of the American High School* (Houghton Mifflin, 1984); John I. Goodlad, *A Place Called School: Prospects for the Future* (McGraw Hill, 1984); and Powell, Farrar, and Cohen, *Shopping Mall High School*.

39. Coleman, Hoffer, and Kilgore, *High School Achievement*.

40. The fury of the attack on Coleman, Hoffer, and Kilgore is illustrated by full-issue critiques of their work in two major education journals: *Sociology of Education*, vol. 55 (April–July 1982); and "Report Analysis: Public and Private Schools," *Harvard Educational Review*, vol. 51 (November 1981), pp. 481–545.

41. The best critical summary of this work remains Stewart C. Purkey and Marshall S. Smith, "Effective Schools: A Review," *Elementary School Journal*, vol. 83 (March 1983), pp. 427–52.

42. These characteristics are summarized in Purkey and Smith, "Effective Schools"; and Thomas B. Corcoran, "Effective Secondary Schools," in Regina M. J. Kyle, ed., *Reaching for Excellence: An Effective Schools Sourcebook* (Washington: National Institute of Education, 1985).

43. Generally, see Paul R. Lawrence and Jay W. Lorsch, *Organization and Environment: Managing Differentiation and Integration* (Harvard University, Graduate School of Business Administration, 1967). On education, see especially Charles E. Bidwell, "The School as a Formal Organization," in James G. March, ed., *Handbook of Organizations* (Rand McNally, 1965); and Karl E. Weick, "Educational Organizations as Loosely Coupled Systems," *Administrative Science Quarterly*, vol. 21 (March 1976), pp. 1–19.

44. For example, E. Mark Hanson, *Educational Administration and Organizational Behavior* (Boston: Allyn and Bacon, 1979); and Frederick M. Wirt and Michael W. Kirst, *Schools in Conflict: The Politics of Education* (Berkeley: McCutchan, 1982). The latter is notable for its unusually sensitive treatment of the political environment.

45. See especially Weick, "Educational Organizations"; John Meyer, W. Richard Scott, and David Strang, "Centralization, Fragmentation, and School District Complexity," *Administrative Science Quarterly*, vol. 32 (June 1987), pp. 186–201; and John W. Meyer and Brian Rowan, "Institutionalized Organizations: Formal Structure as Myth and Ceremony," *American Journal of Sociology*, vol. 83 (September 1977), pp. 340–63.

46. This approach falls under the rubric of what is generally referred to as the "new institutionalism." See James G. March and Johan P. Olsen, *Rediscovering Institutions: The Organizational Basis of Politics* (Free Press, 1989).

47. Coleman, Hoffer, and Kilgore, *High School Achievement*.

48. See note 29.

Chapter Two

1. Max Weber, *The Theory of Social and Economic Organization* (Free Press, 1947); and Charles Perrow, *Complex Organizations: A Critical Essay*, 3d ed. (Random House, 1986).

2. This administrative fact of life is well recognized in the general literature on public administration. See, for example, Harold Seidman and Robert Gilmour, *Politics, Position, and Power: From the Positive to the Regulatory State*, 4th ed. (Oxford University Press, 1986). The role of politics is also taken seriously in a small amount of the literature on school administration, for example, Frederick M. Wirt and Michael W. Kirst, *Schools in Conflict: The Politics of Organization* (Berkeley: McCutchan, 1982); Roald F. Campbell

and others, *The Organization and Control of American Schools* (Columbus, Ohio: Charles E. Merrill, 1980); and Laurence Iannaccone, *Politics in Education* (New York: Center for Applied Research in Education, 1967).

3. Although many education scholars are aware that politics is important to an understanding of schools, empirical research on schools has been dominated by two approaches anchored not in politics but in sociological organization theory. The mainstream approach, which includes effective schools research, sees schools as open systems that operate in a complex environment of which politics is an integral part. Yet research on school performance is approached as if it is the school—its goals, leadership, and internal organization—that really matters and not the environment. See, for example, the literature reviewed in Stewart C. Purkey and Marshall S. Smith, "Effective Schools: A Review," *Elementary School Journal*, vol. 83 (March 1983), pp. 427–52. See also Charles E. Bidwell, "The School as a Formal Organization," in James G. March, ed., *Handbook of Organizations* (Chicago: Rand McNally, 1965). The second approach, whose theoretical logic is quite outside the mainstream, sees schools as components of systems that are "loosely coupled"—fragmented and decentralized; by this view school operations are largely independent of the administrative and political structure imposed by the environment. Karl E. Weick, "Educational Organizations as Loosely Coupled Systems," *Administrative Science Quarterly*, vol. 21 (March 1976), pp. 1–19. Our intellectual sympathies are with the mainstream. Among other things, while the educational system is obviously fragmented and decentralized, we agree with the mainstream that formal structure has important consequences for school performance.

4. Based on data for the years, 1985–87, the United States has 84,945 public elementary and secondary schools, and 27,639 private elementary and secondary schools—or 24.5 percent private schools. National Center for Education Statistics, Office of Educational Research and Improvement, *Digest of Education Statistics, 1988* (Department of Education, 1988), p. 83.

5. On the merits of politics and markets generally, see especially Charles E. Lindblom, *Politics and Markets: The World's Political Economic Systems* (Basic Books, 1977). On the government use of markets, see Charles L. Schultze, *The Public Use of Private Interest* (Brookings, 1977); and on privatization, see E. S. Savas, *Privatizing the Public Sector: How to Shrink Government* (Chatham, N.J.: Chatham House Publishers, 1982).

6. Strictly speaking, the government establishes a legal framework in which private schools must operate, and this framework may include certain standards of operation such as graduation or teacher certification requirements. But the government must, according to a long-standing interpretation of the U.S. Constitution, permit private schools to operate. See *Pierce v. Society of Sisters*, 268 U.S. 510 (1925). Government, nonetheless, regulates private schools to some extent. See Neal E. Devins, ed., *Public Values, Private Schools* (Falmer Press, 1989).

7. The reasons for this are the basis for many now-classic works on the foundations of American politics, such as Grant McConnell, *Private Power*

and American Democracy (Knopf, 1966); Theodore J. Lowi, *The End of Liberalism: The Second Republic of the United States,* 2d ed. (W. W. Norton, 1979); E. E. Schattschneider, *The Semi-Sovereign People* (Holt, Rinehart and Winston, 1960); and Mancur Olson, *The Logic of Collective Action: Public Goods and the Theory of Groups* (Harvard University Press, 1965).

8. This reason is emphasized most often by economists, for example, Milton and Rose Friedman, *Free to Choose: A Personal Statement* (Avon, 1981), pp. 140–78.

9. The concept of exit is developed generally in Albert O. Hirschman, *Exit, Voice, and Loyalty: Responses to Decline in Firms, Organizations, and States* (Harvard University Press, 1970).

10. The importance of natural selection in economic markets was first explicated in Armen A. Alchian, "Uncertainty, Evolution, and Economic Theory," *Journal of Political Economy,* vol. 58 (June 1950), pp. 211–21.

11. See Charles M. Tiebout, "A Pure Theory of Local Expenditures," *Journal of Political Economy,* vol. 64 (October 1956), pp. 416–24; and Paul E. Peterson, *City Limits* (University of Chicago Press, 1981).

12. Attempts to correct market imperfections require the use of public bureaucracy and are themselves subject to "political failures." Government remedies may therefore be less desirable than the imperfections they sought to correct. See, for example, George J. Stigler, "The Theory of Economic Regulation," *Bell Journal of Economics,* vol. 2 (Spring 1971), pp. 3–21.

13. On the crucial importance of what goes on inside of schools—and how little is known about this by administrators and policymakers—see especially John I. Goodlad, *A Place Called School: Prospects for the Future* (McGraw-Hill, 1984); David S. Seeley, *Education through Partnership: Mediating Structures and Education* (Ballinger, 1981); Michael W. Sedlack and others, *Selling Students Short: Classroom Bargains and Academic Reform in the American High School* (New York: Teachers College Press, 1986). On the distinctive and variable needs of schools for the educationally disadvantaged—needs that central administrators are often too inflexible to meet—see James P. Comer, "Educating Poor Minority Children," *Scientific American,* vol. 259 (November 1988), pp. 42–48.

14. On the importance of professionalism, see Carnegie Forum on Education and the Economy, Task Force on Teaching as a Profession, *A Nation Prepared: Teachers for the 21st Century* (Washington, 1986); Ernest L. Boyer, *High School: A Report on Secondary Education in America* (Harper and Row, 1983); Holmes Group Executive Board, *Tomorrow's Teachers: A Report of the Holmes Group* (East Lansing: Holmes Group Executive Board, 1986); Linda Darling-Hammond and Arthur E. Wise, "Teaching Standards, or Standardized Teaching?" *Educational Leadership,* vol. 41 (October 1983), pp. 66–69; Linda Darling-Hammond, "The Over-Regulated Curriculum and the Press for Teacher Professionalism," *NASSP Bulletin* (April 1987), pp. 87–89; and more generally, Eliot Freidson, *Professional Powers: A Study of the Institutionalization of Formal Knowledge* (University of Chicago Press, 1986).

15. On the measurement problems in regulating teaching and schooling,

see Sedlack and others, *Selling Students Short*, chap. 8; and especially, Eric A. Hanushek, "The Economics of Schooling: Production and Efficiency in Public Schools," *Journal of Economic Literature*, vol. 24 (September 1986), pp. 1141–77.

16. The experiences of school districts with merit pay illustrate the difficulties of arriving at performance measures that are mutually agreeable to school authorities and teachers. See, for example, David K. Cohen and Richard J. Murnane, "The Merits of Merit Pay," *Public Interest*, no. 80 (Summer 1985), pp. 3–30; and Harry P. Hatry and John M. Greiner, *Issues and Case Studies in Teacher Incentive Plans* (Washington: Urban Institute Press, 1985).

17. This is especially true where family circumstances deviate from the professional mainstream, such as in ghettos. See especially Comer, "Educating Poor Minority Children."

18. Although local governments (school districts, for example) are creatures of the state and could be eliminated by state action, we take these governments as given. As a practical matter, they have long histories and are not about to be eliminated unilaterally by the states. But more important, if we assumed that local governments are not a fixed part of the public institutional structure, we would soon conclude that local governments, or some entity much like them, would be created by the states as they tried to administer state policies and impose statewide values on their various localities.

19. These problems and the measurement problems referred to earlier are problems of agency. See, for example, Oliver E. Williamson, *The Economic Institutions of Capitalism* (Free Press, 1985); and Terry M. Moe, "The New Economics of Organization," *American Journal of Political Science*, vol. 28 (November 1984), pp. 739–77.

20. We should point out that, because of tenure laws, civil service restrictions, unions, and collective bargaining agreements, officials at state and even local levels find themselves in much the same bind.

21. In fact, these local authorities are organized forces in national politics—playing the role of interest groups—and they use their political power to press for greater local discretion. What they are demanding is much the same as what other groups (usually, advocates for specialized programs) are demanding: the power to use public authority to further their own views of what the schools should be doing. Because they are not the only groups that count, they are only partially successful, and thus find themselves burdened with "excessive" federally imposed bureaucracy. On the problem of bureaucratization in the federal government's largest education program, Chapter 1, see John E. Chubb, "Effective Schools and the Problems of the Poor," in Denis P. Doyle and Bruce S. Cooper, *Federal Aid to the Disadvantaged: What Future for Chapter 1?* (London: Falmer Press, 1988), chap. 12; and Richard F. Elmore, "The Problem of Quality in Chapter 1," in Doyle and Cooper, *Federal Aid to the Disadvantaged*, chap. 8. On the logic of bureaucratization

in federal grant programs generally, see John E. Chubb, "The Political Economy of Federalism," *American Political Science Review*, vol. 79 (December 1985), pp. 994–1015. In fiscal 1989 there were seventy-six categorical grant programs officially designated for elementary, secondary, and vocational education. These (U.S. Budget subfunction 501) grants do not include, moreover, programs that work through schools—breakfast and lunch programs, "Headstart," bus driver training, and more—that are not strictly educational. Advisory Commission on Intergovernmental Relations, *A Catalog of Federal Grant-In-Aid Programs to State and Local Governments: Grants Funded FY 1989* (Washington, October 1989), p. 4.

22. National Center for Education Statistics, *Digest, 1988*, p. 85.

23. On the concept of political uncertainty and its relation to the bureaucratic structure of government more generally, see Terry M. Moe, "The Politics of Bureaucratic Structure," in John E. Chubb and Paul E. Peterson, eds., *Can the Government Govern?* (Brookings, 1989), pp. 267–330; and Terry M. Moe, "The Politics of Structural Choice: Toward a Theory of Public Bureaucracy," in Oliver E. Williamson, ed., *Organization Theory: From Chester Barnard to the Present and Beyond* (Oxford University Press, 1990). For a similar line of reasoning, see Murray J. Horn and Kenneth A. Shepsle, "Commentary on 'Administrative Arrangements and the Political Control of Agencies': Administrative Process and Organizational Form as Legislative Responses to Agency Costs," *Virginia Law Review*, vol. 75 (March 1989), pp. 499–508.

24. *United States Statutes at Large*, 1965, 1966, 1968, 1970, 1974, 1978, 1981, 1983; vols. 79, 80, 82, 84, 88, 92, 95, 97 (Government Printing Office); and *United States Code Service* P. L. 100-297, no. 5 (Rochester, N.Y.: Lawyers Co-operative Publishing Co., 1988), pp. 1864–2156.

25. On the politics of professionalism, see generally Jack H. Knott and Gary J. Miller, *Reforming Bureaucracy: The Politics of Institutional Choice* (Prentice-Hall, 1987); and on the control of education by professionals, see Raymond E. Callahan, *Education and the Cult of Efficiency: A Study of the Social Forces That Have Shaped the Administration of the Public Schools* (University of Chicago Press, 1962); and David B. Tyack, *The One Best System: A History of American Urban Education* (Harvard University Press, 1974).

26. The courts have obviously played important roles over the years in imposing bureaucracy on schools and local districts, but we have chosen not to devote special attention to them here. In part, this is just a matter of economy; we cannot cover everything, and we have to draw the line somewhere. There is a theoretical rationale behind our priorities, however, that we should be clear about. Our concern is to try to set out, as simply as we can, the political foundations of democratic control, and we think this is best done by focusing on politicians, bureaucrats, and interest groups and constituents. For the most part, the courts proceed on the basis of the laws—usually

legislative or administrative in origin, sometimes constitutional—that these other types of actors have designed and imposed. The courts specify what these laws mean or require in particular circumstances. From our standpoint, the fundamental task is to understand the political institutions and processes that give rise to these laws in the first place.

27. The importance of school organization is demonstrated foremost in the effective schools literature, as summarized in Purkey and Smith, "Effective Schools." The most notable studies in this line of research are Michael Rutter and others, *Fifteen Thousand Hours: Secondary Schools and Their Effects on Children* (Harvard University Press, 1979); William Brookover and others, *School Social Systems and Student Achievement: Schools Can Make a Difference* (Praeger, 1979); Theodore R. Sizer, *Horace's Compromise: The Dilemma of the American High School* (Houghton Mifflin, 1984); Goodlad, *A Place Called School*; and Arthur G. Powell, Eleanor Farrar, and David K. Cohen, *The Shopping Mall High School: Winners and Losers in the Educational Marketplace* (Houghton Mifflin, 1985).

28. On teachers' unions, see Myron Lieberman, *Public-Sector Bargaining: A Policy Reappraisal* (Lexington Books, 1980); Myron Lieberman, *Beyond Public Education* (Praeger, 1986); Susan Moore Johnson, *Teacher Unions and the Schools* (Harvard University, Institute for Educational Policy Studies, 1982); and Randall W. Eberts and Joe A. Stone, "Teacher Unions and the Cost of Public Education," *Economic Inquiry*, vol. 24 (October 1986), pp. 631–43.

29. "Agreement between the Board of Education, School District of Philadelphia and the Philadelphia Federation of Teachers, Local 3, American Federation of Teachers, AFL-CIO, September 1, 1985-August 31, 1988" (Philadelphia Federation of Teachers).

30. According to the ATS data, tenure is offered in 24 percent of Catholic high schools, 39 percent of elite high schools, and 17 percent of other independent and sectarian private high schools. John E. Chubb and Terry M. Moe, "Politics, Markets, and the Organization of Schools," *American Political Science Review*, vol. 82 (December 1988), pp. 1065–87, cited on p. 1075.

31. While most public schools are unionized, only about 10 percent of all Catholic schools are unionized. Other private schools appear to be not unionized at all. Chubb and Moe, "Politics, Markets, and the Organization of Schools," p. 1075.

32. An enlightening account of just how complex the goal structures of public agencies tend to be—including not just their mandated goals, but goals thrust on them indirectly by virtue of their public status—see James Q. Wilson, *Bureaucracy: What Government Agencies Do and Why They Do It* (Basic Books, 1989).

33. All may not be well in homogeneous communities either, for all local school systems are embedded in state and federal "communities" that are far more heterogeneous. As higher levels of government, especially the states, take on increasing authority for running local schools, governing weight will shift toward much more heterogeneous polities and increase the pressures

for bureaucratization in even the most homogeneous communities. On the growing influence of higher levels of government, see Wirt and Kirst, *Schools in Conflict*, chaps. 9–11.

34. See, for example, Charles Murray, *Losing Ground: American Social Policy 1950–1980* (Basic Books, 1984); and Richard P. Nathan and Charles F. Adams, Jr., "Four Perspectives on Urban Hardship," *Political Science Quarterly*, vol. 104 (Fall 1989), pp. 483–508.

35. On this vicious circle, see John E. Chubb, "Why the Current Wave of School Reform Will Fail," *Public Interest*, no. 90 (Winter 1988), pp. 28–49.

36. In principle, one should be able to learn still more by taking advantage of institutional variation across nations—by comparing, for instance, the American system of public education with the educational systems of Japan or France. This is not our purpose here, of course; and even if we were inclined to move in this direction, an enormous amount of new research would have to be carried out to provide a solid basis for making the right kinds of comparisons. In the meantime, we think it is important not to jump to conclusions about how our analysis of American education might generalize to—or be modified by—the experiences of other nations. The most obvious such inference is that, because the educational systems of Japan and France (among others) seem to do a better job of promoting academic excellence despite being "highly bureaucratic," bureaucracy is not the kind of problem we claim it is. This may seem plausible on the surface, but it begs all the important questions. For instance, to what extent do their bureaucracies constrain the discretionary behavior of teachers and principals? More generally, how do the fundamental features of their political systems—which are very different from ours—condition the *kinds* of bureaucracies they develop, and thus the organization and performance of their schools? As James Q. Wilson points out, American public bureaucracies tend to be far more constraining and formally complex than bureaucracies in parliamentary systems, which, despite their forbidding appearance, give great reign to administrative discretion and informal arrangements. Nations are different—and appearances can be deceiving. See his *Bureaucracy: What Government Agencies Do and Why They Do It*, chap. 16. For discussions of the school systems of other nations, see, for example, Edmund J. King, *Other Schools and Ours: Comparative Studies for Today*, 5th edition (London: Holt, Rinehart, and Winston, 1979); and Thomas P. Rohlen, *Japan's High Schools* (University of California Press, 1983).

Chapter Three

1. On the intellectual roots of administrative centralization, see David B. Tyack, *The One Best System: A History of American Urban Education* (Harvard University Press, 1974), pp. 126–76. On the shortcomings of effective schools research—small, nonrandom samples, impressionistic measures, cross-sectional designs—see Stewart C. Purkey and Marshall S. Smith, "Effective

Schools: A Review," *Elementary School Journal*, vol. 83 (March 1983), pp. 427–52. Other important critiques of effective schools research include Larry Cuban, "Transforming the Frog into a Prince: Effective Schools Research, Policy, and Practice at the District Level," *Harvard Educational Review*, vol. 54 (May 1984), pp. 129–51; and Michael Rutter, "School Effects on Pupil Progress: Research Findings and Policy Implications," *Child Development* vol. 54 (February 1983), pp. 1–29.

2. The data used in this study are fully described in appendix A.

3. On the late nineteenth and early twentieth centuries, see especially Tyack, *One Best System*. On the more recent decades, see Diane Ravitch, *The Troubled Crusade: American Education, 1945–1981* (Basic Books, 1983).

4. Student achievement is not the only measure of school quality that we will pay some attention to, however. In discussing the organization of effective and ineffective schools we will look at a range of indicators of school quality— graduation requirements, disciplinary policies, classroom practices, teacher attitudes, and many others—that have long been used by accrediting organizations, government agencies, and researchers (especially those skeptical of standardized tests) to measure the caliber of schools. Unlike student academic achievement, however, these indicators will not be used as final measures of school outcomes in our statistical analysis of school performance. On the history of the measurement of school effectiveness see Brian Rowan, "The Assessment of School Effectiveness," in Regina M. J. Kyle, ed., *Reaching for Excellence: An Effective Schools Sourcebook* (Washington: National Institute of Education, 1985), pp. 99–116.

5. There is considerable controversy about how secondary school performance should be measured—for example, Rutter, "School Effects on Pupil Progress"; and Joan Lipsitz, *Successful Schools for Young Adolescents* (New Brunswick, N.J.: Transaction Books, 1984). But despite all the controversy, academic achievement is almost invariably accepted as an important indicator. Moreover, the major association devoted to the promotion of more effective schools, the National Council for Effective Schools, employs achievement— its level, distribution, and breadth—as its sole criterion of school success. Finally, achievement is associated with lifetime earnings. See Sherwin Rosen, "Human Capital: A Survey of Empirical Research," in Ronald G. Ehrenberg, ed., *Research in Labor Economics*, vol. 1 (Greenwich, Conn.: JAI Press, 1977).

6. All of the indicators and measures employed in this study are reported and defined in appendix B.

7. The tests were designed by the Educational Testing Service specifically for the High School and Beyond survey. The tests administered to the sophomore cohort in 1980 and 1982 were intended to measure both high school achievement and aptitude or basic skills. As it turned out, students registered as much if not more progress over the high school years on "aptitude" items as on "achievement" items. This suggests that all of the items are valid measures of the learning that takes place in high school. Basic skills such as reading and writing that are used to gauge "aptitude" continue to be honed

in high school—in all academic courses—and therefore stand to improve perhaps as much as skills developed explicitly by the high school curriculum. The design of the tests is detailed and justified in Barbara Heyns and Thomas L. Hilton, "The Cognitive Tests for High School and Beyond: An Assessment," *Sociology of Education*, vol. 55 (April-July 1982), pp. 89-102.

8. Calculated on the basis of "formula scores" corrected for guessing, the reliabilities of the tests given to the sophomore cohort in 1980 and 1982 are respectively as follows: vocabulary .80, .84; reading .77, .80; math .87, .90; science .74, .76; writing .80, .83; and civics (excluded from this study) .52, .60. The tests are also high in validity: they are related to one another in strong and sensible ways, characterized by prominent math and verbal factors as well as a powerful general factor. The relationships among the tests are stable over time. And the items and the tests appear to tap the same student abilities regardless of sex, race, or ethnicity. The psychometric properties of the tests are thoroughly analyzed in Donald A. Rock and others, "A Study of Excellence in High School Education: Educational Policies, School Quality, and Student Outcomes: Psychometric Analysis," Princeton, N.J., Educational Testing Service, 1985.

9. One-factor solutions of factor analyses of 1980 and 1982 sophomore test scores explained 81 percent and 83 percent of the reliable test variance respectively. Two-factor solutions, distinguishing verbal and quantitative factors, increased the explained reliable variance only marginally, to 86 percent and 87 percent respectively. Little is lost therefore by combining the five tests into a general index of achievement. For the factor analyses, see Rock and others, "Study of Excellence," pp. 59-66.

10. Because the students in the merged Administrator and Teacher Survey-High School and Beyond (ATS-HSB) data set are a 40 percent subset of the students in the HSB sophomore cohort panel, test scores and other characteristics reported in this study may differ slightly from reports based on all of the HSB students.

11. Factor analysis indicates that the five tests can be well characterized by two factors, one quantitative and one verbal, and that all of the tests except science load predominantly on one factor or the other. While science loads significantly on both factors, we chose to group it with mathematics because of the traditionally close curricular relationship between the two. In any case, the subsequent analysis does not examine quantitative and verbal achievement separately.

12. There is the possibility that the tests do not adequately measure high school curricula and therefore underrepresent high school learning. But since all high schools are equally disadvantaged if the tests have such a shortcoming, the tests will still provide valid comparative measures of performance. On this point, see also Heyns and Hilton, "Cognitive Tests for High School and Beyond"; and Rock and others, "Study of Excellence."

13. The calculation of the IRT (item response theory) scores is described in Rock and others, "Study of Excellence," pp. 80-115.

14. The IRT log gain scores, which we shall call "achievement log gain

scores," were supplied to us by the National Center for Education Statistics, and were calculated for each test as follows:

Achievement log gain score $= X_2 - X_1$

Where:
$$X_1 = -LN\left(1 - \frac{Y1 + 13}{N + 14}\right)$$

$$X_2 = -LN\left(1 - \frac{Y2 + 13}{N + 14}\right)$$

And where: $Y1$ is the pretest IRT score
$Y2$ is the posttest IRT score
N is the number of items in the test

15. Compare James Bryant Conant, *The American High School Today: A First Report to Interested Citizens* (McGraw-Hill, 1959); and Mortimer Adler, *The Paideia Proposal: An Educational Manifesto* (Macmillan, 1982).

16. John Meyer, W. Richard Scott, and David Strang, "Centralization, Fragmentation, and School District Complexity," *Administrative Science Quarterly*, vol. 32 (June 1987), pp. 186–201.

17. On the virtues of large high schools see the literature reviewed in Anthony S. Bryk, Valerie E. Lee, and Julia B. Smith, "High School Organization and Its Effects on Teachers and Students: An Interpretative Summary of the Research," paper presented at the Conference on Choice and Control in American Education, University of Wisconsin, 1989, pp. 10–14.

18. See especially Theodore R. Sizer, *Horace's Compromise: The Dilemma of the American High School* (Houghton Mifflin, 1984); and Arthur G. Powell, Eleanor Farrar, and David K. Cohen, *The Shopping Mall High School: Winners and Losers in the Educational Marketplace* (Houghton Mifflin, 1985).

19. See especially National Commission on Excellence in Education, *A Nation at Risk: The Imperative for Educational Reform* (Washington, 1983); and reports discussed in Paul E. Peterson, "Did the Education Commissions Say Anything?" *Brookings Review*, vol. 2 (Winter 1983), pp. 3–11.

20. See William A. Firestone, Susan H. Fuhrman, and Michael W. Kirst, *The Progress of Reform: An Appraisal of State Education Initiatives*, Research Report Series RR-014 (Rutgers University, Center for Policy Research in Education, 1989).

21. On test scores and their possible relationship to requirements see Congressional Budget Office, *Educational Achievement: Explanations and Implications of Recent Trends* (Washington, August 1987).

22. The principal's questionnaire did not specify how the principal of a high school that housed only the final three years of high school (grades 10–12) should gauge its requirements, though the questionnaire assumed that all principals would employ the normal four-year definition of high school as a baseline. It appears that the lack of specificity in the directions did not cause a problem and that virtually all principals included grades 9–12 in their graduation requirements. The reported requirements for English demonstrate

this. Although the overwhelming majority of schools reported four years of English as a graduation requirement, ninety-one schools (23.3 percent) reported only three years, suggesting that perhaps grade 9 was being excluded from the requirements. But of the ninety-one schools, seventy-six were four-year high schools, leaving only thirteen three-year schools that might have underreported their graduation requirements. Of the thirteen, moreover, two reported increased graduation requirements between 1982 and 1984, indicating that the original response was valid. The remaining eleven schools, only 3 percent of the sample, that might have underreported requirements are equally divided between the high and low performance school categories and are therefore unlikely to bias our analysis.

23. Contrary to such remedial views, our research on effective schools for the poor also emphasizes the importance of high expectations. See Purkey and Smith, "Effective Schools."

24. Our measures of goal clarity and most other characteristics of school organization are based on the responses of principals and teachers to survey questions that gauge attitudes on various kinds of scales—for example, six-point scales of agreement or disagreement. In and of themselves these scales are difficult to interpret. For example, is a one-point difference on a six-point scale big or small? Instead of reporting scale scores, we will therefore report throughout this study the proportion of schools or students in the group of interest—say, high performance schools—with scale scores that are above the average for all schools or students.

25. For a thorough empirical study of the demands on the time of principals, see Van Cleve Morris and others, *Principals in Action: The Reality of Managing Schools* (Columbus, Ohio: C. E. Merrill, 1984).

26. On leadership see especially Sara Lawrence Lightfoot, *The Good High School: Portraits of Character and Culture* (Basic Books, 1983); Joan Lipsitz, *Successful Schools for Young Adolescents* (New Brunswick, N.J.: Transaction Books, 1984); Douglas Carnine, Russell Gersten, and Susan Green, "The Principal as Instructional Leader: A Second Look," *Educational Leadership*, vol. 40 (December 1982), pp. 47–50; and Arthur Blumberg and William Greenfield, *The Effective Principal: Perspectives on School Leadership* (Allyn and Bacon, 1980).

27. There are lively debates about how teacher education might be reformed and about how teachers might be rewarded for their performance, but there is little evidence that effective schools have teachers with different educational backgrounds or that effective schools employ different economic incentives. See Eric A. Hanushek, "The Economics of Schooling: Production and Efficiency in Public Schools," *Journal of Economic Literature*, vol. 24 (September 1986), pp. 1141–77; and Carnegie Forum on Education and the Economy, Task Force on Teaching as a Profession, *A Nation Prepared: Teachers for the 21st Century* (Washington, 1986).

28. This is especially clear in Michael Rutter and others, *Fifteen Thousand Hours: Secondary Schools and Their Effects on Children* (Harvard University Press, 1979); Sizer, *Horace's Compromise*; and John I. Goodlad, *A Place*

Called School: Prospects for the Future (McGraw-Hill, 1984); but it is stressed almost universally, as explained in Purkey and Smith, "Effective Schools."

29. On the problems of the bureaucratic model of teaching, see especially Fred M. Newmann and Donald W. Oliver, "Education and Community," *Harvard Educational Review*, vol. 37 (Winter 1967), pp. 61–106; and William A. Firestone and Sheila Rosenblum, "Building Commitment in Urban Schools," *Educational Evaluation and Policy Analysis*, vol. 10 (Winter 1988), pp. 285–300.

30. Although discipline is handled inside and outside the classroom, it is influenced in the ATS schools in the same way as matters that are typically handled outside the classroom. Discipline is therefore included, along with other "outside matters," in our index of teacher influence while matters that are typically handled inside the classroom—selecting topics and assigning homework, for example—are influenced differently and are excluded from the index.

31. See especially Carnegie Forum, *A Nation Prepared.*

32. See especially Bryk, Lee, and Smith, "High School Organization," pp. 55–59.

33. This very important characteristic of tracking has come in for a lot of criticism over the last decade. See especially Powell, Farrar, and Cohen, *Shopping Mall High School*; and Sizer, *Horace's Compromise.*

34. Valuable reviews of this literature include T. L. Good, "Classroom Research: A Decade of Progress," *Educational Psychologist*, vol. 18, no. 3 (1983), pp. 127–44; and Walter Doyle, "Effective Secondary Classroom Practices," in Kyle, ed., *Reaching for Excellence*, pp. 55–70.

35. On class time, see especially Sizer, *Horace's Compromise*; and Powell, Farrar, and Cohen, *Shopping Mall High School.*

36. James S. Coleman and Thomas Hoffer, *Public and Private High Schools: The Impact of Communities* (Basic Books, 1987); and James S. Coleman, Thomas Hoffer, and Sally Kilgore, *High School Achievement: Public, Catholic, and Private Schools Compared* (Basic Books, 1982).

37. Strictly speaking, this is an estimate of time spent on administrative matters *outside* of class, but it is strongly related to complaints about interferences within class.

38. High performance schools expel and suspend a lower proportion (12.6 percent) of their students each year than low performance schools do (16.9 percent). But this difference may be because the two types of schools have different problems with student behavior and not because the sanctions in high performance schools are any less swift, certain, or severe than those in low performance schools. Moreover, if disciplinary policies are working effectively, as they appear to be in high performance schools, suspension and expulsion rates will be reduced, not raised, as the actual rates in fact suggest.

Chapter Four

1. The seminal study of the influence of family background on achievement is James S. Coleman and others, *Equality of Educational Opportunity*

(Department of Health, Education and Welfare, 1966). More than one hundred additional studies are reviewed in Eric A. Hanushek, "The Economics of Schooling: Production and Efficiency in Public Schools," *Journal of Economic Literature*, vol. 24 (September 1986), pp. 1141–77.

2. Hanushek, "Economics of Schooling."

3. These statistics are calculated and documented in John E. Chubb and Terry M. Moe, "Educational Choice: Answers to the Most Frequently Asked Questions about Mediocrity in American Education and What Can Be Done about It," *Wisconsin Policy Research Institute Report*, vol. 2 (March 1989), pp. 3–5. For the most recent figures on public school expenditures, see Tom Snyder and W. Vance Grant, "1989 Back to School Forecast," press release, National Center for Education Statistics, August 24, 1989.

4. On the methodological weaknesses of effective schools research, see Stewart C. Purkey and Marshall S. Smith, "Effective Schools: A Review," *Elementary School Journal*, vol. 83 (March 1983), pp. 427–52.

5. The magnitude of the difference can also be appreciated with reference to national trends. From 1970 to 1988 the ratio of teachers to students in the nation's public elementary and secondary schools fell from 22.4 to 17.4, a decline that is generally viewed as substantial. The difference in staffing ratios between high and low performance schools is nearly half as large as the change in staffing ratios nationwide over the last two decades. (The national figures are higher than those in the Administrator and Teacher Survey (ATS) data because the ATS data include only high schools, which are more intensively staffed than elementary schools.) National Center for Education Statistics, *Digest of Education Statistics, 1988* (Department of Education, 1988), p. 67; Jo Anne Davis and Elaine Price, "Public Elementary and Secondary State Aggregate Nonfiscal Data by State for School Year 1988–1989 and School Revenue and Current Expenditures for Fiscal Year 1988," National Center for Education Statistics, 1990.

6. A fair amount of research indicates that significant economies of scale result from increasing school size. See, for example, Richard L. Daft and Selwyn W. Becker, "Managerial, Institutional, and Technical Influences on Administration: A Longitudinal Analysis," *Social Forces*, vol. 59 (December 1980), pp. 392–413; and William F. Fox, "Reviewing Economies of Size in Education," *Journal of Education Finance*, vol. 6 (Winter 1981), pp. 273–96.

7. On the pros and cons of specialization and tracking, see James Bryant Conant, *The American High School Today: A First Report to Interested Citizens* (McGraw-Hill, 1959); and Jeannie Oakes, *Keeping Track: How Schools Structure Inequality* (Yale University Press, 1985). Notwithstanding the strong stances that have been taken regarding the large, comprehensive high school, research on the academic (as opposed to the economic) effects of school size has produced very ambiguous results. See Charles E. Bidwell and John D. Kasarda, "School District Organization and Student Achievement," *American Sociological Review*, vol. 40 (February 1975), pp. 55–70; and Noah E. Friedkin and Juan Necochea, "School Size and Performance: A Contingency

Perspective," *Educational Evaluation and Policy Analysis* vol. 10 (Fall 1988), pp. 237–49.

8. The most recent, thoroughgoing critique of the large, comprehensive high school is Arthur G. Powell, Eleanor Farrar, and David K. Cohen, *The Shopping Mall High School: Winners and Losers in the Educational Marketplace* (Houghton Mifflin, 1985). On the empirical effects of program specialization and student stratification, see especially Karl L. Alexander, Martha Cook, and Edward L. McDill, "Curriculum Tracking and Educational Stratification: Some Further Evidence" *American Sociological Review*, vol. 43 (February 1978), pp. 47–66; James E. Rosenbaum, *Making Inequality: The Hidden Curriculum of High School Tracking* (John Wiley and Sons, 1976); and A. B. Sorenson, "The Organizational Differentiation of Students in Schools as an Opportunity Structure," in Maureen T. Hallinan, ed., *The Social Organization* (Plenum Press, 1987).

9. In the unweighted sample, which is roughly representative of the schools attended by a random sample of American students, schools are on average much larger than they are in the weighted sample, and low performance schools (average enrollment, 1,291) are about 10 percent larger than high performance schools (average enrollment, 1,176).

10. Bureau of the Census, *Statistical Abstract of the United States, 1982–83*, 103d ed. (Department of Commerce, 1982), pp. 436, 417. The poverty level is for an average family of four.

11. Parental expectations are an especially problematic indicator of family influence because they are so strongly influenced by the actual achievement of students. As a consequence, differences in observed expectations may represent little more than differences in parental predictions of achievement.

12. Technically, we do not believe it is possible to identify a system of simultaneous equations that includes equations for all variables that are substantially endogenous. It is difficult to conceive of unique exogenous causes of each endogenous variable and in our view it is impossible to find suitable measures of such causes in the ATS-HSB data set.

13. If variables are highly correlated with one another—the problem of multicollinearity—the estimates of their effects will be subject to large margins of error. In models with high levels of multicollinearity, adding or subtracting a variable can lead to substantial changes in parameter estimates.

14. The mean IRT index scores for students in high and low performance schools are 11.4 and 8.14 respectively.

15. On the virtues of using panel data to study achievement, and on the methods for doing so, see Hanushek, "Economics of Schooling."

16. See especially James S. Coleman and Thomas Hoffer, *Public and Private High Schools: The Impact of Communities* (Basic Books, 1987).

17. We also exclude family expectations of student college attendance, despite its moderately strong association with achievement gains, for two reasons: the question may not measure normative expectations at all but instead gauge parent predictions about college attendance, which are probably more a result of student achievement than a cause of it; and only 80 percent

of the students were able to answer the survey questions about parent expectations.

18. Coleman and others, *Equality of Educational Opportunity*; and Robert L. Crain and Rita E. Mahard, "The Effects of Research Methodology on Desegregation-Achievement Studies: A Meta-Analysis," *American Journal of Sociology*, vol. 88 (March 1983), pp. 839–54.

19. On the importance of the contextual influence of families and social groups, see especially James M. McPartland and Edward L. McDill, "Control and Differentiation in the Structure of American Education," *Sociology of Education*, vol. 55 (April-July 1982), pp. 77–88.

20. Although the bivariate analysis of school size indicated that its relationship with achievement might be complex rather than nonexistent, preliminary multivariate analysis showed that, all things being equal, school size is not a significant determinant of achievement. We consequently dropped school size from this stage of the analysis. We will reexamine it in chapter 5 as a determinant of school organization.

21. Although the measures of school organization examined in chapter 3 are clearly associated with student achievement gains in the ATS schools, it is not immediately clear that these measures should be candidates to explain achievement gains. Most of the organizational measures were obtained from the ATS questionnaires, which were administered in 1984, two years after the final achievement tests were administered. If schools changed between 1982 and 1984, the 1984 measures of school organization might not provide valid measures of school organization for the years 1981 and 1982, when the students in this analysis were in school. As we explain in appendix A, schools did not change systematically during the two years after student achievement was measured, so the 1984 measures of school organization can be used with little risk of bias to explain achievement in 1980 and 1982.

22. John I. Goodlad, *A Place Called School: Prospects for the Future* (McGraw-Hill, 1984).

23. Michael Rutter and others, *Fifteen Thousand Hours: Secondary Schools and Their Effects on Children* (Harvard University Press, 1979); and Michael Rutter, "School Effects on Pupil Progress: Research Findings and Policy Implications," *Child Development*, vol. 54 (February 1983), pp. 1–29.

24. Wilbur J. Brookover and others, *School Social Systems and Student Achievement: Schools Can Make a Difference* (Praeger, 1979).

25. Ronald Edmonds, "Effective Schools for the Urban Poor," *Educational Leadership*, vol. 37 (October 1979), pp. 15–24.

26. Organizational interdependence also means that it does not make a great deal of sense to model the influence of school organization as if it were neatly ordered—for example, principals influencing school objectives and staff behavior, and those variables affecting classroom operations, which in turn affect student achievement. Attempts to so model the structure of schools, using the ATS data, have revealed this organizational interdependence clearly. See, for example, Fred M. Newman, Robert A. Rutter, and Marshall S. Smith, "Organizational Factors Affecting School Sense of Efficacy, Commu-

nity, and Expectations," University of Wisconsin, School of Education, August 12, 1988.

27. This approach has also been used in an analysis of the merged ATS-HSB data by Anthony S. Bryk and Mary Driscoll, "An Empirical Investigation of School as a Community," University of Chicago, 1988.

28. In fact, only three school qualities examined in the school profiles are not represented in the index: the experience of teachers, the amount of writing assigned by teachers—which showed no relationship whatsoever to student achievement—and the amount of classroom disruption—which we deemed too dependent on the makeup of the student body to use as an independent indicator of school organization. In addition, classroom effectiveness is well measured by other indicators in the comprehensive index.

29. The coefficient on school economic resources is also nonsignificant when percent black is in the model.

30. The coefficient on percent black is also nonsignificant when school resources are in the model.

31. Research on the effects of race on achievement has actually produced very mixed results. If nonracial causes of achievement are specified adequately, it is not unusual to find that black-white distinctions do not add significantly to statistical explanations of achievement. See especially Crain and Mahard, "Effects of Research Methodology on Desegregation-Achievement Studies."

32. The unstandardized coefficients are difficult to interpret directly because the dependent variable is measured in terms of IRT log gains, a metric that lacks straightforward meaning.

33. Consistent with the small standardized coefficients, the R^2 value for the model is small too. The model explains 5 percent of the variance in achievement gain scores. This would be troubling if it signified the omission of some important independent variable. But theory suggests that this is not the case. In addition, the model's error variance, albeit sizable, appears to be randomly distributed. The regression coefficients should therefore be unbiased and efficient. It is important to note, moreover, that the low R^2 value is a price we pay for our double control on sophomore scores. In preliminary analyses we modeled senior scores as a function of sophomore scores and other independent variables, and we obtained R^2 values of roughly .70. Our coefficients for school effects were less conservative, however.

34. Generally speaking, standardized coefficients are useful for comparing the effects of variables with different units of measurement and different variances; unstandardized coefficients are useful for making substantive interpretations and for gauging the strength of relationships independent of sample variations. Our preference is for the interpretations provided by the unstandardized coefficients, but here those coefficients are based on variables with arbitrary or technically complicated units of measurement. And to interpret unstandardized coefficients, we must rely on a unit of measurement— years of achievement—that is dependent on variation in the ATS-HSB sample. Nevertheless, the unstandardized coefficients have more substantive meaning than the standardized coefficient, and we rely primarily on them.

35. This explanation is stressed in Anthony S. Bryk, Valerie E. Lee, and Julia B. Smith, "High School Organization and Its Effects on Teachers and Students: An Interpretative Summary of the Research," paper presented at the Conference on Choice and Control in American Education, University of Wisconsin, 1989.

36. This explanation is stressed in Purkey and Smith, "Effective Schools."

37. Coleman and Hoffer, *Public and Private High Schools*, argues that this is the best proximate explanation of why Catholic high schools are more successful than public high schools in promoting academic achievement.

38. The calculations of these effects are described in appendix C and table C-4.

39. The only exception to this procedure was our handling of the index of school harmony. Because this index is itself a fairly heterogeneous and quite comprehensive measure, we disaggregated it, and examined the effects of each of its components on the importance of school organization separately.

40. Coleman and Hoffer, *Public and Private High Schools*.

Chapter Five

1. In 1989 there were seventy-six federal grant programs for elementary, secondary, and vocational education. Advisory Commission on Intergovernmental Relations, *A Catalog of Federal Grant-In-Aid Programs to State and Local Governments: Grants Funded FY 1989* (Washington, 1989), p. 4. In 1985–86, 49.4 percent of all public elementary and secondary school revenue came from state funds, 43.9 percent from local funds, and 6.7 percent from federal funds. National Center for Education Statistics, Office of Educational Research and Improvement, *Digest of Education Statistics 1988* (Department of Education, 1988), p. 124. In 1945–46 the United States contained 101,382 public school districts; in 1986–87 it contained 15,713. National Center for Education Statistics, *Digest, 1988*, p. 83. On the rapid rise of administrative costs see John E. Chubb and Terry M. Moe, "Educational Choice: Answers to the Most Frequently Asked Questions about Mediocrity in American Education and What Can be Done about It," *Wisconsin Policy Research Institute Report*, vol. 2 (March 1989), pp. 3–6.

2. The tension between rational bureaucracy and effective school organization was first crystalized in the classic paper by Charles E. Bidwell, "The School as a Formal Organization," in James G. March, ed., *Handbook of Organizations* (Rand McNally, 1965). The tension has since been explored by many scholars, including especially those who have developed the effective schools literature, as reviewed in Stewart C. Purkey and Marshall S. Smith, "Effective Schools: A Review," *Elementary School Journal*, vol. 83 (March 1983), pp. 427–52. There are, however, some education scholars who regard this tension as only a minor problem because schools are "loosely coupled"

and able to overcome it—for example, Karl E. Weick, "Educational Organizations as Loosely Coupled Systems," *Administrative Science Quarterly*, vol. 21 (March 1976), pp. 1–19; and Jane Hannaway and Susan Abramowitz, "Public and Private Schools: Are They Really Different?" in Gilbert R. Austin and Herbert Garber, eds., *Research on Exemplary Schools* (Orlando: Academic Press, 1985), chap. 2. The controversy has recently been discussed in Paul Hechinger, "Does School Structure Matter?" *Educational Researcher*, vol. 17 (August-September 1988), pp. 10–13.

3. Although the comprehensive index of school organization has a weaker influence on achievement than the condensed index (see chap. 4), the comprehensive index is the appropriate focus for this next step in our analysis. The comprehensive index is based on our four-dimensional conceptualization of effective school organization and on our analysis of the relationships among the indicators that might conceivably be used to measure it. The index turns out to have a significant and substantial effect on student achievement. The condensed index, which measures the same dimensions and essentially the same concept of organization, has a stronger effect on achievement. But the primary value of the condensed index is in demonstrating that the influence of school organization, which is inherently difficult to measure, may be greater than the comprehensive index estimates it to be. The condensed index does not have the independent validity of the comprehensive index, and in another sample of schools it might not have superior predictive power either.

4. The research surrounding this controversy is reviewed most recently in Anthony S. Bryk, Valerie E. Lee, and Julia B. Smith, "High School Organization and Its Effects on Teachers and Students: An Interpretative Summary of the Research," paper presented at the Conference on Choice and Control in American Education, University of Wisconsin, 1989.

5. The best review of this literature is Eric A. Hanushek, "The Economics of Schooling: Production and Efficiency in Public Schools," *Journal of Economic Literature*, vol. 24 (September 1986), pp. 1141–77.

6. Schools that did not report either no problems or only minor problems reported either moderate or serious problems.

7. As we will explain later in this chapter, there is one other reason to be cautious about concluding that student bodies are responsible for school organization. That is, the caliber of students in a school may be a consequence of school organization and not just a cause. Schools with good organization and reputations for success certainly attract better students than schools that are known to be academically inferior. This is true of good private schools and also of good public schools that affect parents' decisions about residence.

8. The other potential sources of influence that principals were asked about include teachers at the school, parents, school boards or governing boards, and teacher associations or unions.

9. We did not use the mean of the two administrative influences because in instances where administrative constraints were strong, but were being imposed by the superintendent or the central office alone, the mean would underestimate the administrative influence that the school was experiencing.

10. Principals were asked about several other barriers too, such as low pay. But the other barriers were not related to the indicators of personnel constraint and therefore were not included in this part of the analysis.

11. Virtually all private schools in our sample are governed by school boards of some sort.

12. Another important problem is that several of the variables that we believe affect school organization directly—student ability, parent-school contacts, and parent-school relationships—are strongly influenced by a variable, parent SES, that may also affect school organization, but mostly indirectly. If parent SES and the three variables that it influences are all included as independent variables in a regression equation for school organization, parent SES will be estimated to have a larger direct effect on school organization than it actually has. Student ability, parental contacts, and parental relationships will be estimated to have smaller effects than they actually have. To avoid such bias, we estimated a regression equation in which parent SES was the dependent variable and student ability, parent contacts, and parental relationships were the independent variables. We retrieved the residuals from the estimates for that equation, and used the residuals as our measure of parent SES in the model of school organization. Parent SES will therefore receive credit for only that portion of its influence that works directly on school organization and not indirectly through these three other variables that are likely to influence school organization directly themselves.

13. We exclude teacher salaries from the models because the relationship between school organization and teacher salaries is thoroughly confounded by reciprocal causality. Schools with difficult students and troubled organizations often have to pay high wages to attract teachers. As a result, our estimates of the effects of teacher salaries on school organization are negative. This, however, is misleading because higher salaries are unlikely to undermine school organization.

14. We also explored the possibility that board influence is different, and perhaps more favorable, in rural and suburban areas where school systems are smaller. The results, however, were negative.

15. The direct influence of parents on school organization is even weaker than it may appear since the variables that measure it do not have to compete with the indirect influences that parents of differing levels of SES exert on school organization. As we explained in note 12, the parent SES measure is a residual measure, controlling for parent-school contacts and parent-school relationships. We have thereby given the direct parental role in schools every opportunity to demonstrate its importance, and it has failed to make much of a difference for school organization.

16. See Frederick H. Brigham, Jr., *United States Catholic Elementary and Secondary Schools 1988–89: A Statistical Report on Schools, Enrollment, and Staffing* (Washington: National Catholic Education Association, 1989); and National Center for Education Statistics, *Digest, 1988*, p. 85.

17. For example, of the fifty largest school systems in the United States, thirty-two are centered in urban areas, as defined by the High School and

Beyond (HSB) survey. See National Center for Education Statistics, *Digest, 1988*, p. 85.

18. As defined in the HSB survey, urban schools are in central cities within standard metropolitan statistical areas (SMSAs). Suburban schools are within SMSAs but outside of central cities. Rural schools are outside of SMSAs.

19. While it may be surprising to see that large percentages of both high and low control schools are rural, these percentages are close to the percentage of rural schools in the sample as a whole. It is important to bear in mind that we are analyzing a random sample of American high schools and not a sample of schools weighted to be representative of the schools attended by random American students.

20. In preliminary analyses we estimated models with three locations—urban, suburban, and rural—but we never found significant differences in constraint between any location other than those between urban and nonurban schools.

21. In research that we conducted prior to launching the analysis that occupies this book—research that inspired the line of analysis followed in this book—we found that private schools of all types tend to have significantly higher levels of virtually all effective school characteristics than public schools. Those findings, however, did not allow for the many alternative causes of school organization that have concerned us here. See John E. Chubb and Terry M. Moe, "Politics, Markets, and the Organization of Schools," *American Political Science Review*, vol. 82 (December 1988), pp. 1065–87.

22. For the sake of completeness, we estimated other models with other controls, including school location. In the presence of these additional controls, school sector continued to have an enormous influence.

23. The exact predicted percentiles are 56.0 for public schools and 82.8 for private schools.

24. It would take us too far afield here to present an adequate analysis of the direct effect of school control (or school sector) on student achievement. We have conducted such an analysis, however, and will provide our results upon request. In essence, we find that students in private schools register significantly larger total achievement log gain scores than students in public schools, when all of the factors (except school organization) considered in our chap. 4 analysis of student achievement are held constant. The achievement difference associated with private schooling is not as large, however, as the achievement difference associated with school organization in the original analysis of chap. 4. This suggests that the immediate key to private school success is not any elusive quality of "privateness," but rather school organization, which tends to be more effective in the private sector than in the public sector.

Chapter Six

1. For a review and evaluation of the early wave of reforms, see Denis P. Doyle and Terry W. Hartle, *Excellence in Education: The States Take Charge*

(Washington: American Enterprise Institute for Public Policy Research, 1985); and William Chance, *"the best of educations": Reforming America's Public Schools in the 1980s* (Washington: John D. and Catherine T. MacArthur Foundation, 1986).

2. Among the more influential calls for a second wave of reform are Carnegie Forum on Education and the Economy, Task Force on Teaching as a Profession, *A Nation Prepared: Teachers for the 21st Century* (New York, 1986); and National Governors' Association, *A Time for Results: The Governors' 1991 Report on Education* (Washington, National Governors' Association, 1986).

3. For an overview of the 1980s reforms that includes an assessment of the limited achievements (thus far) of second-wave proposals, see William A. Firestone, Susan H. Fuhrman, and Michael W. Kirst, "The Progress of Reform: An Appraisal of State Education Initiatives," Research Report Series, RR-014 (Rutgers University, Center for Policy Research in Education, 1989). See also Jane L. David, *Restructuring in Progress: Lessons from Pioneering Districts* (Washington, National Governors' Association, 1989); and Richard F. Elmore, *Early Experience in Restructuring Schools: Voices from the Field* (Washington, National Governors' Association, 1988).

4. In the aggregate, expenditures on elementary and secondary education rose at least $50 billion during the 1980s. Expenditures per pupil rose 50 percent in real terms, reaching $5246 per child in 1989–90. Tom Snyder and W. Vance Grant, "1989 Back to School Forecast," press release, National Center for Education Statistics, August 24, 1989; and National Center for Education Statistics, Office of Educational Research and Improvement, *Digest of Education Statistics, 1988* (Department of Education, 1988), pp. 124, 132.

5. See Eric A. Hanushek, "The Economics of Schooling: Production and Efficiency in Public Schools," *Journal of Economic Literature*, vol. 24 (September 1986), pp. 1141–77.

6. For spending figures on public and private schools, see C. Emily Feistritzer, *Cheating Our Children: Why We Need School Reform* (Washington: National Center for Educational Information, 1985). For a comparative analysis of public and private school performance, see James S. Coleman, Thomas Hoffer, and Sally Kilgore, *High School Achievement: Public, Catholic, and Private Schools Compared* (Basic Books, 1982); and James S. Coleman and Thomas Hoffer, *Public and Private High Schools: The Impact of Communities* (Basic Books, 1987).

7. It is also relatively inexpensive, easy to do, widely popular among people in and out of the educational community—and, not surprisingly, far-and-away the most common of educational reforms to be adopted in the 1980s. Some forty-five states either adopted new requirements or strengthened their existing ones. See Firestone, Fuhrman, and Kirst, "Progress of Reform," pp. 17–20.

8. In most states, reforms have only recently gone into effect, so it is difficult to evaluate their effects with much confidence. At this point, however, the available evidence is not heartening. A recent study by the General

Accounting Office based on a sample of 61,000 students in four states, concludes that stricter graduation requirements have had no significant effect. See "High School Graduation Requirements Said Not to Affect Achievement Test Scores," *Chronicle of Higher Education*, October 4, 1989, p. A20. For a more general discussion of the available evidence and the issues involved in assessing it, see William H. Clune with Paula White and Janice Patterson, *The Implementation and Effects of High School Graduation Requirements: First Steps toward Curricular Reform* (Rutgers University, Center for Policy Research in Education, 1989).

9. This assumes that within feasible salary ranges, salaries are not contingent on teacher performance—which is generally true of teacher compensation today. On the relationship between salaries and performance, see Hanushek, "Economics of Schooling;" and Myron Lieberman, "Are Teachers Underpaid?" *Public Interest*, no. 84 (Summer 1986), pp. 12–28.

10. For discussions of state efforts in strengthening certification requirements, see Firestone, Fuhrman, and Kirst, "Progress of Reform"; Denis P. Doyle and Terry W. Hartle, *Excellence in Education*; and Linda Darling-Hammond and Barnett Berry, *The Evolution of Teacher Policy* (Santa Monica, Calif.: Rand Corporation, Center for Policy Research in Education, 1988).

11. See C. Emily Feistritzer, *Teacher Crisis: Myth or Reality? A State-by-State Analysis* (Washington: National Center for Educational Information, 1986).

12. See Carnegie Forum on Education and the Economy, *A Nation Prepared*.

13. Perhaps the most widely touted statewide experiment in merit pay, adopted by Florida in 1983, collapsed of its own bureaucratic weight when implementation produced little more than confusion, dissatisfaction, and conflict. It was discontinued in 1986. See Firestone, Fuhrman, and Kirst, "Progress of Reform," p. 32. More generally, on the problems of implementing merit pay schemes, see David K. Cohen and Richard J. Murnane, "The Merits of Merit Pay," *Public Interest*, no. 80 (Summer 1985), pp. 3–30; Harry P. Hatry and John M. Greiner, *Issues and Case Studies in Teacher Incentive Plans* (Washington: Urban Institute Press, 1985); and Henry C. Johnson, Jr., ed., *Merit, Money, and Teachers' Careers: Studies on Merit Pay and Career Ladders for Teachers* (Lanham, Md.: University Press of America, 1985).

14. For an overview of the kinds of tests that states have adopted, see *Creating Responsible and Responsive Accountability Systems*, Report of the OERI State Accountability Study Group (Department of Education, 1988).

15. For more extensive treatments than we can provide here, see Daniel Koretz, "Arriving in Lake Wobegon: Are Standardized Tests Exaggerating Achievement and Distorting Instruction?" *American Educator*, vol. 12 (Summer 1988), pp. 8–15; Doug A. Archbald and Fred M. Newmann, *Beyond Standardized Testing: Assessing Authentic Academic Achievement in the Secondary School* (Reston, Va.: National Association of Secondary School

Principals, 1988); and Craig E. Richards and Mwalimu Shujaa, "The State Education Accountability Movement: Impact on Schools?" Rutgers University, Center for Policy Research on Education, 1988.

16. To the extent that these ideas have been put into practice, most of the action has taken place at the district rather than the state level, with the states' role largely restricted to providing encouragement and seed money for local reforms. Districts that have been most aggressive in restructuring, moreover, have often been those facing serious problems or crises.

17. On Chicago, see Herbert J. Walberg and others, *We Can Rescue Our Children: The Cure for Chicago's Public School Crisis—With Lessons for the Rest of America* (Chicago: Heartland Institute, 1988). On Rochester, see Adam Urbanski, "Public Schools of Choice and Education Reform," in Joe Nathan, ed., *Public Schools by Choice* (St. Paul: Institute for Learning and Teaching, 1989), pp. 225–38; Ellen Graham, "Starting from Scratch: Rochester Wipes the Slate Clean, Gives Teachers New Responsibility," *Wall Street Journal*, March 31, 1989, pp. R4–6; and Jerry Buckley, "A Blueprint for Better Schools," *U.S. News and World Report*, January 18, 1988, pp. 60–65. On Dade County, see Lynn Olson, "The Sky's the Limit: Dade Ventures Self-Governance," *Education Week*, December 2, 1987, p. 1; and Lynn Olson, "Dade's School Restructuring: A Trip into Uncharted Territory," *Education Week*, December 2, 1987, p. 19.

18. For general discussions of the basic features of school-based management and some of the problems and issues that it raises, see James W. Guthrie and Rodney J. Reed, *Educational Administration and Policy: Effective Leadership for American Schools* (Prentice-Hall, 1986); James W. Guthrie, "School-Based Management: The Next Needed Education Reform," *Phi Delta Kappan*, vol. 68 (December 1986), pp. 305–09; Ted Kolderie, "School-Site Management: Rhetoric and Reality," University of Minnesota, Public Services Redesign Project, Humphrey Institute of Public Affairs, 1988; and Betty Malen, Rodney T. Ogawa, and Jennifer Kranz, "What Do We Know about School-Based Management? A Case Study of the Literature—A Call for Research," paper presented at the Conference on Choice and Control in American Education, University of Wisconsin, 1989.

19. See Kolderie, "School-Site Management."

20. The dangers of instability are greatest in the early years and should decline over time. If the new structures do manage to survive for an extended period of time, those benefited and empowered by them will tend to organize, marshal their resources, and defend the system against change. The real question is whether these kinds of decentralizing reforms can count on withstanding political vicissitudes long enough for this to happen.

21. Carnegie Forum on Education and the Economy, *A Nation Prepared.*

22. For a discussion of the ideas behind teacher empowerment and some of the efforts to put them into effect in districts around the country, see Darling-Hammond and Berry, *The Evolution of Teacher Policy*; Firestone,

Fuhrman, and Kirst, "Progress of Reform"; and Susan Moore Johnson, "Teachers, Power, and School Change," paper presented at the Conference on Choice and Control in American Education, University of Wisconsin, 1989.

23. See Blake Rodman, "N.E.A. Pursues Its Plan to Establish State Boards Controlled by Teachers," *Education Week*, April 29, 1987, p. 1.

24. Carnegie Forum on Education and the Economy, *A Nation Prepared*.

25. American Federation of Teachers, "School Based Management," *Radius*, vol. 1 (May 1988), pp. 1–5. For the origin of this proposal, see Myron Lieberman, "A Foundation Approach to Merit Pay," *Phi Delta Kappan*, vol. 41 (December 1959), pp. 118–22.

26. See, for instance, Kenneth J. Meier, *Regulation: Politics, Bureaucracy, and Economics* (St. Martin's Press, 1985).

27. Rodman, "N.E.A. Pursues Its Plan To Establish State Boards Controlled by Teachers."

28. For overviews of the recent choice movement within the public sector, including applications to desegregation, see Nathan, ed., *Public Schools by Choice*; "The Call for Choice: Competition in the Educational Marketplace," *Education Week*, June 24, 1987, pp. C1–C24; and Chester E. Finn, Jr., "Education That Works: Make the Schools Compete," *Harvard Business Review*, vol. 65 (September-October 1987), pp. 63–68.

29. A Times Mirror nationwide survey conducted by the Gallup Organization in January 1988 found that 49 percent of the country is "more likely" and only 27 percent "less likely" to vote for a presidential candidate who supports giving parents vouchers to pay for their kids' education, Times Mirror Center for the People and the Press, "The People, the Press, and Politics: Survey II," January 8–17, 1988. Throughout the 1980s, national polls showed that the public overwhelmingly endorses the general concept of parental choice. In 1987, 71 percent of the public said yes, parents in this community should have the right to choose which local schools their children attend. Alec M. Gallup and David L. Clark, "The 19th Annual Gallup Poll of the Public's Attitudes toward the Public Schools," *Phi Delta Kappan*, vol. 69 (September 1987), pp. 17–30. On parent and public reactions to particular choice plans, see Joe Nathan, "Results and Future Prospects of State Efforts to Increase Choice among Schools," *Phi Delta Kappan*, vol. 68 (June 1987), pp. 746–52.

30. National Governors' Association, *Time for Results*.

31. See, for example, Carnegie Forum on Education and the Economy, *A Nation Prepared*; David T. Kearns and Denis P. Doyle, *Winning the Brain Race: A Bold Plan to Make Our Schools Competitive* (San Francisco: Institute for Contemporary Studies, 1988); James S. Coleman, "Choice, Community, and Future Schools," paper presented at the Conference on Choice and Control in American Education, University of Wisconsin, 1989; and David S. Seeley, *Education through Partnership: Mediating Structures and Education* (Ballinger, 1981).

32. See, for example, Committee for Economic Development, *Investing in Our Children*; and City Club of Chicago, *Educational Choice: A Catalyst for*

School Reform, prepared by Edward Marciniak, a report of the Task Force on Education of the City Club of Chicago (August 1989).

33. See *Education Week*, "Call for Choice." Note also that support for choice is highest among the poor and racial minorities. In a January 1988 Times Mirror poll, 61 percent of the "partisan poor" said they would be more likely to support a presidential candidate "who supports giving parents vouchers to pay for their kids' education," Times Mirror Center for the People and the Press.

34. "Call for Choice"; and Adam Urbanski, "Public Schools of Choice and Education Reform," in Nathan, ed., *Public Schools by Choice*, pp. 225-38.

35. See Mary Anne Raywid, "The Mounting Case for Schools of Choice," in Nathan, ed., *Public Schools by Choice*, pp. 13-40.

36. Rolf K. Blank, "Educational Effects of Magnet Schools," paper presented at the Conference on Choice and Control in American Education, University of Wisconsin, 1989.

37. See *Education Week*, "Call for Choice," pp. C6-C9. See also Joe Nathan, "Progress, Problems, and Prospects with State Choice Plans," in Nathan, ed., *Public Schools by Choice*, pp. 203-24; and Mary Haywood Metz, *Different by Design: The Context and Character of Three Magnet Schools* (New York: Routledge and Kegan Paul, 1986).

38. For reviews of what is now a rather extensive empirical literature, see Raywid, "Mounting Case for Schools of Choice"; Mary Anne Raywid, "A Synthesis of Research on Schools of Choice," *Educational Leadership*, vol. 41 (April 1984), pp. 70-78; and Richard F. Elmore, "Choice as an Instrument of Public Policy: Evidence from Education and Health Care," paper presented at the Conference on Choice and Control in American Education, University of Wisconsin, 1989. For a more critical treatment, see Henry M. Levin, "The Theory of Choice Applied to Education," paper presented at the Conference on Choice and Control in American Education, University of Wisconsin, 1989.

39. For discussions of the Minnesota reforms and early evidence on their effects, see Jessie Montano, "Choice Comes to Minnesota"; and Joe Nathan, "Progress, Problems, and Prospects with State Choice Plans," in Nathan, ed., *Public Schools by Choice*, pp. 165-80, 203-24. At this writing, six other states—Arkansas, Idaho, Iowa, Nebraska, Ohio, and Utah—have also adopted statewide systems of public school choice.

40. On the design, operation, and recent history of the Cambridge system, see Robert Peterkin and Dorothy Jones, "Schools of Choice in Cambridge, Massachusetts," in Nathan, ed., *Public Schools by Choice*, pp. 125-48; and Christine H. Rossell and Charles L. Glenn, "The Cambridge Controlled Choice Plan," *Urban Review*, vol. 20 (Summer 1988), pp. 75-94.

41. Applications are not, of course, uniform across all schools. As one would expect, the best schools (by reputation) get more than their share, the worst get less. Cambridge officials have taken applications as a signal in determining which schools need attention and improvement—in one case, appointing a new principal and giving him the flexibility to transform the school to enhance its appeal. In subsequent years, applications to that school

rose dramatically. See Rossell and Glenn, "Cambridge Controlled Choice Plan."

42. For evidence on test scores, enrollments, and other indicators of improvement, see especially Peterkin and Jones, "Schools of Choice in Cambridge," p. 129; and Rossell and Glenn, "Cambridge Controlled Choice Plan." For discussions of racial balance in particular, see Michael J. Alves, "Cambridge Desegregation Succeeding," *Integrated Education*, vol. 21 (January-December 1983), pp. 178–87; and Ross Zerchykov, "A Context Note: Choice, Diversity, and Desegregation in Massachusetts," *Equity and Choice*, vol. 2 (May 1986), pp. 9–16.

43. The most comprehensive accounts of the East Harlem system are Sy Fliegel, "Parental Choice in East Harlem Schools," in Nathan, ed., *Public Schools by Choice*, pp. 95–112; and Raymond J. Domanico, "Model for Choice: A Report on Manhattan's District 4," *Education Policy Paper*, no. 1 (New York: Manhattan Institute for Policy Research, 1989). This system has also received extensive attention in the media, both because it is such a radical departure from tradition and because it has proven so successful. See, for example, Catherine Foster, "Junior High Choice in Harlem," *Christian Science Monitor*, April 5, 1989, p. 12; and Jane Perlez, "Year of Honor in East Harlem Schools," *New York Times*, June 27, 1987, p. 29.

44. The descriptive information we provide here and in following notes is taken from Fliegel, "Parental Choice in East Harlem"; and Domanico, "Model for Choice."

45. For the complete list, see Domanico, "Model for Choice," p. 9.

46. On the nature of the scandals, see Joyce Purnick, "2 Who Made Loans to Alvarado Got Extra School Pay," *New York Times*, March 8, 1984, p. 1; and Neil A. Lewis, "School Officials Being Ousted over Funds," *New York Times*, December 8, 1988, p. B1.

47. Edward B. Fiske, "The Alternative Schools of Famous District 4: Accolades and Better Attendance Are Not Enough," *New York Times*, November 1, 1989, p. B8.

48. For an overview of recent reformist thinking that nicely illustrates how choice fits into the grab-bag of second-wave reforms, see "Call for Choice." For a succinct statement, see "Not By Choice Alone," *Washington Post*, October 21, 1989, p. A24.

49. One of the best examples is Rochester, New York, which has adopted virtually every reform imaginable, including choice. For sympathetic discussions, see Adam Urbanski, "Public Schools of Choice and Education Reform"; Ellen Graham, "Starting from Scratch: Rochester Wipes the Slate Clean, Gives Teachers New Responsibility"; and Jerry Buckley, "Blueprint for Better Schools."

50. The classic argument for vouchers is developed in Milton and Rose Friedman, *Free to Choose: A Personal Statement* (Avon, 1981), pp. 140–78. A similar argument is now prominently made in Myron Lieberman, *Privatization and Educational Choice* (St. Martin's Press, 1989), though Lieberman also endorses other market options such as contracting out for educational

services. The Friedmans' argument is of course associated by educators with political conservatism. But vouchers have also been proposed by social democrats on the left, who seek to enlist markets in the cause of justice and equal opportunity for the poor. Perhaps the most influential of these proposals has come from Christopher Jencks, who, along with like-minded colleagues, urged administrators within the Office of Economic Opportunity (within both the late Johnson and early Nixon presidencies) to take vouchers seriously and encourage experimentation by states and districts. Their most tangible success, if it can be called that, is the ill-fated Alum Rock experiment—which, because of poor design and implementation (arising in part from the resistance of established interests), cannot meaningfully be considered a test of anything. See David K. Cohen and Eleanor Farrar, "Power to the Parents? The Story of Educational Vouchers," *Public Interest*, no. 48 (Summer 1977), pp. 72–97. Probably the most widely recognized voucher proposal since that time has been offered by Coons and Sugarman, who, to our knowledge, cannot readily be placed in an ideological camp. See John E. Coons and Stephen D. Sugarman, *Education by Choice: The Case for Family Control* (University of California Press, 1978).

51. State legislatures and governors must retain the basic authority to govern their educational systems. Yet they, too, will come under pressure in the future to use their authority to control the schools from above—and thus to destroy what they are trying to create. There is ultimately no solution to this dilemma. A good way of mitigating it, however, would be to design institutions around fully decentralized authority and then install them through constitutional amendment. The legal foundation of the new system would then be very difficult to change or violate once put in place. And, because state constitutions are the ultimate authorities in state government, they have the power to constrain what future legislatures and governors (and the political groups that pressure them) can do in controlling the schools.

52. To the extent that district governments must make political decisions about taxation and perhaps other matters in representing all citizens within their boundaries, they should be allowed to cover these expenses with local tax money or state subsidies. The point is that, in covering the costs of running their own schools, districts must rely only on student scholarships.

53. One way to arrange transportation would be for the Choice Office to operate a system of buses for getting students to drop-off points throughout the district, where schools (or contractors hired by the schools) would then pick them up. The state would pay for all this, reimbursing schools on a per child basis (just as they do for scholarships). Many and perhaps most children, however, would probably choose a school close to their home or would be driven by a parent; and this would limit the state's transportation job, as well as its expense. Moreover, if the number and quality of schools increased, as we fully expect they would in a choice system, most students could have attractive options near their homes.

54. Desegregation plans may call for additional rules, quotas for example. On the compatibility of choice and desegregation plans, see Patricia M. Lines,

"The Denial of Choice and *Brown* v. *Board of Education,*" *Metropolitan Education,* no. 4 (Spring 1987), pp. 108–27.

55. For example, they might be assigned by lottery to schools in reasonable proximity to their homes; and all schools, as a precondition for becoming public, would then be required to run the risk of having an occasional student assigned to them.

56. There is little reason to believe that expulsions (or even denials for readmission) will be common. In the first place, schools and students have voluntarily chosen one another; most of the time, they will be happy together. Second, expulsions are quite infrequent in the existing private sector, where schools have long been free to expel at will. Third, schools that frequently expel students will acquire a reputation for doing so, which will hurt them in the application process; knowing this, they should be very hesitant to expel except in the most egregious cases. And finally (although we think this is unnecessary), special rules might be set up to discourage expulsions: for example, a rule requiring an expelling school to fill that slot with a student who has been expelled from another school.

57. This implies, among other things, that the state will do nothing to impose teacher professionalism on the schools. Teacher professionalism will emerge from below as teachers are granted the autonomy to control their own schools and their own work, and as schools develop their own structures for governing themselves and pursuing their missions.

Appendix A

1. National Center for Education Statistics, *High School and Beyond 1980 Sophomore Cohort First Follow-up (1982): Data File User's Manual* (Department of Education, 1983); and National Center for Education Statistics, Office of Educational Research and Improvement, *High School and Beyond Administrator and Teacher Survey (1984): Data File User's Manual* (Department of Education, 1988). The information in the first section of this appendix is drawn from the Administrator and Teacher Survey (ATS) user's manual, pp. 1–12, 18, 19.

2. See National Center for Education Statistics, *High School and Beyond 1980,* pp. 19–22.

3. The weights were also adjusted to preserve the original sample sizes. The original weights were divided by a constant obtained by dividing the weighted sample size by the unweighted sample size. The constants were 37.398 for all schools, 37.01 for public schools only, 149.843 for all students, and 158.609 for public school students only.

4. The question wording was a compromise—necessitated by the length of the questionnaire—between two objectives, one to determine whether schools had changed after the HSB students graduated, and the other to determine whether school changes had influenced student achievement.

Appendix C

1. Richard A. Berk, "An Introduction to Sample Selection Bias in Sociological Data," *American Sociological Review*, vol. 48 (June 1983), pp. 386–98.

2. The rates of transfer and early graduation were virtually identical in high and low performance schools: 6.7 percent transfers in both types of schools, and 3.4 percent and 3.8 percent early graduation in high and low performance schools respectively.

3. The seminal paper on this procedure is James J. Heckman, "Sample Selection Bias as a Specification Error," *Econometrica*, vol. 47 (January 1979), pp. 153–61. The method followed in this appendix is described in Berk, "An Introduction."

Appendix D

1. Public schools admit 98.4 percent of the students that come to them. The private schools are more selective, but they are not as selective as some people might imagine. The Catholic schools accept 85.9 percent of their applicants, the elite schools 52.0 percent, and the other private schools 74.5 percent. Moreover, private schools are not especially aggressive in getting rid of students who are troublesome. Perhaps this is because the threat of expulsion from private school encourages troublesome students to improve their behavior. But whatever the cause, private schools hold on to more of their problem students than public schools do. We found that private schools retained through their senior year 84.9 percent of their students who as sophomores reported that they had disciplinary problems or were suspended. Public schools retained only 72.7 percent of their sophomores who reported such difficulties.

2. On the many problems allegedly associated with joint analyses, see the collections of criticisms assembled in response to Coleman, Hoffer, and Kilgore's analysis of the first wave of the High School and Beyond data: *Sociology of Education*, vol. 55, nos. 2, 3 (April, June 1982), pp. 63–161; and "Report Analysis: Public and Private Schools," *Harvard Educational Review*, vol. 51 (November 1981), pp. 481–545.

3. In analyses that we do not report here we found that the race (and sex) of the individual student did not have a significant independent effect on student achievement in public schools.

4. The apparently larger effect of school size in public schools, as compared with all schools, is primarily a result of the wide variation in school size among public schools and not the marginal effect of school size, which is roughly the same in public schools as in all schools.

Index